The Teradata Database

Implementation for Performance

Brian Marshall

Published By

Education In Parallel
Rancho Palos Verdes, California

Published By
Education In Parallel
Rancho Palos Verdes, California 90275-1705
www.EducationInParallel.com
Email: brianmar@netcomuk.co.uk

To Larry Rex

*For his pioneering work in this subject,
and for the endless hours we spent locked
in "Personal Research".*

SPECIAL ACKNOWLEDGEMENTS

To Paul Sinclair

*For his patience, technical help, and explaining it
in a way that even I could understand.*

To Mark Jahnke

*For his continued enthusiasm and unfailing support.
An early employee of the Teradata Corporation, NCR, three major
customers, and an active contributor to the Teradata Partners' Group,
Mark has proven invaluable in spreading the word.*

ISBN 0-9665493-2-5

Table of Contents

Chapter 6
Write Operations and Disk Management

Chapter 7
The Primary Index

Chapter 11
Sizing the Data Warehouse

Chapter 12
The Parser

Chapter 13
Statistics

Chapter 14
The EXPLAIN

Chapter 15
JOIN Processing

Chapter 16
JOIN Analysis

Chapter 17
Final Index Choice

Chapter 18
Denormalization and Sub-Entities

The Teradata Database

Implementation for Performance

Brian Marshall

1 | Simply a Wild Guess

"We don't have time for analysis". "Just go ahead and load the tables so we can start writing some code. Besides, if anything goes wrong, we can always fix it later". These words may sound all too familiar in today's frantic business world, with its insatiable thirst for instant results and its insistence on setting unattainable deadlines.

Although the Teradata Database is often able to deliver surprisingly good results, even under the most adverse conditions, the RDBMS (Relational Database Management System) can always benefit from the skill and expertise of the team responsible for its physical implementation. Despite this, we are all tempted to undervalue our own ability and rely instead on the ever increasing power of the juggernaut computer to smooth our minor imperfections as it rolls relentlessly forward. In the half-believed tenet that we are saving precious time, we tend to throw caution to the wind and rush blindly ahead, fortified by a little knowledge, a great deal of hope and a logical data model, pristine and perfect in its third normal form.

The Logical Data Model

A logical data model provides a remarkably accurate way of representing a complete, or partial, business enterprise as a series of two dimensional tables with horizontal rows and vertical columns. Tables in a relational database cross-reference each other using matching columns in each table, designated as "keys". Other important elements of information (Attributes) are assigned to the appropriate tables by applying the three rules of normalization. If the placement of Attributes in a table complies with all three rules, the tables are said to be in "third normal form".

Figures 1-1(a) and 1-1(b) depict seven sample tables extracted from the RENTS database. Each table has:

> A unique name (within the database).
> A brief description of its purpose, type and anticipated number of rows.
> Columns uniquely named within the table.
> Sample Data.

Entities

The ORDER table *(Figure 1-1(a))* is described as, "An order for merchandise placed by a customer", and it is identified as an "Entity" (a real-world person, place, thing or idea of interest to the organization). Each individual order is distinguished from all others by being allocated a unique Order Number. The Order Number column is marked "PK", which indicates that the column has been designated as the Primary Key of the table.

Each relational table is required to have a column, or group of columns, designated as the Primary Key, and this column, or group of columns, must be have three distinct properties. It must be unique. It must always have a value (never NULL), and it must never be subject to change. Since the physical implementation procedure chosen by the user calls for values in the Order Number column to be automatically generated by the RDBMS, it is also marked "SA" (System-assigned).

Domains and Keys

Values in different columns, which may be logically added, subtracted or compared, are said to be in the same "domain". Columns which may be logically multiplied or divided by each other (price by quantity, for example), always refer to different real world persons, places, things or ideas, and must therefore be in different domains. There is however, one exception to this rule. On the rare occasion when two columns in a like domain may be logically multiplied together (length by length), the result is always in a different domain (area).

The Location Number, Customer Number, Status Code and User ID columns in the ORDER table are marked "FK" (Foreign Key). This indicates that all non-NULL values in these columns must have matching values in the PK column of the same, or another, table. If this is true, both the PK and FK columns must refer to the same real world person, place, thing or idea and must, in consequence, be from the same domain. Thus, non-NULL values which appear in the Location Number column of the ORDER table (marked FK), must appear as valid values in the PK column (Location Number) of the LOCATION table *(Figure 1-1(b))*. Similarly, non-NULL values in the Customer Number column of the ORDER table must also have matching values in the PK column of the CUSTOMER table, and so on. If this relationship between FK and PK columns is properly maintained, the tables are said to preserve "referential integrity".

Associative Tables

In contrast with the Entity tables, each of which has a single-column PK, The PK of the ORDER ITEM table has multiple components, consisting of Order Number and Item Number. Each of these is designated as a Foreign Key. This unique kind of key structure, where each component of a multiple-column PK is also marked "FK", allows the table to be identified as an "Associative" table. Associative tables are used to model many-to-many relationships between the entities referenced by the FK columns. The ORDER ITEM table therefore, permits one order to reference many distinct items, and one type of item to appear on many different orders.

TABLE NAME : **ORDER**
DESCRIPTION: AN ORDER FOR MERCHANDISE PLACED BY A CUSTOMER
ROW COUNT: 30K   TABLE TYPE: ENTITY

Order Number	Location Number	Customer Number	From Date	To Date	Status Code	Update Date	Update Time	User ID
PK,SA	FK, NN	FK, NN	NN	NN	FK,NN	NN	NN	FK,NN
2002	367	2002	10/08/98	10/08/98	O	09/21/98	1030	RC
2005	998	2006	09/25/98	09/30/98	C	09/21/98	1045	RC
2007	1611	2002	10/22/98	10/27/98	O	09/21/98	1310	RW

TABLE NAME : **ORDER ITEM**
DESCRIPTION: ITEMS ON AN ORDER
ROW COUNT: 170K   TABLE TYPE: ASSOCIATIVE

Order Number	Item Number	Quantity	Status Code	Update Date	Update Time	User ID
PK,SA						
FK	FK	NN	NN	NN	NN	
2002	23905	100	X	09/21/98	1030	RC
2002	24001	25	O	09/21/98	1030	RC
2005	23910	500	S	09/21/98	1310	RW

TABLE NAME : **ITEM**
DESCRIPTION: MERCHANDISE AVAILABLE FOR RENTAL
ROW COUNT: 20k   TABLE TYPE: ENTITY

Item Number	Category Number	Description	On Hand Quantity	Daily Rental Amount
PK,SA		NN	NN	
23905	103	Plastic Chairs	1200	2.00
23910	107	Folding Wood Chairs	1500	2.50
24001	103	Round Plastic Tables	600	4.00

Figure 1-1(a)

TABLE NAME : **CUSTOMER**
DESCRIPTION: SOMEONE TO WHOM WE SELL MERCHANDISE
ROW COUNT: 30K   TABLE TYPE: ENTITY

Customer Number	Customer Name	Billing Location Number	Area Code	Phone Number
PK,SA	NN	FK, NN		
2002	ABC INC	1611	310	444 1000
2005	Smith Assoc.	367	213	221 3455
2006	Adams	998	310	653 2950

TABLE NAME : **LOCATION**
DESCRIPTION: PLACE OF INTEREST TO THE ORGANIZATION
ROW COUNT: 100K   TABLE TYPE: ENTITY

Location Number	Street	City	State Code	Zip Code
PK,SA	NN	NN		
367	1234 Main Street	Santa Monica	CA	90243
998	50, Richmond Plaza	Manhattan Beach	CA	92011
1200	500 Route 7	Dayton	OH	45405
1611	200 Elm	Los Angeles	CA	90066

TABLE NAME : **STATUS**
DESCRIPTION: THE STATUS OF AN ORDER
ROW COUNT: 8   TABLE TYPE: ENTITY

Status Code	Description
PK	
C	CLOSED
O	OPEN
S	SUBSTITUTED
X	CANCELLED

TABLE NAME : **USER**
DESCRIPTION: EMPLOYEE USER IDs
ROW COUNT: 50   TABLE TYPE: ENTITY

Status Code	Last Name
PK	
JL	LIVINGSTONE
RC	COLLINS
RW	WILLIAMS

Figure 1-1(b)

5

The Three Rules of Normalization

Every table must have a Primary Key. Moreover, if other columns in the table directly relate to the PK column(s) of the same or another table, these columns are identified as Foreign Keys. In addition to PK and FK columns however, tables will almost always have one or more columns not marked "PK" and "FK". These non-key columns are known as "Attributes" and while their inclusion in tables might appear relatively innocent and inconsequential, their specific location becomes fraught with meaning.

For example, in *Figure 1-1(a)*, the Daily Rental Amount column, located in the ITEM table, permits no more than a single amount to be stored for each item. This implies that the Daily Rental Amount for an item remains constant for all orders, without regard to the size of the order or the customer who placed it. On the other hand, many business organizations prefer to offer lower prices or discounts to their best customers, and the Daily Rental Amount might vary according to the customer placing the order, the size of the order itself or some other qualification of importance to the business. In this event, the Daily Rental Amount should, more properly, be placed in the ORDER ITEM table, since this would provide the ability to record a different Daily Rental Amount for each item on each order.

While there may be several tables in which a given attribute may logically be placed, only one will correctly reflect the true day-to-day business operations of the organization. The three rules of normalization are therefore needed to determine the appropriate table for each Attribute column, based on its particular shade of meaning to the specific business enterprise.

Rule 1: The attribute must describe the instance or row uniquely referenced by the Primary Key.

In the ORDER table, values in the From Date, To Date, Status Code columns, etc. all contain information which refers to one specific Order Number, and no other. These columns comply with the first rule of normalization and the table is said to be in "first normal form". The first rule of normalization also forbids the inclusion of repeating groups of columns in a table, such as "Item1", "Item2", "Item3", etc.

Rule 2: The attribute must describe all the components of the Primary Key, and not just some.

This rule applies only to tables, such as the ORDER ITEM table which have multiple-component PK values. Since values in the Quantity column indicate the number of items on the order, they describe both components of the PK and conform to the second rule of normalization. If attributes obey both the first and second rules, the table is said to be in "second normal form".

Rule 3: Attributes must only describe the PK column and not each other.

This is the rule which forbids placing both the Customer Number and the Customer Name columns in the ORDER table since Customer Name would qualify Customer Number and not the PK column (Order Number). In this example, a violation of the third rule might well result in a loss of data integrity, since the Customer Number column could easily be updated to reference a customer other than the one listed in the Customer Name column.

If attributes columns obey the first three rules of normalization, the tables are said to be in "third normal form".

While the abstractions of pure mathematics might permit additional rules of normalization, from the perspective of the typical commercial relational database implementation, these are generally considered unreasonably eccentric, and are ignored.

Sample Data

The final component of the logical data model is the sample data. Frequently dismissed as being of little importance, the sample data is, to the contrary, the most important single element of the logical model. Without sample data we can only speculate whether the model is capable of delivering the information we need. With sample data, we can prove it. For example, using the sample data provided in *Figures 1-1(a) and (b)*, we can determine the answers to an almost infinite number of questions:

> How many customers placed orders in October, 1998?
> Which employee handled the most orders?
> What was the most popular item ordered during1998?
> Which was the most productive state?
> And so on ....

Sample data is essential in proving the efficiency of the logical data model but is, of course, discarded in favor of real data during the physical implementation process.

Keys and Indexes

While Primary Keys and Foreign Keys have a great deal of relevance to the logical data model, their only role in the physical model involves the maintenance of referential integrity. Of considerably more concern to the RDBMS are the physical issues of where each data row should be physically stored on disk and how it can be quickly located and retrieved in response to a query. For this purpose, the RDBMS uses indexes rather than keys. The Teradata Database supports various types of indexes, of which the most important are:

> Unique Primary Index (UPI).
> Non Unique Primary Index (NUPI).
> Unique Secondary Index (USI).
> Non Unique Secondary Index (NUSI).

Unlike the Primary Key, which must be unique, never NULL and never changed, a Primary Index may be unique or non-unique, may contain NULLs and may be changed (although this is discouraged as an "unreasonable update"). The Teradata Database uses a computation or hashing algorithm, based on the value of the Primary Index column(s) to calculate the logical storage address of a row on disk. Anything lost can be easily found if its last location is remembered. In the same way, if the original value used to determine the logical storage address of a row is later provided in an SQL request, a procedure, identical to that used to place the row, can be used to find it.

As a result, Teradata recommends that the Primary Index column(s) be chosen, not purely on the basis of uniqueness, as with the Primary Key, but rather as the column(s) most frequently referenced as a literal or join condition in the SQL. While the Primary Key is used to uniquely *identify* a row, the Primary Index is used to physically *access* the row on disk.

Despite the clear difference in function, the terms "Primary Key" and "Primary Index" are frequently mistaken as synonyms, even though the presumed relationship between them is obscure, inexact and unreliable. Nevertheless the simple similarity of terms is often sufficient to prove an irresistible temptation to a physical implementation team, faced with impossible time constraints. To save the relatively short amount of time needed to properly analyze and plan the application activity against the tables, the over-stressed team becomes attracted by a series of simple shortcuts for assigning indexes, which we will refer to as the "SWAG" method (Simply a Wild Guess).

The "SWAG" Method

The "SWAG" method is, all too often, used to choose Primary Index columns for table, based purely on the Primary Key. The rules are simple:

> If a table has a single-column Primary Key, it is given a Unique Primary Index on the PK column.
>
> If a table has a multiple-column Primary Key, it is allocated a Non Unique Primary Index based on one of the FK components of the Primary Key.

The Teradata Database was built ground-up to handle massive relational tables modeled in third normal form, and SWAG method of choosing indexes, based purely on keys, produces good results up to ninety percent of the time. Unfortunately this also implies that the "SWAG" method fails at least ten percent of the time. On the basis of a similar success-to-failure ratio, a pedestrian who regularly crosses a street twice each day might expect to be involved in a nasty accident at least once per week.

The tables shown in *Figures 1-1(a) and (b)* are of two distinct types, Entity and Associative. Entities may be divided into 2 main categories, major and minor. Major entities may be characterized as the important dynamic tables of the database, subject to frequent change, such as ORDER or ITEM. Major entities generally have a large number of rows and, if properly normalized, no more than 12 columns. Minor entities, like the STATUS table, are easily recognized as typically small, static, validation tables, with fewer than 100 rows, and seldom more than three columns. Major or Minor entity tables always have a single-column Primary Key. Conversely, any table with a single column Primary Key can be readily identified as an Entity.

In a similar way, any table (such as ORDER ITEM) with a double-component Primary Key, each constituent of which is a Foreign Key, can be instantly recognized as an Associative table used to model a many-to-many relationship.

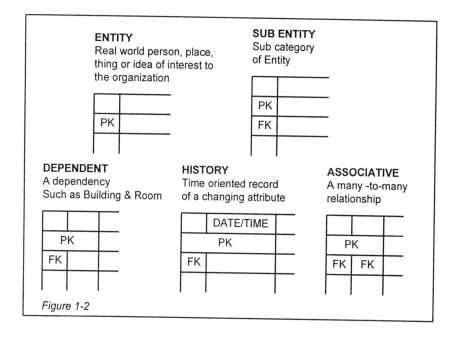

Figure 1-2

In addition to Entity and Associative tables, there are a number of other variations which might be encountered in a logical data model, some of which are shown in *Figure 1-2*. Like the Entity and Associative tables, each kind of table can be readily identified by its PK/FK structure and the SWAG method can, in consequence, be used to provide each table with a reasonably good choice of Primary Index *(Figure 1-3)*.

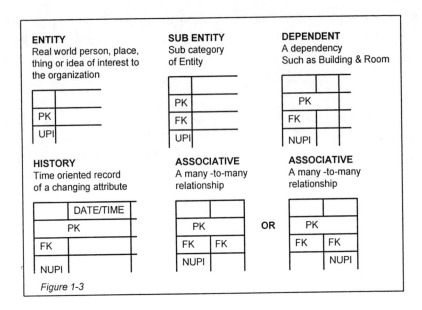

Figure 1-3

Conclusion

If computer systems could be unfailingly relied upon to handle all tasks equally well, there would be no effective barrier to simply taking a logical data model, using the "SWAG" method to convert keys to indexes and submitting SQL statements to create the tables for the data warehouse. Although the Teradata Database is unique, in that it will often perform remarkably well, even with a poor choice of indexes, it offers spectacular rewards to those who invest the time and effort necessary to take advantage of its strengths and steer clear of its weaknesses.

If the user of the system has no clear sense of direction or purpose, the RDBMS cannot help. It needs instructions in the form of indexes on tables, established not by mere chance alone, but by science and a thorough understanding and analysis of the specific tasks the system will be required to perform. Using the "SWAG" method of choosing indexes for a mission-critical application, and being right 90% of the time, is rather like taking off in a fully loaded 747, with no particular destination in mind, and with enough fuel to cover most of the journey.

Despite the temptation for haste therefore, we must inevitably bow to good sense and acknowledge the need for an intermediate step between the development of the logical model and implementation of the physical tables, known as "Application Analysis", an alternative process which produces impressive rewards for surprisingly little effort.

2 | Application Analysis

Unlike the "SWAG" method, described in the previous chapter as most frequently used in the "real world", Application Analysis is often summarily dismissed in the myopic view that any activity of this kind must inevitably result in "analysis paralysis". At the same time, few application designers would consider attempting to write SQL to access the database without first identifying the specific tables involved in the transaction and giving some degree of thought to the amount of work needed to achieve the desired result. In one case therefore, we might "SWAG" the indexes, design the applications and prepare the SQL, and in the other, design the applications using Application Analysis, choose the indexes and write the code. In other words, the primary difference between the "SWAG" method of choosing indexes and Application Analysis is little more than a simple re-ordering of events.

While "SWAG" is simple to implement, it is a one-size-fits-all solution. By ignoring the applications which will access the tables, "SWAG" is of little help in identifying secondary index candidates and often results in disappointing results, which require an expensive fix after the applications have been designed, coded and implemented. Application Analysis, on the other hand, results in an ordered approach to application design, allowing tables to be implemented for top performance, based on how they will be used *within the organization*. Moreover by providing justification and support for all index and denormalization decisions, Application Analysis elevates the physical implementation process from a mysterious "black art" to a well-documented science.

The end product of Application Analysis is the addition to the logical data model of statistical information between the *intention* of the table (*Figure 2-1*) (that part of the table which includes the column names and key structure), and the *extension* of the table (the data rows) to create the Extended Logical Data Model (ELDM). The ELDM thus becomes the necessary "bridge" between the Logical Data Model and the Physical or Implemented Data Model.

EXTENDED LOGICAL DATA MODEL

TABLE NAME: ORDER

DESCRIPTION:AN ORDER FOR MERCHANDISE PLACED BY A CUSTOMER

ROW COUNT: 30,250   TABLE TYPE: ENTITY

INTENTION

ORDER

ORDER NUMBER	CUSTOMER NUMBER	LOCATION NUMBER	FROM DATE	TO DATE	STATUS CODE	UPDATE DATE	UPDATE TIME	USER ID
PK,SA	FK ,NN	FK	NN	NN	FK ,NN	NN	NN	FK

STATISTICAL INFORMATION

EXTENSION

200010	657	11092	7/3/97	7/6/97	O	6/10/97	10:20	RC

Figure 2-1

In gathering the statistical information needed to complete the ELDM, it is important to recognize that every employee in the business organization is, to some degree, a specialist. As a result, it is unlikely that the physical implementation team will be as familiar with the day-to-day operations of the organization as the eventual users or the operating departments, who will be the ultimate beneficiaries of the database. Statistical information is only as reliable as its source, and finding a dependable source within a large organization is often more difficult than gathering the statistics themselves.

Some rewarding areas for investigation might include:

> Pre-existing systems.
> General knowledge of the business.
> Past Performance Records.
> Future Performance Estimates.
> Cost-justification for installation of the system.

Recognizing that averages seldom tell the truth, the interview questions should be carefully phrased to uncover statistical maximums or typicals. For example:

> What is the *maximum* number of orders we process in the course of a year (*including peak periods*)?
>
> What is the projected *rate of increase* over the next year(s)?
>
> What is the *maximum* number of orders expected to be open at any one time?
>
> How frequently do we intend to archive closed orders?
>
> What is the *maximum* number of items in inventory?
>
> What is the *most frequently* requested item and how many of them are on order during the *heaviest* trading period?
>
> What is the *maximum* number of items permitted on a single order?
>
> How many items *typically* appear on an order?

In the improbable event that, despite the best efforts of the implementation team, reasonably reliable statistics are not available somewhere in the organization, it becomes unfortunately necessary to cautiously tread the perilous path of an educated guess.

The Scope of Application Analysis

The statistics which result from application analysis are used to correctly assign Primary and Secondary Indexes to the tables in the data warehouse, and support subsequent denormalization decisions.

In any large data warehouse, typical of Teradata installations, as many as 95% of the tables may be classified as "minor " entities. Minor entities, as described in Chapter 1, are small validation or look-up tables, with fewer than 100 rows and seldom more than two or three columns. Since it is almost unknown for the Primary Index of minor entity tables to be based on anything other than the Primary Key, minor entities may be effectively excluded from the statistical analysis. What remains for consideration therefore, is the relatively small number of important and volatile tables in the database.

The Demographics

For each of the columns in every table subject to analysis, we must eventually generate a total of nine statistics. The first four deal with the demographics of the tables and columns themselves. For each qualifying column, we need to determine:

The number of distinct data values (DISTINCT VALUES).

The maximum number of rows having any one value (MAXIMUM ROWS/VAL).

The maximum number of rows with no value (MAX ROWS NULL).

The typical (not average) number of rows per value (TYPICAL ROWS/VAL).

ORDER									
30,250 ROWS	ORDER NUMBER	CUSTOMER NUMBER	LOCATION NUMBER	FROM DATE	TO DATE	STATUS CODE	UPDATE DATE	UPDATE TIME	USER ID
PK/FK	PK, UA	NN							
DISTINCT VALUES	30.25K	20K	24K	700	700	10K	N/A	N/A	N/A
MAXIMUM ROWS/VAL	1	50	100	100	100	5K	N/A	N/A	N/A
MAX ROWS NULL	0	0	20	0	0	5K	N/A	N/A	N/A
TYPICAL ROWS/VAL	1	1	7	30	40	10K	N/A	N/A	N/A

Figure 2-2

Figure 2-2 shows the first four statistics already calculated for the ORDER table. Since the Status Code and User ID columns reference minor entity tables, and the Update Date and Update Time columns are excluded from analysis, we are left with five columns - Order Number, Customer Number, Location Number, From Date and To Date.

A study of pre-existing applications combined with the interview process has provided the following information used to complete the first four demographics in the ELDM:

Order Number

The ORDER table is required to maintain two years of current data before obsolete rows are committed to archive.

The organization presently processes a maximum of 15,000 orders per year, including peak periods, and expects this figure to increase by about 250 orders next year. The total number of rows in the table over the next 2 years period is calculated to be 30,250 (30.25K).

Order Number is the PK of the ORDER table and PK values must be unique and never NULL. The total number of distinct values is therefore equal to the number of rows, and both the maximum and typical number of rows per value must be equal to 1.

Customer Number

Approximately 20,000 distinct customers are expected to place orders during the next 2 years, generally at the rate of one order per customer, although the best customers may place as many as 50.

This column is marked "NN" which prohibits NULLs in the Customer Number column.

Location Number

Each customer may have multiple locations to which orders may be shipped, and the expected 30,250 orders may be shipped to as many as 24,000 different locations.

On rare occasions (no more than 20 at any one time), values in this column may be NULL.

The Access Statistics

Following the calculation of table and column demographics, the remaining five statistics needed to complete the ELDM are derived from an enterprise-wide analysis of each application which will access the data. For each relevant column in each major table, we must determine:

1. The Value Access Frequency (VALUE ACC FREQ)
   The number of times per year this table is accessed using a literal value in the SQL.
   The maximum number of rows returned on each occasion.

2. Value Access Rows * Frequency (VALUE ACC R*F)
   Calculate the maximum number of rows accessed using a literal value by the annual frequency of the application.

3. The JOIN Access Frequency (JOIN ACC FREQ)
   The number of times per year this table is accessed by a join to this column from another table.
   The maximum number of rows returned on each occasion.

4. JOIN Access Rows * Frequency (JOIN ACC R*F)
   Calculate the maximum rows returned by a join on this column by the annual frequency of the application.

5. Change Rating
   An indication of how frequently values in this column change during processing. The values are somewhat arbitrary in nature and range from zero to 9.

      0 (never changes)
      1 (changes only once)
      5 (changes approximately half the time)
      9 (changes with every access).

Application Analysis

To show how these statistics are derived, we will analyze five sample applications:

Application 1 - Process a New Order.
Application 2 - Process up to 10 Items on an Order.
Application 3 - Cancel an Order.
Application 4 - Change up to 9 Items on an Order.
Application 5 - Weekly Billing for up to 200 Completed Orders.

Application 1 - Process a New Order

The organization processes a maximum of 15.25K new orders per year, which involves inserting a new row into the ORDER table. We use the Customer's Phone Number to retrieve customer details from the CUSTOMER table. We use the Customer Number to join with the LOCATION table and identify the customer's Location Number to which the order is to be sent. (Each customer has up to 5 locations listed in the LOCATION table). Finally, we always perform a referential integrity check of the User ID.

There is probably no clearer way of explaining this application than by providing a diagram *(Figure 2-3)* in which we show:

The tables and columns accessed by the application.

The maximum number of rows affected by the each instance of the application.

The type of access (VALUE or JOIN).

From this diagram we can clearly see:

How one row of the CUSTOMER table is accessed by way of a phone number contained as a literal value in the SQL.

How the derived Customer Number is used to retrieve up to 5 rows from the LOCATION table by way of a JOIN.

How this information is used to insert a new row in the ORDER table.

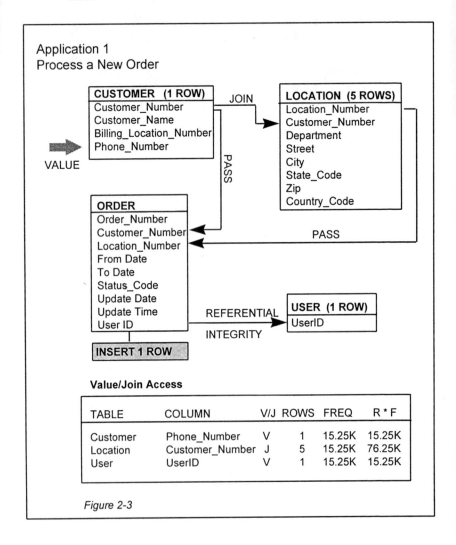

Figure 2-3

In the summary of Value/Join Access, it should be emphasized that we are only concerned with the column(s) used to access the table(s), the maximum number of rows selected, and the number of times per year this application is run. The INSERT operation is not included in the statistics since INSERTS are not affected by index choices.

Application 2 - Process Items on an Order

For each new order, the customer may choose up to 10 individual items *(Figure 2-4)*. An item is first selected by category, and each category may include up to 100 distinct items. Each time an item is selected, the ORDER/ITEM table must be accessed to determine all the outstanding ORDERS for that particular item, and the rows for those orders examined to determine the dates during which the item is not available. There are generally no more than 30 open orders for any one item:

> Each new ORDER selects up to 10 rows from the CATEGORY table.

> Each CATEGORY has up to 100 ITEMS (1000 rows).

> For each ITEM ordered, we must compare up to 30 rows from ORDER ITEM table with 30 rows in the ORDER table to ensure the ITEM is available on the dates requested (10 * 30 = 300 rows each).

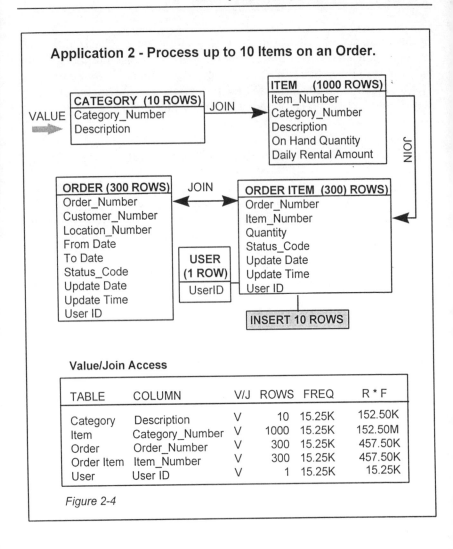

Figure 2-4

Application 3 - Cancel an Order

A maximum of 5,000 orders per year are cancelled by the customer which requires the UPDATE of the Status Code column for 1 row in the ORDER table and up to 10 rows in the ORDER ITEM table *(Figure 2-5)*.

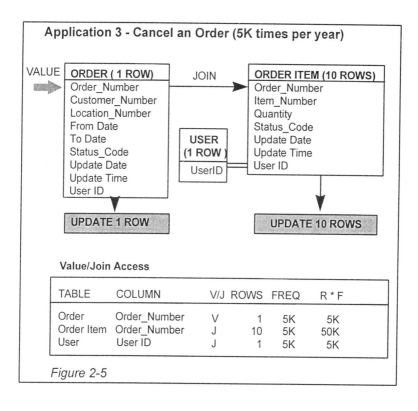

Figure 2-5

Application 4 - Change Items on an Order

Up to 5,000 times per year a customer may wish to change up to 9 items on an order *(Figure 2-6)*. The relevant Order Number is supplied as a literal in the SQL. The application is then required to verify the item being changed by joining Item Number in the ORDER ITEM table to Item Number in the ITEM table, before processing an UPDATE to the Status Code column of the ORDER ITEM table. Once this is complete, the application must process up to 9 new items on the order. (This is similar to the process of a new order in Application 2, but for 9 items instead of 10).

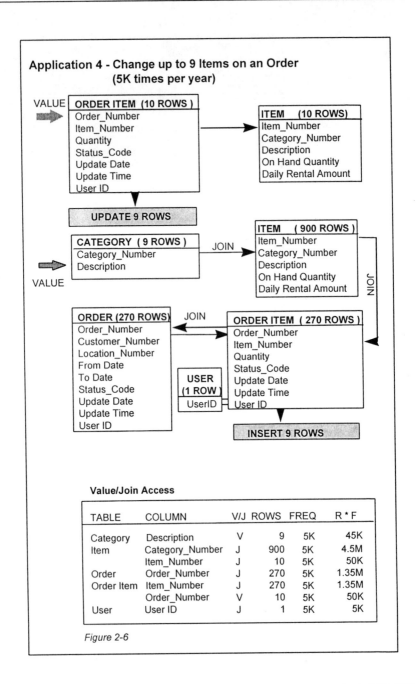

**Application 4 - Change up to 9 Items on an Order
(5K times per year)**

VALUE

ORDER ITEM (10 ROWS)
Order_Number
Item_Number
Quantity
Status_Code
Update Date
Update Time
User ID

ITEM   (10 ROWS)
Item_Number
Category_Number
Description
On Hand Quantity
Daily Rental Amount

UPDATE 9 ROWS

CATEGORY (9 ROWS)
Category_Number
Description

JOIN

ITEM   (900 ROWS)
Item_Number
Category_Number
Description
On Hand Quantity
Daily Rental Amount

VALUE

JOIN

ORDER (270 ROWS)
Order_Number
Customer_Number
Location_Number
From Date
To Date
Status_Code
Update Date
Update Time
User ID

JOIN

ORDER ITEM (270 ROWS)
Order_Number
Item_Number
Quantity
Status_Code
Update Date
Update Time
User ID

**USER
(1 ROW)**
UserID

INSERT 9 ROWS

Value/Join Access

TABLE	COLUMN	V/J	ROWS	FREQ	R * F
Category	Description	V	9	5K	45K
Item	Category_Number	J	900	5K	4.5M
	Item_Number	J	10	5K	50K
Order	Order_Number	J	270	5K	1.35M
Order Item	Item_Number	J	270	5K	1.35M
	Order_Number	V	10	5K	50K
User	User ID	J	1	5K	5K

Figure 2-6

Application 5
Weekly Billing for up to 200 Completed Orders.

Each week, a billing statement *(Figure 2-7)* is issued for up to 200 completed orders, identified by the Status_Code in the ORDER table. Customer Number in the ORDER table is joined to Customer Number in the CUSTOMER table *(Figure 2-8)* and Billing Location Number in the Customer table is joined to Location Number in the LOCATION table.

Customer_Name   Current Date
Department
Street
City, State_Code, Zip

Re: Order Number ___ From (date)____ To _(date)___
Rental of:
Quantity Description Quantity   Amount
(up to 10 times)

       Plus delivery charge

              Total Amount Due   _____

       Figure 2-7

Order Number in the ORDER table is joined to Order Number in the ORDER ITEM to retrieve the items on order, and ITEM is accessed for the Description and Daily Rental Amount.

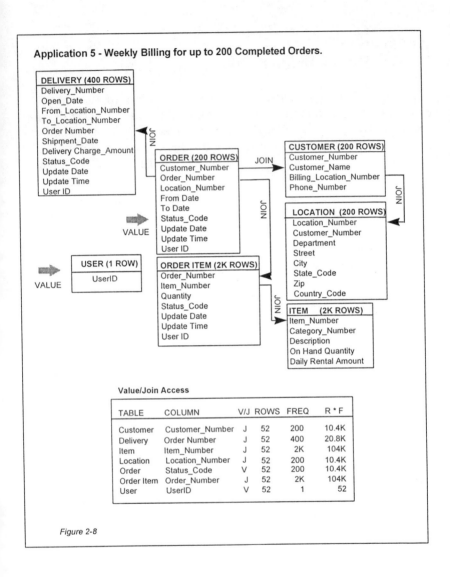

Application 5 - Weekly Billing for up to 200 Completed Orders.

DELIVERY (400 ROWS)
Delivery_Number
Open_Date
From_Location_Number
To_Location_Number
Order Number
Shipment_Date
Delivery Charge_Amount
Status_Code
Update Date
Update Time
User ID

ORDER (200 ROWS)
Customer_Number
Order_Number
Location_Number
From Date
To Date
Status_Code
Update Date
Update Time
User ID

CUSTOMER (200 ROWS)
Customer_Number
Customer_Name
Billing_Location_Number
Phone_Number

LOCATION (200 ROWS)
Location_Number
Customer_Number
Department
Street
City
State_Code
Zip
Country_Code

USER (1 ROW)
UserID

ORDER ITEM (2K ROWS)
Order_Number
Item_Number
Quantity
Status_Code
Update Date
Update Time
User ID

ITEM   (2K ROWS)
Item_Number
Category_Number
Description
On Hand Quantity
Daily Rental Amount

Value/Join Access

TABLE	COLUMN	V/J	ROWS	FREQ	R * F
Customer	Customer_Number	J	52	200	10.4K
Delivery	Order Number	J	52	400	20.8K
Item	Item_Number	J	52	2K	104K
Location	Location_Number	J	52	200	10.4K
Order	Status_Code	V	52	200	10.4K
Order Item	Order_Number	J	52	2K	104K
User	UserID	V	52	1	52

Figure 2-8

Combining the Results

Having analyzed all the known applications on an enterprise-wide basis, the results from all applications are incorporated into a single spreadsheet *(Figure 2-9)*, ordered by:

Table Name.
Column Name.
Value or Join (V/J).

APP ID	TABLE	COLUMN	V/J	ROWS	FREQ	R*F	ELDM FREQ	R*F
2	Category	Description	V	10	15.25K	152.50K		
4			V	9	5K	50K	20.25K	202.50K
5	Customer	Customer_Number	J	200	52	10.4K	52	10.4K
1		Phone_Number	V	1	15.25K	15.25K	15.25K	15.25K
5	Delivery	Order_Number	J	400	52	20.8K	52	20.8K
2	Item	Category_Number	V	1000	15.25K	152.5M	15.25K	152.5M
4			J	900	5K	4.5M	5K	4.5M
4		Item Number	J	10	5K	50K		
5			J	2K	52	104K	5K	154K
1	Location	Customer_Number	J	5	15.25K	76.25K	15.25K	76.25K
5		Location_Number	J	200	52	10.4K	52	10.4K
2	Order	Order_Number	V	300	15.25K	457.5K		
3			V	1	5K	5K	20.25K	462.5K
4			J	270	5K	1.35M	5K	1.35M
5		Status_Code	V	200	52	10.4K	52	10.4K
2	Order ITEM	Item_Number	V	300	15.25K	457.5K	15.25K	457.5K
4			J	270	5K	1.35M	5K	1.35M
3		Order_Number	J	10	5K	50K		
5			J	2K	52	104K	5K	154K
3			V	10	5K	50K	5K	50K
1	User	UserID	V	1	15.25K	15.25K		
2			V	1	15.25K	15.25K		
3			V	1	5K	5K		
4			V	1	5K	5K		
5			V	1	52	52	40.6K	40.6K

Figure 2-9

The total values for FREQ and ROWS * FREQ (R*F) for each distinct Table Name, Column Name and V/J Access combination are calculated and projected to the ELDM for each major table in the database. *(Figure 2-10),* and with the statistics in place, we may now safely discard the sample data.

APP ID	TABLE	COLUMN	V/J	ROWS	FREQ	R*F	ELDM FREQ	R*F
2	Order	Order_Number	V	300	15.25K	457.5K		
3			V	1	5K	5K	20.25K	462.5K
4			J	270	5K	1.35M	5K	1.35M
5		Status_Code	V	200	52	10.4K	52	10.4K

ORDER

30,250 ROWS	ORDER NUMBER	CUSTOMER NUMBER	LOCATION NUMBER	FROM DATE	TO DATE	STATUS CODE	UPDATE DATE	UPDATE TIME	USER ID
PK/FK	PK, SA	FK,NN	FK	NN	NN	FK,NN	NN	NN	NN
VALUE ACC FREQ	20.25K	0	4K	0	0	52	0	0	0
VALUE ACC R*F	462.5K	0	0	0	0	10.4K	0	0	0
JOIN ACC FREQ	5K	0	0	0	0	0	0	0	0
JOIN ACC R*F	1.35M	10	0	0	0	0	0	0	0
DISTINCT VALUES	30.25K	20K	4K	700	700	10K	N/A	N/A	N/A
MAXIMUM ROWS/VAL	1	50	100	100	100	5K	N/A	N/A	N/A
MAX ROWS NULL	0	0	20	0	0	5K	N/A	N/A	N/A
TYPICAL ROWS/VAL	1	1	7	30	40	10K	N/A	N/A	N/A
CHANGE RATING	0	0	2	3	3	7	9	9	9
SAMPLE DATA	200010	657	11092	7/3/97	7/6/97	O	6/10/97	10:20A	RC

Figure 2-10

Conclusion

Figure 2-11 illustrates the major design components needed to support a successful physical implementation of the data model:

A good logical relational model reduces application workload.

Application analysis produces reliable demographics.

Reliable demographics are needed to make sound index choices.

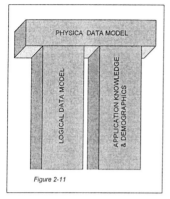

Figure 2-11

With the statistics of the completed Extended Logical Data Model as our preliminary blueprint, all we now need is a little knowledge of the internal workings of the Teradata Database to ensure a successful implementation of the data warehouse based on fact not fantasy, experience not experiments.

3 | The Physical Architecture

Once a lone voice crying in the wilderness, Teradata pioneered the now universal "shared-nothing" architecture necessary to support the huge data warehouse projects which drive today's industry and influences the lives of every man, woman and child in the western world in ways of which they remain largely unaware. In the late 1970s when, outside of the military and the aerospace industry, the newly developed micro chip was still seen as little more than a fascinating toy, and the term "Personal Computer" (PC) had yet to be coined, Teradata was quick to realize the potential of joining hundreds or even thousands of these tiny processors together in parallel to challenge, and ultimately defeat, the then mighty main frame. Where once the architecture was physical and proprietary, it is now open and virtual. Either way, the underlying principles of parallelism remain the same.

If we measure the amount of time required by a single PC or processor to perform a task, and we then divide the workload equally between two processors, allowing each of them to perform their portion of the task in parallel, the entire task should be completed in half the time required by one processor working alone. If we similarly divide the same workload evenly amongst one hundred processors, the task should be completed in one percent of the time required by a single processor, and so on.

Where the simplicity of such a system tends to fail, however is in the assumption that combining the results from multiple processors operating in parallel requires no additional time. What propelled the former Teradata Corporation to greatness therefore, was its invention and patent of an intelligent interconnect, known as the Ynet, to efficiently merge the results from multiple processors working in parallel and deliver the results to the user in an ordered and coherent stream. This kind of multiple-processor system, where each individual processor remains exclusively responsible for maintaining its own portion of the data on its own dedicated disk, is known as a "shared-nothing" architecture.

In its original configuration, known as the DBC/1012, the Teradata Corporation relied on proprietary hardware consisting of physical processor boards, each with its own dedicated Central Processor Unit (CPU), its own copy of the RDBMS and its exclusive access to between one and four physical disks. Although the DBC/1012 was initially positioned as a powerful peripheral device designed to relieve the main frame of the massive workload inherent in managing large relational databases, Teradata was quick to realize the possibilities of the newly emerging network and open systems environment. In partnership with NCR therefore, Teradata, began the long evolutionary process which would eventually allow it to shed the shackles of its proprietary architecture and emerge into the bright new world of open systems as a purely software product, free at last to expand into new and exciting UNIX and Windows NT environments.

In its latest incarnation as "Version 2", the Teradata Database is presently supported on a variety of hardware systems, including the NCR 3550, 4100, 4300, 4700 and the powerful WorldMark 5150M with more planned in the near future. As a result, it now becomes possible to offer the massive processing power of the Teradata Database to customers large and small with data needs which range from a few gigabytes of data to many terabytes. Despite its startling metamorphosis from proprietary hardware to open systems, Teradata's logical architecture remains fundamentally unchanged *(Figure 3-1)*.

The Symmetric Multi-Processing Unit (SMP)

The standard open systems hardware used by Teradata Version 2 software is the SMP unit, which is powered by up to 16 powerful Intel micro-processors, tightly coupled together to share gigabytes of memory and other resources. The SMP has its own UNIX operating system which allows it to be used, in the foreground as a stand alone unit and in the background as a database server, with both network and channel connects.

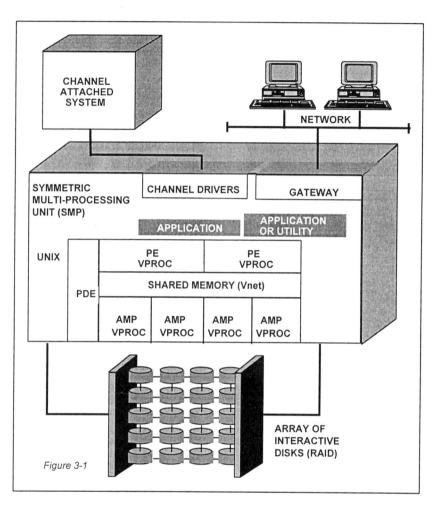

Figure 3-1

While the Teradata Version 2 RDBMS runs on a near-standard UNIX platform, it still requires minor changes to the UNIX kernel, known as the PDE (Parallel Database Extensions). The physical processors of Teradata Version 1 are effectively emulated in Version 2 software as virtual processes (Vprocs), which run on top of the UNIX operating system. Vprocs communicate with each other using a shared memory interconnect known as the Vnet (virtual net).

Virtual Processes (Vprocs)

Teradata Version 2 systems feature two distinct kinds of Vprocs, known as Parsing Engines (PEs) and Access Module Processors (AMPs). While there are no theoretic limits as to the number of Vprocs which may be initiated on a single SMP unit, it is unfortunate that while the power of a state-of-the-art CPU seems to double on average every eighteen months, inter-processor and other communications technology is evolving at a much slower rate. As a result, the number of Vprocs which can be efficiently supported within a single SMP unit becomes, in effect, regulated by the massive output of the powerful processors and the limited bandwidth of the inter-connect. For this reason, NCR/Teradata recommend a maximum of 4 AMP Vprocs with probably one or fewer Parsing Engines (depending on processing needs) for each SMP unit of the powerful WorldMark 5150M system.

PEs are primarily responsible for:

> Management of multiple users submitting multiple processing sessions in parallel.
> Input Data Conversion from the user's server to ASCII.
> Parsing and Optimizing the SQL.
> Compiling and dispatching processing instructions over the Communications Layer to other parts of the system.
> Communications Layer Interface.

Consistent with the requirements of a shared-nothing architecture, each AMP assumes sole responsibility for providing a number of important services for the data assigned to it:

> Communications Layer Interface.
> Database Management.
> Locking.
> Joins.
> Sorting.
> Output Data Conversion (to conform to the requirements of the user's system).
> Output Data Formatting.
> Disk Space Management.

Accounting.
Disk Interface.

Disk Arrays

Unlike Teradata Version 1 systems where each AMP had exclusive access to dedicated disks, the disk arrays used in Version 2 are shared by all the virtual AMPs of an SMP unit. However the Teradata Database maintains the shared-nothing characteristics of its architecture by subdividing the disk array units into equal Logical Units (LUNS) or virtual disks (Vdisks) *(Figure 3-2)* which are then treated as if they were independent disks and assigned equally and exclusively to the AMP Vprocs running in the SMP.

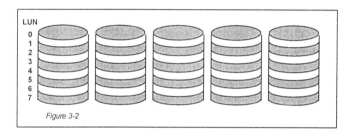

Figure 3-2

Disk Arrays, from various manufacturers, are standard in Teradata Version 2 systems and provide automatic data protection from single disk failure with little or no interruption in processing. They are available in a number of different configurations. The configuration most commonly supported by Teradata consists of as many as 20 disks organized in 4 ranks of 5 disks per rank. Data protection becomes the sole responsibility of the dual disk array controllers and effectively improves the performance of the RDBMS by freeing it from this time-consuming task. Of the ingenious data protection mechanisms in general use two, RAID 1 (Random Array of Interactive Disks) and RAID 5, are generally considered most suitable for the Teradata Database.

RAID 1 protects data by mirroring. While this still consumes double the disk, data recovery is automatically handled by the disk array controller and results in little or no loss of processing time.

RAID 5 protects data using parity to automatically reconstitute missing or damaged data. Data is spread block-by-block amongst four randomly selected disks in a rank and the fifth is used to maintain the parity information. In the event of a failure of any disk in a rank, the parity information is used in conjunction with the data on the remaining disks by the array disk controller to calculate the value of the missing data using "XOR" (Exclusive OR) logic:

Each of the four data bits are compared top to bottom.

If there is an even number of 1s or 0s, (0000, 1111, 1001, 0011, etc.), the parity bit is set to 0.

If there is an odd number of 1s and 0s (1110, 0001, 0111 etc.), the parity bit is set to 1.

For Example:

Disk 1	0101	0100	T
Disk 2	0100	0100	D
Disk 3	0100	0001	A
Disk 4	0101	0100	T
	EEEE	EOEO	(E=Even, O=Odd)
Disk 5	0000	0101	Parity

When the Teradata Database is running on multiple-SMP units (nodes) such as the WorldMark 5150M nodes are grouped into *cliques (Figure 3-3)* - a collection of individual nodes with shared access to disk arrays using SCSI interfaces such that *each node has access to every disk array.* This shared access provides a powerful level of hardware protection and permits the system to continue operating even with the loss of:

One disk in every rank,
One controller in every array,
One Bynet and three nodes.

The system not only continues to operate, but in addition, automatically reconfigures itself for transparency.

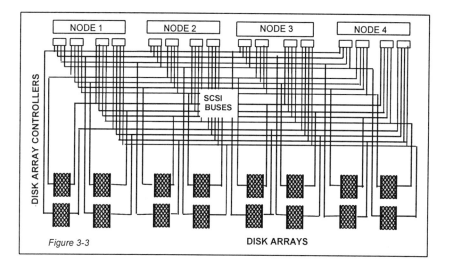

Figure 3-3   **DISK ARRAYS**

Apart from the unlikely event of multiple disk failures within the same rank, RAID 5 offers a high level of data protection at the hardware level at the reasonable cost of only 25% more disk, and has no detrimental effect on over-all system performance.

Massively Parallel Processing (MPP)

While a single standard SMP unit will permit most open systems RDBMS vendors to support a departmental data mart or even a small data warehouse reasonably well, almost all have encountered extreme difficulty in providing the robust and efficient connectivity between the hundreds of SMP units required for massively parallel processing today or the thousands of SMP units which will needed in the near future. It is here that Teradata's long experience with the Ynet makes a substantial difference. While the Ynet had proved extremely efficient in managing the heavy communications traffic between physical processors on the DBC/1012, it offered only a single communications path between any two physical processors, this limitation became apparent in Teradata systems larger than a few hundred AMPs.

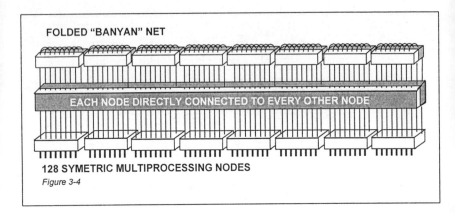

FOLDED "BANYAN" NET

EACH NODE DIRECTLY CONNECTED TO EVERY OTHER NODE

128 SYMETRIC MULTIPROCESSING NODES

Figure 3-4

To combat this phenomenon for its Version 2 systems, Teradata developed the Bynet *(Figure 3-4)* by which all the SMP units on the system are interconnected in such a way that there are as many possible communications paths between SMP units as there are SMP units in the system. In this way the Bynet becomes fully scaleable as the number of SMPs expands and with a bandwidth of 20 Megabytes per second for each node, provides the Teradata Database with all the capacity required for handling the heavy demands expected of it in the foreseeable future.

4 | Disk Space and Data Recovery

The stock-in-trade of the Teradata data warehouse is storage space. The owner of the warehouse, called "DBC" (the Data Base Computer), retains some of the space for administration purposes and "rents" the remainder to other "users". Each user is provided with a password which permits limited access to the data warehouse. Under the ultimate control of DBC, any user may share rights of access, or even sublet space, to any other person of the user's choosing. Anyone granted access rights, or space in this way, is automatically accorded the full status of "user".

The space owned by any user of the data warehouse is known as a "database", and is used to store a logical collection of zero or more tables, views and macros. Not all users require space in the data warehouse. Some may simply require access to objects owned by somebody else. Nevertheless, whether or not a user is allocated space for storage of data in tables, we might still simplistically define a user as," a database with a password".

In order to perform any task on the Teradata Database, the user must have the necessary permissions or "access rights" recorded in the Data Dictionary. These rights may be acquired by default from the direct owner or by a specific grant from DBC, or any other user who already has ownership of the access rights being granted. (Ownership and Access Rights are discussed at length in Chapter 11 of "The Teradata Database-SQL".)

With the appropriate level of access rights therefore, any user may:

> Create any number of other users.
> Subdivide any owned space into additional databases.
> Grant other users ownership of sub-divided space.
> Share any access rights with other users.

Users, Databases and Space

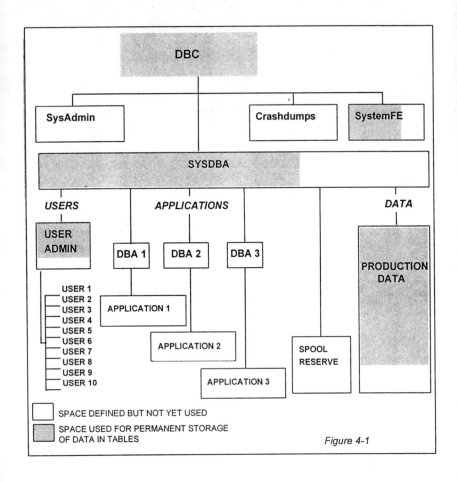

Figure 4-1

Figure 4-1 represents the total amount of disk space available to the Teradata Database. It shows a production-level, hierarchical structure of users and databases optimized for ease of maintenance and control. Initially, all of the space in the system is owned by DBC which is also known as Data Dictionary (DD). DBC retains a certain amount of space to maintain the tables, views and macros needed by the RDBMS to locate, manage and control all users, databases, tables views and macros stored on the system. For example, the following SQL statement will create a database structure "A" with 1 megabyte of space:

CREATE DATABASE A AS PERM=1000000;

To create an identical structure with a LOGON capability, "A" must be defined as a USER:

CREATE USER A AS PERM=1000000, PASSWORD = mother;

In addition to being able to log on, a user requires functionality to define the priority levels, the primary database for access, accounting parameters, etc. which are necessary for a live user of the system, but not required of an inanimate data structure such as a database. The main differences between a database and a user are illustrated in *Figure 4-2.*

FUNCTION	USER	DATABASE
Unique name		
PERM space definition		
FALLBACK/NO FALLBACK		
Permanent Journal definitions		
SPOOL space definition		DEFAULT
Accounting information		DEFAULT
Password		
Priority		
Startup string		
Default database		
Collation Sequence		

Figure 4-2

Hierarchical Structure

Despite the implication that a relational database is free from the encumbrances of hierarchy, the Teradata Database observes a strict structure of ownership. Initially all the space on the disks belongs to DBC, and it is from the sub-division of the space originally owned by DBC that all other databases and users are created. When a new Teradata system arrives from the factory, User DBC and three important descendants have already been created:

Object Name	Database/User	Main Purpose
SysAdmin	User	Maintains Utility Restart Logs.
CrashDumps	Database	Captures Diagnostic Information.
SystemFE	User	Maintains Diagnostic tables and macros needed by the Field Engineer.

The first task of the Teradata System Administrator, on taking delivery of a new system, is to create a user beneath DBC in the hierarchy, with the suggested name of "SYSDBA". SYSDBA may then become the base from which all the resources and all user access to the system can be effectively managed and controlled. Thus, SYSDBA becomes, in effect, the source of all other non-system user/database objects in the data warehouse.

Since DBC is the user from which all other objects are created, it is known as an "owner" or "parent" of all other objects on the system. All objects below DBC in the hierarchy are described as "descendants" or "children" of DBC. From the perspective of any other user or database, any object in a direct lineage higher in the hierarchy is an "owner" or "parent" (synonyms), while any object directly below is a "descendant" or "child" (synonyms).

Returning to *Figure 4-1* for example, USERADMIN has two parents, SYSDBA and DBC. It also has ten children, USER 1 through USER 10. Database Administrator 1 (DBA1) also has two parents, but only one child, APPLICATION 1. A user or database object may therefore have any number of owners or parents, and there is no restriction on the number of descendants or children. Even so, ownership or parenthood is not for ever, and can be changed using an SQL "GIVE" statement. The following statement transfers ownership of APPLICATION 1 from DBA1 to DBA2:

GIVE Application1 TO DBA2;

As a result, DBA1 has now relinquished custody of its only descendant to DBA 2.

In addition to maintaining the tables needed by the RDBMS to catalog all objects in the Teradata system, the Data Dictionary also contains the views and macros needed by the administrator or other users to derive meaningful DD information in a reasonably user-friendly fashion.

The DD view DBC.Children can be used to display a non-sequenced list of the parents or children of any user or database using the following SQL:

SELECT Parent FROM DBC.Children
WHERE Child = USER;

SELECT Child FROM DBC.Children
WHERE Parent = USER;

In dividing up the space between the users and applications (PERMANENT SPACE or PERM), and in allowing sufficient SPOOL for temporary work-space and interim results of queries, the System Administrator should remain aware that the Teradata Database is unusual amongst RDBMS vendors in that it does not require the allocation of *contiguous* disk space for databases or users.

A user or a database might therefore be alternatively defined as "a *statement* of space maintained in the DD", since the physical disk space is allocated only on an "as needed" basis for storage of data in tables. In the meantime space defined for users, but not yet being physically used, can be made available to DBC or any other user, as temporary work space or SPOOL. In this way, Teradata users are able to get double-mileage from temporarily unused disk space.

Permanent Space (PERM)

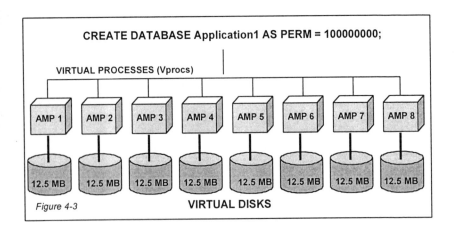

Figure 4-3   **VIRTUAL DISKS**

When a USER or database is created, the permanent space is deducted from that of the owner, and evenly divided amongst all the AMPs on the system. In *Figure 4-3* for example, APPLICATION 1 is created with 100 MB of permanent space drawn from that of the owner, no matter which user created the object. The 100 MB is then evenly divided amongst the 8 AMPs of the system so that each AMP is allocated 12.5 MB. Since Teradata uses a shared-nothing architecture, AMPs are not permitted to borrow space from each other. As a result if, in this example, the 12.5 MB per AMP limit is exceeded on any AMP, applications attempting to access APPLICATION 1 will begin to encounter (perhaps premature) "out of database space" errors. Thus, an even distribution of data amongst all the AMPs of the system becomes crucial to economical space management.

For most RDBMS vendors a "database out-of-space" condition might well result in a time-consuming interruption of production for a complete reorganization (re-org) of the data. The Teradata RDBMS does not require disk space allocated to a user or database to have contiguous disk addresses, and permits the PERM space for an object to be dynamically modified, on-line, with little or no interruption in processing.

Spool

Spool space is defined as temporary space acquired automatically by the system for intermediate query results or answer sets. Like permanent space, each database or user is specifically granted, or inherits, a spool space allocation. This becomes the limit of temporary work space that applications submitted by the user, or his/her descendants, may consume before being required to prematurely terminate. Unlike permanent space, spool is initially limited by that of the immediate owner (user or database), but is granted in *addition* to the owner's spool, not deducted from it.

For example, the following SQL statement creates User A with 100 MB of permanent space and 100 MB of spool:

```
CREATE USER  B  FROM A
              AS  PERM = 100000000,
              SPOOL = 100000000,
              PASSWORD = mother;
```

In order to successfully submit this statement, User A must initially have at least 100 MB of unused permanent space and 100 MB of spool. As a result of creating User B, the PERM space of the User A will be reduced by 100 MB, but the spool allocation will remain unchanged.

Spool, like permanent space, is equally divided amongst all the AMPs in the system, and this becomes a per AMP limit which cannot be exceeded. As a result, when the user's spool limit has been exhausted on one AMP, regardless of how much spool may be available on other AMPs, the application terminates. "Insufficient Spool" errors often result from poorly distributed data, or joins on columns with large numbers of non-unique values. Keeping spool rows small and few in number reduces spool I/O and improves system performance.

Data Distribution

Rows of every table, user or system-defined, require PERM space defined at the user/database level. Rows of every table are distributed evenly and (apparently) randomly across all AMPs, provided the Primary Index of the table is unique or nearly unique. Each AMP is responsible for the maintenance of rows on its dedicated physical or virtual disk and, provided there are more rows than AMPs, each table has some rows on every AMP *(Figure 4-4)*. Even distribution of the rows permits data on each AMP to be accessed in parallel and provides excellent performance for full table scans and other all-AMP operations.

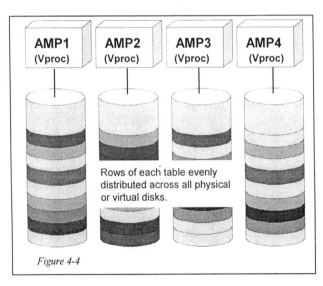

Figure 4-4

No matter how robust or reliable the RDBMS may be however, hardware failures must, sooner or later, become inevitable. Electronic components such as processor boards seldom fail, and rarely if ever result in permanent loss of valuable data. Disk drives, on the other hand, involve high-precision mechanical components, which must eventually fail, and might result in data loss. It therefore becomes incumbent upon the RDBMS to provide the user with affordable protection against unforeseen hardware failure resulting in:

> Loss of Transaction Integrity.
> Loss of Data.

Transaction Protection

A transaction can be defined as "one or more SQL statements which take a database from one consistent state to another". Imagine the situation where a sale is processed but a system failure occurs before the item sold has been removed from inventory. Since the data shows the item still in inventory, even though it is physically no longer there, the organization will eventually suffer embarrassment and confusion when it later attempts to sell the same item to another customer. Had the partially completed transaction been backed out as soon as the failure was detected, the confusion could have been avoided. Proper recognition of transaction boundaries therefore becomes of crucial importance to data integrity and, with this in mind, the Teradata RDBMS maintains two distinct kinds of journal:

> The Transient Journal
> The Before-Image Permanent Journal

The Transient Journal

The Transient Journal (or the Transaction Journal) is automatically maintained by the Teradata Database as a table in the Data Dictionary to ensure against partial completion of individual transactions. For each single or multiple statement transaction, the Transient Journal captures a copy of the data row(s) before any change has occurred. In the event of transaction failure, the "before-change" copy of the row is super-imposed over any new value, and the change is effectively nullified. Once the transaction successfully completes, the rows are automatically removed from the journal.

The BEFORE IMAGE Permanent Journal

While the Transient Journal is automatic and temporary, the BEFORE IMAGE journal is optional and permanent, in that rows are captured or discarded only by specific authorization from the user. BEFORE IMAGE journals created on a table-by-table basis and, in connection with the SQL CHECKPOINT statement, can be used to roll badly corrupted tables back to some earlier (consistent) moment in time. This has the net effect of undoing all changes made to the table, by any user, since the checkpoint statement was processed. Since this option is time-oriented, rather than transaction-oriented, it should be used with extreme caution to ensure that any previously successful transactions processed after the checkpoint, but before the recovery, are re-submitted following the ROLLBACK operation. Permanent Journals are provided as an option of the Teradata Archive/Recovery utility.

Data Protection

Apart from the automatic data protection offered at the hardware level by the RAID 1 and RAID 5 Disk Arrays, The Teradata Database provides its users with two optional software solutions:

FALLBACK Protection.

The Teradata Archive and Recovery Utility.

FALLBACK Protection

Tables in the Teradata Database may be defined as "FALLBACK" or "NO FALLBACK" when the table is initially created, or may be changed at some later time with an "ALTER TABLE" SQL statement. If a table is not provided with the automatic data protection afforded by RAID 1 or RAID 5 disk arrays and is not defined as FALLBACK, any disk failure is likely to result in some data loss, and will almost certainly involve a time-consuming recovery procedure of some kind. With FALLBACK protection however, the data remains available and processing can continue largely uninterrupted.

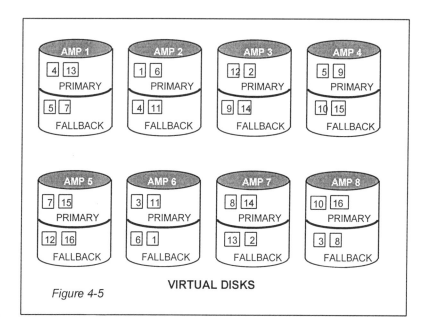

Figure 4-5

VIRTUAL DISKS

Figure 4-5 illustrates a system where each primary row (represented by numbered squares) is protected by a duplicate row on some other virtual AMP/DISK. Imagine that the system has 100 AMPs. If the Disk on AMP3 becomes unreadable, a copy of each row on that disk is maintained by another AMP in the *system.* (Row 12 is protected on AMP 5, and Row 2 on AMP 7). All the data is still available, but 99 AMPs are now doing the work of 100. Over-all performance of the system is therefore expected to degrade by $1/99^{th}$ (about one percent), a negligible amount.

On the other hand, if AMP 7 were now to additionally fail, we could no longer be certain that all rows were still protected. (Row 2 for example, would have been lost). Thus we can say that while FALLBACK protects against the loss of a single disk in the system, a failure of *more than one* results in missing data. Since the chances of any *two disks out of one hundred* failing at the same time is probably quite high, this is considered an unreasonable degree of risk.

A better plan might be to organize the AMPs in groups or *clusters* with some small number of AMPs to a cluster, in such a way that the primary rows of each group would be protected on another AMP in the same cluster. This would permit a failure of one (*and no more than one*) AMP per cluster and still allow full access to data. On the other hand, any single failure would be expected to have a significantly greater impact on over-all performance of the system:

AMPs per Cluster	Percent of Tolerated Failures	Performance Degradation
5	20%	25%
4	25%	33%
3	33%	50%
2	50%	100%

The determination of the optimum number of AMPs per cluster clearly involves a trade-off between the level of protection considered necessary and the maximum degree of performance degradation which can be tolerated in the event of failure.

Teradata users seem to agree that four AMPs per cluster *(Figure 4-6)* and a loss of 33% performance represents an acceptable compromise. Thus a 100 AMP system would now have 25 *clusters*, with primary data rows protected, not on another AMP in the *system*, but on another AMP in the *cluster*. At this point, while we would still lose access to data if two disks failed in the same cluster. However, each cluster could experience a single disk failure (a total of 25 for the system), at any one time, and still allow full access to the data.

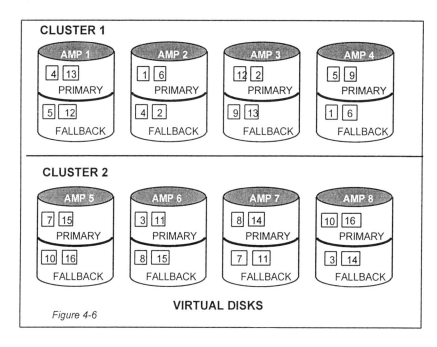

Figure 4-6

In addition to the low-cost automatic data protection afforded by RAID 5 disk arrays, FALLBACK additionally protects against the simultaneous failure of multiple disks in a single rank. As a result, despite the fact that FALLBACK requires double the disk space to accommodate twice the data, and additional CPU workload for write transactions, it is still considered a worth-while investment by many users of the Teradata Database.

Archive and Recovery

No matter how much protection is intrinsically built into the hardware and software, we must always allow for the complete loss of a system due to some kind of major catastrophe. In this event we are faced with the prospect of rebuilding the data from a previously archived copy stored off-site. As the typical tables maintained by Teradata users expand from hundreds of millions to billions of rows, the challenge of initially capturing the archived data, in direct competition with the ever-increasing demands of the production environment, becomes more and more difficult with each passing day. Very large tables take a significant amount of time to load, and a substantial amount of time to archive to tape.

Notwithstanding the difficulties however, the challenge must be met, and even though the Teradata Database provides a fast Archive/ Recovery utility supported on every host platform, it still becomes the most pressing duty of the System Administrator to devise and implement a recovery policy which subordinates the workload to the limited resources available:

> The majority of tables in the database are most likely *minor entities* - small static tables which seldom change. These need generally be archived once, and refreshed only as the need occurs.

> Tables used for decision support are often down-loaded to the Teradata Database from an original tape on the host. Many users rely on being able to repeat this operation from the original source medium.

> Tables which are subject to frequent insert, update or delete generally require archive protection. Since these tables may be very large, the Teradata Archive/Recovery utility needs to offer a high degree of flexibility to archive:

A complete Teradata system (with a single command).

A database (including tables, views and macros) and its descendants.

A table with or without indexes, in full or partitioned over multiple archive sessions.

Day-to-day changes to data using Permanent Journals.

Permanent Journals

Permanent Journals are an optional feature of the Teradata Archive/Recovery utility, and provide the User with the ability to capture *changes to data* (rather than the data itself) as:

After Image journals, which protect against a hardware failure.

Before Image journals permitting a time-oriented rollback following an application failure.

Consider the case where the user has a very large table containing many millions of rows, which is subject to a few hundred thousand updates each evening and needs to be protected against hardware failure. The amount of time needed to archive the complete table to tape each evening exceeds the amount of time available in the assigned maintenance window. By using Permanent Journals to capture daily changes to the data, the user may safely archive the table on a weekly, or even monthly, basis and capture no more than the changes each evening. If the need should arise to recover the table, the weekly or monthly archive is recovered first, followed by a restore and roll-forward of each daily journal archive.

Conclusion

Having completed this brief review of the data structures, ownership hierarchies and data protection mechanisms of the Teradata Database, we are now ready to proceed to the next step on our guided tour through the data warehouse, where we will be shown how Teradata combines its powerful parallel architecture with an ingenious hashing algorithm to initially locate, and unerringly find, any row of any table, however many there might be, with unbelievable speed.

5 | Data Distribution and Location

If there is one thing which sets the Teradata Database apart from all other RDBMS vendors, it is its clever use of a hashing algorithm for the three-fold purpose of evenly distributing rows amongst the processor units (AMPs) of the system, determining where to place the rows on the disk, and locating them again as needed. Moreover, since the number of virtual AMPs running on a Version 2 system is determined by the System Administrator, the hashing algorithm must also be capable of redistributing rows with a minimum of data movement in the event of a change of configuration.

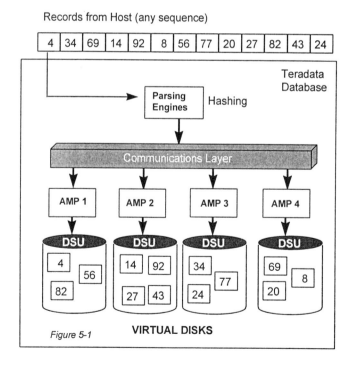

Figure 5-1

Records being loaded to the Teradata Database from a user are streamed to the least busy Parsing Engine where the data is converted to ASCII (Teradata internal format). The value of the Primary Index column is then subjected to a mathematical procedure, known as the hashing algorithm. The hashing algorithm is used to divide the records into one of 65,636 logical groupings or "hash buckets", and each record is individually sent over the Communications Layer (Vnet or Bynet) to the AMP responsible for storing rows with the specific hash bucket value.

The Hashing Algorithm

The Hashing Algorithm is an arithmetic formula that creates a fixed length value from any length input string. The number of 65,636 (a power of 2) was selected as a large number, evenly divisible by an equally large number of factors. Input to the algorithm is the Primary Index (PI) value of a row. The output is a 32 bit binary value known as the "row hash", which:

> Becomes the logical storage address of the row.

> Identifies the cylinder and data block where the row is to be stored.

> Is used for distribution, placement and retrieval of the row.

Good data distribution depends directly on row hash uniqueness, and the degree to which the row hash is unique depends directly on the uniqueness and data type of the Primary Index value of the row. As a result, the same PI value and data type combination always hashes to a similar value, and rows with the same row hash will always be directed to the same AMP. The algorithm produces apparently random, but consistent, row hashes and is specifically designed in such a way that different PI values rarely produce the same row hash (Synonyms).

The Destination Selection Word (DSW)

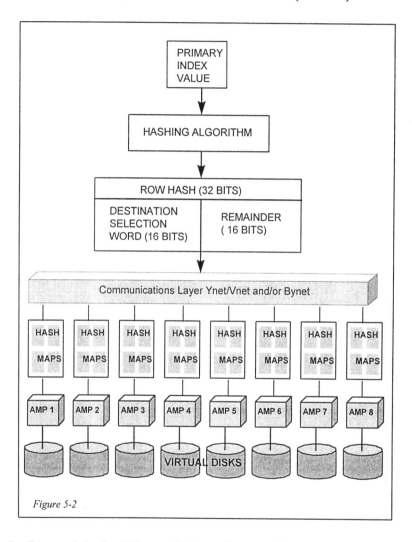

Figure 5-2

In Figure 5-2, the Primary Index column of the row is input to the hashing algorithm. The result is the Destination Selection Word which is affixed to the beginning of the row and becomes the Row ID. The Row ID is then referred to the hash maps contained within the

Communications Layer, which are then used to determine the AMP responsible for the appropriate hash bucket.

Hash Maps

Hash Maps are the mechanism for determining which AMP gets a row and there are four distinct hash maps in every Communications Layer Interface *(Figure 5-3):*

> Primary hash map for the current AMP configuration.
> FALLBACK hash map for the current AMP configuration.
> Primary hash map for a new AMP configuration.
> FALLBACK hash map for a new AMP configuration.

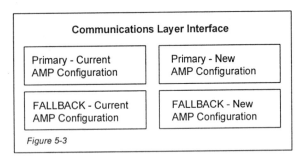

Figure 5-3

Each Hash Map in Teradata Version 2 is an array of 65,536 entries. The Communications Layer Interface checks all incoming messages against the designated Hash Map, and only the AMP whose number appears in the referenced hash map entry *(Figure 5-4)* is interrupted.

The DSW points to one, and only one entry within the hash map, and the cross-referenced value identifies the destination AMP. Hash buckets are equally divided amongst all the AMPs according to a strict regimen. Consequently, the primary hash maps for any two Teradata Version 2 systems, each configured with the same number of AMPs, will be alike. This becomes helpful if data from one hardware system ever needs to be restored to another. FALLBACK hash maps, on the other hand, are configured based on the specifics of AMP clusters, and may differ accordingly.

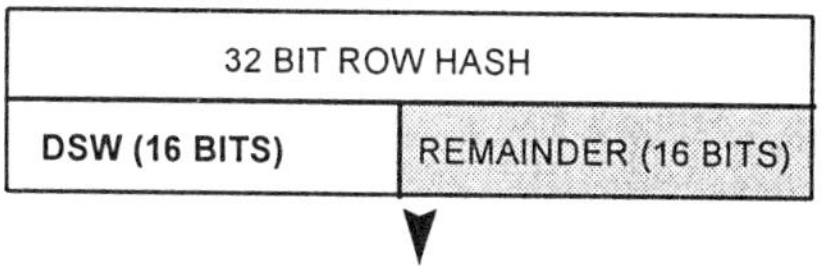

HASH MAP

	0	1	2	3	4	5	6	7	8	9	A	B	C	D	E	F
00	01	02	03	04	05	06	07	08	01	02	03	04	05	06	07	08
01	01	02	03	04	05	06	07	08	01	02	03	04	05	06	07	08
02	01	02	03	04	05	06	07	08	01	02	03	04	05	06	07	08
03	01	02	03	04	05	06	07	08	01	02	03	04	05	06	07	08
04	01	02	03	04	05	06	07	08	01	02	03	04	05	06	07	08
05	01	02	03	04	05	06	07	08	01	02	03	04	05	06	07	08

Figure 5-4

AMP Reconfiguration

Figure 5-5 depicts a change of configuration on a Teradata system where the original configuration shows the 65,536 hash buckets equally shared by the 4 AMPs on the system. After increasing the configuration to 8 AMPs, each AMP now becomes responsible for 8,192 buckets, or almost exactly one half of the buckets (and data) formerly assigned to each AMP of the original configuration.

The Teradata RDBMS creates new hash maps to accommodate the new configuration. The old maps and new maps are compared, and each AMP reads rows of every table and physically moves those which have been reassigned to the virtual disk of the new AMP:

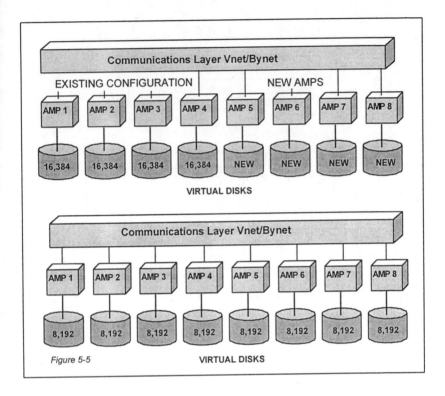

Figure 5-5

$$\text{Rows to migrate} = \frac{\text{Number of AMPs } (\textit{previous})}{\text{Number of AMPs } (\textit{new config})} * 100 = \frac{4 * 100}{8} = 50\%$$

Since the amount of data typically supported by the Teradata Database is extremely large, it is important to note that it is not necessary to off-load data during the reconfiguration process.

Testing Row Hash Distribution

Teradata provides a set of SQL functions which enables users to check how evenly the rows of a given table are distributed by the hashing mechanism and how the rows would be distributed if a different column, or columns, were chosen as the Primary Index:

HASHROW	([< expression-list >])
HASHBUCKET	([< expression >])
HASHAMP	([< expression >])
HASHBAKAMP	([< expression >])

Using Order Number as the Primary Index of the ORDER ITEM table, the following SQL uses the HASHROW function to compute the average number of hash duplicates per row:

```
SELECT (COUNT (*) (FLOAT)) /
       COUNT (DISTINCT HASHROW (Order_Number))
FROM Order_Item;
```

If there are no hash collisions, the result of the statement will be close to the value of 1.0. The larger the value returned by the query, the less efficient the distribution. HASHROW, HASHBUCKET and HASHAMP may be used together to analyze the distribution of primary rows amongst the AMPs. The following query calculates the row distribution of the ORDER ITEM table using Order Number as the Primary Index:

```
SELECT HASHAMP (HASHBUCKET
       (HASHROW (Order_Number )))
       , COUNT (*)
FROM Order_Item
GROUP BY 1
ORDER BY 1;
```

For relatively small tables of a few million rows, efficiency of access by value or join is generally considered more important than evenness of distribution. However, if the table is large and the row distribution between the AMPs is particularly uneven, possible remedial activity might include:

Changing the Primary Index to a more unique column.

Adding a column to the Primary Index to improve uniqueness.

Changing the data type of one or more Primary Index columns.

Locating a Data Block Using the 3-Part Message

SELECT * FROM TableName WHERE PrimaryIndex = value ;

from Parser	from Hashing Algorithm	from SQL Request
TABLE ID	32 BIT ROW HASH	INDEX VALUE
48 BITS	BUCKET	REMAINDER	

Bucket Number is used to identify AMP

TABLE ID	32 BIT ROW HASH	INDEX VALUE
	BUCKET	REMAINDER	

Table ID and 32 Bit Row Hash are used to locate Data Block

TABLE ID	32 BIT ROW HASH	INDEX VALUE
	BUCKET	REMAINDER	

3-Part Pointer Array is used to locate Row

DATA BLOCK

ROW

POINTER ARRAY

| ROW ID | BYTE OFFSET | LENGTH |

Figure 5-6

Figure 5-6, provides a broad overview of the procedure used to select a row based on a primary index literal value supplied in the SQL, using a 3-part message composed of:

> The Table ID resolved from the Data Dictionary.
> The row hash of the literal value (bucket number + remainder).
> The literal value itself.

The bucket number is used to identify the responsible AMP, the row hash is used to identify the appropriate data block and the row is located either by a forward read of the data block or by means of a pointer array. Finally, the literal value is used to filter out hash synonyms.

At a slightly deeper level, as the AMP receives the 3-part message *(Figure 5-7)*, it consults its Master Index, which refers it to the appropriate Cylinder Index. The Cylinder Index, in turn, is used to identify the exact data block where the existing row (or new row) should be located. Since the Master Index is always maintained in AMP memory, the Cylinder Index may be in memory up to 50% of the time and the data block might be in memory, a single row can frequently be located by Primary Index with no more than a *single disk I/O* (Input/Output).

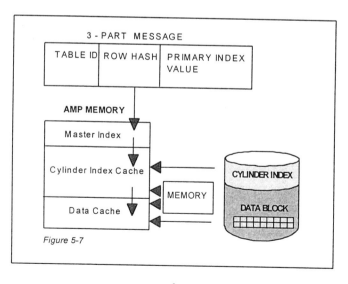

Figure 5-7

The Uniqueness Value

The hashing algorithm has proven highly effective in producing reliable and consistent row hashes. However row hash synonyms (identical row hashes) may occur whether or not the Primary Index of the table is unique. Since the rules of the relational database require that each row must be uniquely identifiable, as Teradata inserts a new row, it stores the data values and the Row ID, and also appends a 32-bit uniqueness value.

If no pre-existing rows are encountered in the block with a row hash value equal to that of the new row, the new row will be allocated a uniqueness value of 1. If, on the other hand, pre-existing rows with the same row hash (row hash synonyms) are found in the block, the RDBMS will increment the maximum uniqueness value of the synonym rows by 1 and assign this as the uniqueness value for the new row. The concatenation of the uniqueness value to the row hash as a Row ID therefore, guarantees each row in the table to be 100% unique. Duplicate Row IDs could however still exist in different tables.

ROW ID = ROW HASH & UNIQUENESS VALUE

Row IDs determine the sort sequence within a data block and unique Row IDs support the performance of Unique Secondary Indexes.

The Table ID

UNIQUE VALUE (From DBC.Next)	SUBTABLE ID
32 Bits	16 Bits

Figure 5-8

The 48-bit Table ID *(Figure 5-8)* is composed of a unique 32-bit value, supplied by the Data Dictionary, which is concatenated with a 16-bit subtable ID and results in a unique ID for:

A normal data table.
Permanent journal table.
Spool table, etc.

While a single table might be thought of as an indivisible unit, the Teradata RDBMS sees it as multiple distinct components. The subtable ID is therefore used to specify the particular component of the table:

Table Header.
Primary data.
FALLBACK data .
First secondary index primary copy.
First secondary index FALLBACK copy etc.

While there is nothing in the RDBMS to prevent rows in different tables from having a similar row hash and uniqueness value, the combination of Table ID and Row ID renders every row in the Teradata Database unique.

The Master Index

Rows in the Teradata database are stored in data blocks sorted ascending by row hash order. Teradata never mixes rows of different tables in the same data block, and rows may never span blocks.

The Master Index, which is used to identify the cylinder containing any specific range of row hash values, is always maintained in memory by every virtual AMP. The Master Index is maintained in two versions, 1 and 0 which are "flipped" whenever a new entry is recorded. Since the immediately earlier version of the Master Index is still available in memory, it can be quickly re-designated as the "current" version in the event of transaction failure. The maintenance of dual versions of the Master Index might therefore be considered analogous to a before change image journal.

The Master Index maintains only one entry for each cylinder on the AMP which is identified by the lowest hash + uniqueness value of rows by Table ID occurring on the cylinder. Empty cylinders are listed on the Free Cylinder List.

If, apart from the uniqueness value, the row hash of the target row appears in the Master Index as the starting row hash for a cylinder, the possibility exists that other rows with the same row hash might also occur on the previous logically adjacent cylinder. (A logically adjacent cylinder is one which appears in the Master Index either immediately before or immediately after the cylinder of interest). If the Continued Hash Flag is set to "1", this indicates that one or more row hash synonyms equal to the Starting Hash are also resident on the previously logically adjacent cylinder.

TABLE ID	ROWHASH	VALUE
100	1000	3250

SELECT ... FROM Order
WHERE Order_Number = 3250;

MASTER INDEX (VERSION 0)					FREE CYLINDER LIST	FREE CYLINDER LIST
TABLE ID	STARTING HASH	CYLINDER NUMBER	INDEX VERSION	CONTINUED HASH FLAG		
.	.	.	.	.	.	.
.	.	.	.	.	.	.
.	.	.	.	.	.	.
078	33012,1	206	0	0	045	350
100	00247,1	025	1	0	059	375
100	00523,1	148	0	0	100	560
100	01261,2	195	0	0	101	668
100	02547,1	684	0	0	107	709
100	03062,1	131	1	0	124	813
100	04223,1	512	0	1	125	935
100	05614,1	310	1	0	126	1170
100	06445,1	055	1	0	183	1235
123	00230,1	601	0	0	189	1350
.	.	.	.	.	.	.
.	.	.	.	.	.	.

TO CYLINDER INDEX

Figure 5-9

Using *Figure 5-9* as an example, in searching for the row which has a Table ID of 100 and a row hash of 1000, we have been directed to a specific AMP by the hash maps on the Communications Layer. We scan the Master Index, first to locate the Table ID (Table IDs are sorted in ascending sequence), and then search within that Table ID for the appropriate range of row hashes. The highest row hash value in Table ID

100 which is less than or equal to the target value of 1000 is 00523,1. The next value, which is 01261,2 is higher than the target value of 1000. Since rows are stored sorted ascending by row hash, we may safely conclude that all rows which have a Row ID equal to or greater than 00523,1 but less than 01261,2 will be found on Cylinder 148. If the target row, which has a Table ID of 100 and a row hash of 1000 does therefore exist, it will be found on Cylinder 148.

The Cylinder Index

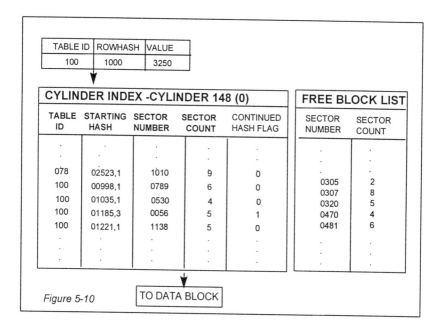

TABLE ID	ROWHASH	VALUE
100	1000	3250

CYLINDER INDEX -CYLINDER 148 (0)

TABLE ID	STARTING HASH	SECTOR NUMBER	SECTOR COUNT	CONTINUED HASH FLAG
.	.	.	.	.
078	02523,1	1010	9	0
100	00998,1	0789	6	0
100	01035,1	0530	4	0
100	01185,3	0056	5	1
100	01221,1	1138	5	0
.	.	.	.	.

FREE BLOCK LIST

SECTOR NUMBER	SECTOR COUNT
.	.
0305	2
0307	8
0320	5
0470	4
0481	6
.	.

Figure 5-10   TO DATA BLOCK

Cylinder Indexes are presented, and may be read in a similar way, to the Master Index. Like the Master Index, Cylinder Indexes are maintained in two versions which are alternately flipped for each write transaction to facilitate efficient recovery from transaction failure. A Cylinder Index contains only one entry with the Row ID of the first row for each data block on the cylinder. Blocks with data appear on the Cylinder Index. Empty blocks are listed in the free Block List.

Continuing with the search for Table ID 100 and row hash 1000, we scan the index for the Table ID. Once found, we then examine the starting row hash values for Table 100 until we encounter a starting row hash equal to, or larger than, the target row hash value of 1000. In this example *(Figure 5-10)*, if the row exists it will be located in the 6 disk sectors beginning at 0789 (in the range of hash values equal to, or greater than, 00998,1 but less than 01035,1).

The Data Block

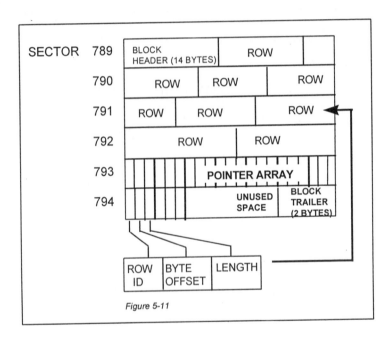

Figure 5-11

The Teradata RDBMS never mixes rows from different tables in the same data block and rows may be accessed either by a forward scan or by the pointer array maintained as a trailer on each block *(Figure 5-11)*. Data blocks vary in size from 512 to 32,768 bytes (1 to 64 disk sectors), and are adjusted dynamically by the RDBMS within tunable parameters set by the System Administrator. Since the space occupied by deleted rows is recaptured with every block write, and blocks are always written to the sector boundary, the unused space in a data block can never exceed 511 bytes.

The Data Row

Like data blocks, rows may be variable in length. In addition to the data values, each row has a 14-byte overhead composed of a leading and trailing row length, the 8 byte Row ID and 2 bytes for overhead (spare byte and presence bits, etc.) *(Figure 5-12)*. Column values are physically stored, not in the order of the CREATE TABLE statements, but with variable length columns first, followed by fixed length data. The order in which columns are stored however, has no effect on the default order in which they are presented to the user. While duplicate rows were not supported by the Teradata Database Version 1, they are offered as an option for Version 2 systems to conform with ASCII standards.

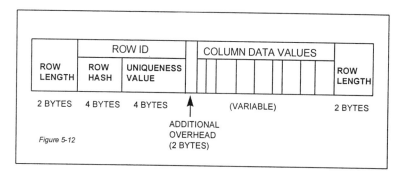

Figure 5-12

The Index Value

The final portion of the 3-part message consists of the literal data value itself. While hash synonyms are relatively rare, even with as many as 64,536 possible hash buckets, they are by no means unknown. In *Figure 5-13* for example, the data block contains two rows (synonyms) with a row hash equal to 1000. Only one of them however has a literal data value equal to the search value of 3250, specified in the SQL.

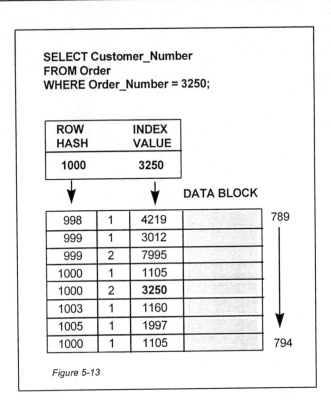

```
SELECT Customer_Number
FROM Order
WHERE Order_Number = 3250;
```

ROW HASH	INDEX VALUE
1000	3250

DATA BLOCK

998	1	4219		789
999	1	3012		
999	2	7995		
1000	1	1105		
1000	2	**3250**		
1003	1	1160		
1005	1	1997		
1000	1	1105		794

Figure 5-13

Conclusion

The Teradata Database distributes the rows evenly and, from the user's perspective, randomly amongst all the AMPs based on the hash of the Primary Index value supplied in the SQL. In its clever use of the hashing algorithm, the Master Index, which is permanently consigned to memory, and the Cylinder Index, which is frequently consigned to memory, Teradata becomes uniquely able to locate rows without the unnecessary expense and overhead of maintaining a Primary Index subtable. As a result, Teradata is able to locate any row in the entire system by Primary Index value with generally one but seldom more than two disk I/Os.

Short of attempting to consign the complete data warehouse to memory (a highly expensive and hazardous solution), locating a single row using only one disk I/O provides the kind of performance which is close to perfect and almost impossible to beat. It is that kind of performance that makes it possible to travel to the far ends of the Earth, insert a card into an automated teller machine and walk away with cash in hand - all in the space of a few seconds.

6	# Write Operations and Disk Management

In Chapter 4, we provided a detailed look at how the Teradata Database is able to locate and retrieve any row of any table by hashing on the Primary Index value. By using the Master Index, which is always in memory, and a Cylinder Index, which is often in memory, locating a row in this way, seldom requires more than a single disk I/O.

All Teradata Version 2 systems are equipped with massive amounts memory, shared between the processors, which is protected by battery in the event of power failure. In this chapter, we shall endeavor to show how the RDBMS uses this protected memory to safely process Primary Index write operations with seldom more than a single disk I/O. At the same time, we shall examine how the RDBMS automatically recaptures poorly distributed or wasted disk space, with little or no interruption in processing.

The Steps and I/O Implications of a Primary Index Write

Whenever a read or write SQL transaction is processed by the Teradata Database, it is first sent to a (virtual) Parsing Engine where the syntax is checked, names are resolved to object IDs and the most efficient course of action is decided upon. Machine-readable instructions, known as "AMP steps" are then generated and transmitted across the Communications Layer to the AMPs based on the hash maps.

Upon receiving AMP steps for a write transaction (INSERT, UPDATE or DELETE), each AMP takes the following steps. (For the purposes of

---

this exercise, we will take the reasonable (but perhaps optimistic) view, that the Cylinder Index is always available in memory).

Access the Master Index (always memory resident).
Read the Cylinder Index (assumed to be in memory).
Read the Data Block, if not in memory
(*generally requires DISK I/O*).
Transmit the steps to the FALLBACK AMP (if appropriate).
Write entries to the Transient Journal memory buffer.
Make the changes to the Data Block in memory.
Determine length of the new Data Block.

If the length of the data block is unchanged:
Re-write the data block to memory buffer.
ELSE, Allocate a new data block.
Put the old data block on the Free Block List of the Cylinder Index.

Write the new data block to memory (unless it is empty).
Change the Cylinder Index version in the Master Index.
Move the Cylinder Index to memory buffer.

These operations happen concurrently on the FALLBACK AMP. The contents of the memory buffer are periodically flushed to disk and the Transient Journal is used to automatically roll back failed or partially complete transactions.

Expanding the Data Block

As we noted in Chapter 4, Teradata stores rows in data blocks sorted ascending by Row ID. Rows of different tables are never accommodated in the same data block and rows never span blocks. As a result the physical position of new rows or expanded variable length data within an existing data block is not arbitrary.

INSERT INTO Order VALUES (3900, ... , . . .);

TABLE ID	ROWHASH	DATA VALUES		
100	1100	3900		

CYLINDER INDEX -CYLINDER 148 (0)

TABLE ID	STARTING HASH	SECTOR NUMBER	SECTOR COUNT	CONTINUED HASH FLAG
.	.	.	.	.
.	.	.	.	.
078	02523,1	1010	.9	0
100	00998,1	0789	6	0
100	01035,1	0530	4	0
100	01185,3	0056	5	1
100	01221,1	1138	5	0
.	.	.	.	.
.	.	.	.	.

FREE BLOCK LIST

SECTOR NUMBER	SECTOR COUNT
.	.
.	.
0305	2
0307	8
0320	5
0470	4
0481	6
.	.
.	.

The Block must be expanded by 1 sector to accommodate the new row

CYLINDER INDEX -CYLINDER 148 (1)

TABLE ID	STARTING HASH	SECTOR NUMBER	SECTOR COUNT	CONTINUED HASH FLAG
.	.	.	.	.
078	02523,1	1010	.9	0
100	00998,1	0789	6	0
100	01035,1	0307	5	0
100	01185,3	0056	5	1
100	01221,1	1138	5	0
.	.	.	.	.
.	.	.	.	.

FREE BLOCK LIST

SECTOR NUMBER	SECTOR COUNT
.	.
.	.
0305	2
0312	3
0320	5
0470	4
0481	6
0530	4
.	.
.	.

Figure 6-1

Figure 6-1 shows how the insert of a new row, which requires the data block to be expanded from 4 to 5 sectors, is accomplished using the Cylinder Index. An SQL insert always provides a value for the column defined as the Primary Index, whether or not the column is NULL. Since an insert must therefore involve a Primary Index access, the responsible AMP is identified from the hash maps and the appropriate Cylinder Index is referenced from the Master Index.

In this example, the insert of a new row (Table ID: 100, Row Hash: 1100) must be inserted in sequence in the 4-sector block which begins in disk sector 0530. The RDBMS calculates that, as a result of this insert, the block must be expanded to 5 sectors. It therefore scans the Free Block List for the first free block with a minimum of 5 contiguous sectors and discovers an available block of 8 contiguous sectors beginning at sector 0307.

The new data block is therefore written at sector 0307 for 5 sectors, and the three remaining sectors beginning at sector 0312, are returned to the Free Block List along with the now-available original 4-sector block at 0530. Finally, once the re-write is fully complete, the "current" Cylinder Index version is flipped in the Master Index.

While the expansion of a data block is generally accomplished in a smooth and orderly fashion, additional complications can arise when the length of the new block exceeds the maximum block size or the relevant cylinder becomes filled to capacity. Block sizes and the Cylinder Fill Factor (CFF) are tunable by the Teradata System Administrator. If the table is used exclusively for decision-support and is never subject to write transactions, the data block size may be set at the maximum and the CFF to 100%. Tables subject to frequent insert, update or delete would benefit from a smaller block size and a lesser CFF.

Block Splits

Block sizes on Teradata Version 2 are variable from 1 to 64 sectors (512 - 32,768 bytes). The block size which the system will attempt to maintain for maximum I/O efficiency is calculated on the basis of:

(Largest block) / 2 (round up) + (512 or 1024)

The largest individual row size is 32,000 bytes, which would be defined as an "oversized" row, since only the one row could be accommodated in a single data block.

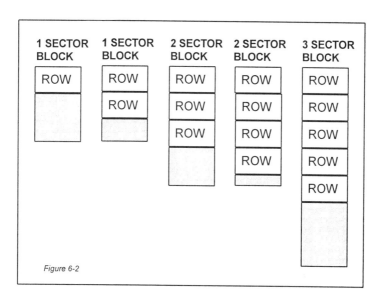

Figure 6-2

Figure 6-2 shows how a data block expands to accommodate new rows and updates. The RDBMS moves rows, as necessary, within the block to maintain Row ID sequence. Large rows require more disk space for the Transient Journal, Permanent Journals and Spool.

When a data block requires more space than the largest block, it splits into two fairly equal parts *(Figure 6-3)* and automatically reclaims any unused space in excess of 511 bytes. Block splits generally require only one disk I/O and rarely have much effect on transaction processing performance.

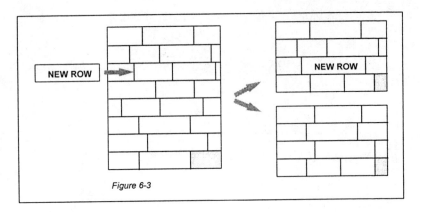

Figure 6-3

An oversized row, on the other hand, requires its own data block and the RDBMS is still obliged to store such rows in Row ID sequence. The data block must therefore be split at the point of insertion (*Figure 6-4*), and this might lead to uneven block sizes and result in poor utilization of the disk.

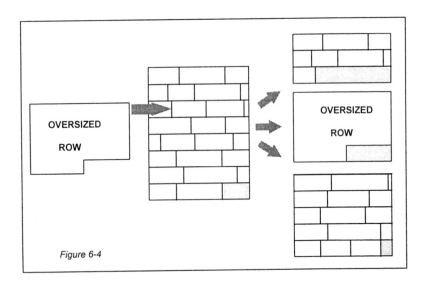

Figure 6-4

Aggregation of Data Blocks and Cylinder Pack (CYLPACK) Operations

The Teradata RDBMS never mixes data and spool on the same cylinders. Cylinders which are free of data become available for temporary spool space. Since even a single block of data on an otherwise empty cylinder renders it unavailable for spool, the RDBMS automatically re-collects and aggregates free data blocks as a normal part of table maintenance *(Figure 6-5)*, and routinely performs Mini-Cylpacks to free additional cylinders for spool.

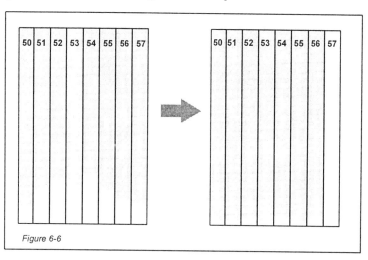

Figure 6-6

The function of a Mini-Cylpack is to progressively move data blocks from one cylinder to the previous physical one until a complete cylinder is freed of data and thereby becomes available for temporary work space.

Figure 6-6 represents disk cylinders 50 through 57, each of which have data, but none of which are packed to capacity. The Mini-Cylpack task begins by moving data blocks from the "top" of cylinder 51 and adding them to the "Bottom" of cylinder 50, until cylinder 50 is packed to its CFF. The task then repeats this operation by moving data blocks from cylinder 52 to 51 until cylinder 51 is packed to the CFF, and so on until one complete cylinder becomes free of data and added to the Free Cylinder List of the Master Index. Spool cylinders themselves are never subject to cylinder packing.

Since Mini-Cylpacks run as a low priority background task, they have little effect on system performance and response times. Repetitive or excessive Mini-Cylpacks however indicate that the system does not have enough disk space, PERM or Spool, to support its current workload. When sizing a system therefore, it becomes highly important to ensure that enough cylinders are available on the system to accommodate both data and spool. Limiting the row size and the number of columns per row can reduce the amount of spool needed.

Conclusion

By not insisting upon contiguous disk space for data storage and in its efficient use of background tasks to recapture fragmented and poorly distributed disk space, the Teradata Database has effectively freed its users from the time-consuming drudgery of the frequent re-orgs required by most other RDBMS vendors with little or no impact on system performance. In this way, not only does the Teradata RDBMS demonstrate the superiority of its file system, but it does so with a length of experience no other vendor can match.

7	The Primary Index

Having examined the role of the Primary Index in determining the logical disk address of the data, we are now ready to contemplate the nature of the Primary Index itself. In this chapter we will weigh the differences between Unique and Non Unique Primary Indexes and describe the kind of SQL constructs which always result in a full table scan. Finally, we will begin to discuss how possible Primary Index candidates can be identified using the distribution demographics from the application analysis process described in Chapter 2.

Primary Indexes for tables in the Teradata RDBMS must be chosen on the basis of three, occasionally conflicting, considerations:

ACCESS	To maximize one-AMP operations.
DISTRIBUTION	To optimize parallel processing.
VOLATILITY	To minimize expensive I/O operations.

The ideal Primary Index should therefore be selected as the column most frequently used to access the data, a column which provides excellent distribution of the data and a column with stable data values.

Performance

To reiterate from Chapter 1, a Primary Index is different from a Primary Key. A Primary Key must be unique, must never be NULL and should never be changed. A Primary Index may be unique or non-unique, may be NULL and may change, although this is considered an unreasonable update and is strongly discouraged.

Every table in the Teradata Database is required to have a column, or combination of columns, designated as the Primary Index. Each table has one, and only one, Primary Index and a single-value Primary Index access requires only one AMP and typically one disk I/O.

If the Primary Index is unique, only one row is returned and since the response buffer is large enough to accommodate the largest single row, no spool file is ever required. If the Primary Index for a table is defined as unique, each row in the table must also be unique, which the Teradata RDBMS is able to automatically enforce based on a check of the index values alone.

If the Primary Index is non-unique, duplicate values are hashed to the same AMP and, if possible, assigned to the same data block. If all the rows with an identical row hash are able to fit within a single data block, only one I/O is needed to return all the rows and no spool file is required. However, if the Teradata RDBMS is required to enforce the uniqueness of the rows and there is no unique secondary index defined for the table, it must resort to a duplicate data check of the complete row.

Distribution

The net efficiency of a parallel processing system depends directly on an even division of workload between the multiple processor units. If one processor is required to process more data than others, the less burdened processors must stand idle while they wait for the overloaded processor to complete, and this degrades the performance of the entire system. The Teradata RDBMS uses the hashing algorithm to distribute rows amongst the AMPs based on the value of the Primary Index - the more unique the Primary Index, the more even the distribution.

Figure 7-1, first shows the distribution of rows based on a Primary Index column of Customer Number. If we are familiar with Vilfred Paretto's law (1848-1923), it comes as no surprise that 20% of the customers typically place 80% of the orders and the distribution amongst the AMPs is very uneven. Not only does this result in poor performance, but since the PERM space is allocated to the AMPs on an equal basis and this becomes the threshold which cannot be exceeded on any AMP, heavily populated AMPs will tend to experience "out of space" conditions while others have plenty of space remaining. As a result, SQL queries which "touch" the AMP which is "out of space" may prematurely terminate, while identical queries directed at other AMPs may succeed. Conversely, a Primary Index based on the unique Order Number will provide even distribution of rows and applications will be less likely to encounter premature "out of space" conditions.

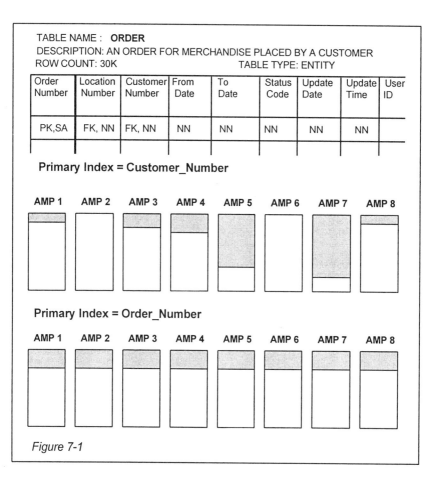

TABLE NAME : **ORDER**
DESCRIPTION: AN ORDER FOR MERCHANDISE PLACED BY A CUSTOMER
ROW COUNT: 30K   TABLE TYPE: ENTITY

Order Number	Location Number	Customer Number	From Date	To Date	Status Code	Update Date	Update Time	User ID
PK,SA	FK, NN	FK, NN	NN	NN	NN	NN	NN	

Primary Index = Customer_Number

Primary Index = Order_Number

Figure 7-1

Locating Data Rows

Locating or processing data rows by supplying a value for the Primary Index column(s) in the SQL is, by far, the most efficient operation the Teradata RDBMS can perform. Apart from the insert, which is always a Primary Index operation, the syntax of all SQL Data Manipulation

Language (DML) statements provides for the inclusion of a "WHERE" clause:

```
SELECT [expression] FROM tablename WHERE . . .
UPDATE tablename SET ColumnName=[expression] WHERE . . .
DELETE FROM tablename WHERE . . .
```

In each case the row or rows to be acted upon must first be physically located. Values in the WHERE clause determine the set of rows to be accessed, and if no WHERE clause is supplied, the RDBMS becomes obliged to read all the rows in the table. By limiting the number of rows which must participate in an application, we lessen the workload of the RDBMS and improve the over-all performance of the system.

Equality comparisons in the WHERE clause permit the RDBMS to use Primary or Secondary indexes to select the rows, depending on the type and selectivity of the index. Examples of equality conditions include:

```
ColumnName = value
ColumnName IS NULL
ColumnName IN (subquery)
ColumnName IN (explicit list of values)
ColumnName = ANY, SOME
T1.Col1 = T1.Col2
Condition1 AND Condition2
Condition1 OR Condition2
```

Range testing and aggregate processing can take advantage of Value-Order "Covering" indexes:

```
ColumnName BETWEEN... AND...
Aggregates (SUM, MIN, MAX, AVG, COUNT, DISTINCT)
```

Non-equality comparisons and string searches in the WHERE clause always cause Full Table Scans:

```
ColumnName IS NOT NULL
ColumnName NOT IN (explicit list of values)
ColumnName NOT IN (subquery)
```

Join condition1 OR Join condition2
NOT (condition1)
TI.Col1 [computation] = value
Ti .Col1 [computation] = T1.Col2
Col1 II Col2 = value
ColumnName LIKE...
INDEX (ColumnName)
SUBSTR (ColumnName)
ANY, ALL
Missing WHERE clause

The following functions effect output only, and have no effect on base row selection:

GROUP BY	ORDER BY
HAVING	UNION
WITH	INTERSECT
WITH...BY...	MINUS

Although the Teradata RDBMS is designed, ground up, to perform full table scans with a grace and efficiency matched by no other RDBMS vendor, the application designer should always be alert to the opportunity to convert a non-equality comparison to an equality condition by a clever rewrite of the SQL. The physical implementation team also should consider that poor relational models severely limit physical design choices and generally force more Full Table Scans.

Duplicate Row Check

If a table has a Non-Unique Primary Index (NUPI), and the Teradata RDBMS is required to enforce uniqueness of the rows, it must read each row in the table which has a similar row hash value (row hash synonyms) to perform the duplicate row check, which must precede the insert of a new row.

Insert of the first row with a specific row hash value *(Figure 7-2)* requires no other rows to be read first. The duplicate row check for the second row requires the prior read of the first row, and so the total accumulated logical read operations for the first and second rows is now equal to 1. By the time the 3rd row is inserted, the cumulative logical reads necessary to insert all 3 rows has climbed to 3. From this point on, however the number of cumulative reads required for each new row begins to climb in alarming fashion. The total number of logical read operations needed to insert 100 rows with the same row hash is 4,950, and this figure climbs to nearly half a million for the insert of the 1000th row. While we should stress that these are *logical* reads rather than physical, and the actual number of disk I/Os will be significantly fewer than the logical reads. Despite this, the performance cost of a very non-unique Primary Index becomes abundantly clear and provides us a reasonable upper limit of 100 rows per value as the maximum degree of non-uniqueness which should be tolerated for a Non-Unique Primary Index.

ROW NBR TO BE INSERTED	ROWS TO BE READ FIRST	CUMULATIVE LOGICAL ROWS READ
1	0	0
2	1	1
3	2	3
4	3	6
5	4	10
6	5	15
7	6	21
8	7	28
9	8	36
10	9	45
20	19	190
30	29	435
40	39	780
50	49	1,225
100	99	4,950
200	199	19,900
500	499	124,750
1000	999	499,500

Figure 7-2

Multiple Column Primary Indexes

At first glance, Primary Indexes composed of multiple columns for uniqueness might be seen as an advantage. Since the index is unique, it would be "strongly selective" (returns a small number of rows) and would result in even data distribution. It is unlikely, however that all the values for a multiple column Primary Index would ever be referenced in the SQL. In this event, since the hashing algorithm cannot be used to locate rows based on partial column values, a full table scan would always result. Multiple column Primary Indexes are only of benefit therefore, if values for all the component columns are typically provided in the WHERE clause of the SQL.

Demographics

The demographics presented in the Extended Logical Data Model allow the physical implementation team to qualify all three index selection determinants and thereby substantiate index choices.

> Access Demographics are needed to identify index candidates that maximize one-AMP operations (the columns most frequently used for access by value or join).

> Distribution Demographics identify index candidates that optimize parallel processing (columns that provide good distribution).

> Volatility Demographics identify index candidates that reduce maintenance I/O (columns with stable data values).

To identify a good Primary Index candidate:

> **Distinct Values** should be a high number compared to the table count - the higher the number, the more unique. In particular, the candidate column should have enough distinct values to allow for distribution to all the AMPs.

Maximum Rows per Value should be few enough to allow all matching rows to fit within a single data block.

Maximum Rows NULL. A very large number indicates a major distribution "spike" which might eventually cause serious space consumption problems.

Typical Rows per Value. Different to an average, this statistic reflects the number of rows which have a common value most of the time.

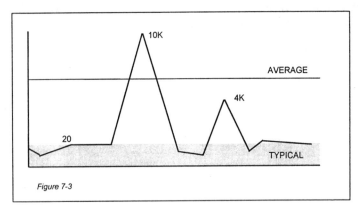

Figure 7-3

In *Figure 7-3*, most of the time there are about 20 rows per value. There is however, a massive "spike" with one value having 10,000 rows. It is significant to note that there are no values close to the average.

Conclusion

The "SWAG" method of choosing indexes, referred to in Chapter 1, is sufficiently accurate to be considered a legitimate "rule of thumb". It states that tables with a single column Primary Key (PK) should have a Unique Primary Index (UPI) based on the PK, and tables with a multiple component PK should have a Non-Unique Primary Index (NUPI) based on one of the Foreign Key (FK) components of the Primary Key. A UPI on the PK will always give excellent distribution, but if it is seldom used to access rows, a large number of full table scans will result and the over-all performance of the system may plummet. "Close enough" is almost certainly not good enough for today's mission-critical data warehouse project. While the physical implementation team will probably receive few accolades if they choose indexes wisely, they will certainly be noticed if they do not.

Practical Exercises

In order to demonstrate how the demographics are used to initially identify and eventually resolve Primary and Secondary indexes, we have provided a short series of practical exercises, the object of which is to make well-documented index choices for the six tables in *Figure 7-4*.

The method uses five simple steps and is somewhat pedestrian in nature:

Exercise 1 identifies all possible Primary Index candidates.

Exercise 2 identifies all possible Secondary Index Candidates.

Exercise 3 eliminates Primary and Secondary candidates based change rating.

Exercise 4 eliminates Non Unique Secondary Index candidates based on Value Access, Join Access and Frequency.

Exercise 5 uses Join Access statistics to make final Primary and Secondary index choices.

While the step-by-step approach is useful in explaining the principles of index selection, once the nature and purpose of each step becomes clear, all five steps may be safely to condensed into one.

In poor weather conditions, an airplane pilot is taught to rely on instruments, since human senses become unreliable when the vision is impaired. A typing student is required to type on a machine with the keys covered to avoid the temptation to "hunt and peck". In a similar way students of physical design are frequently tempted to ignore the statistics of the ELDM, and rely instead on "common sense" and some level of experience gained in a previous situation. Unfortunately the term "common sense" is frequently used to merely justify an unsubstantiated belief, and experience gained in one particular circumstance may be inappropriate in another. To deliver students from temptation therefore, the tables and columns used in the exercises are deliberately presented with generic, rather than meaningful, names. PK/FK structures are however provided.

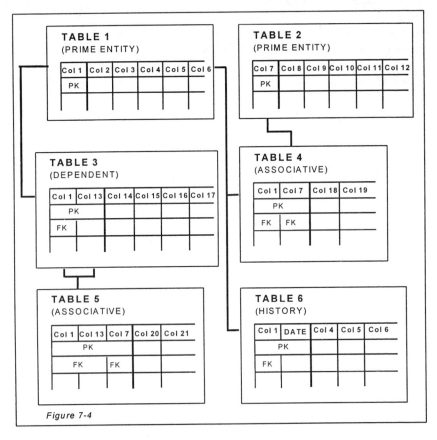

Figure 7-4

The exercises are consecutive, and each begins precisely where the previous one ended. Hence the "answers" to Exercise 1 will be found at the beginning of Exercise 2, and so on.

Students who are concerned about marking the book are strongly encouraged to work with a photo-copy of the exercise pages.

Instructions for Exercise 1

In a normal political election, there are multiple candidates running for the same office. In a similar way, for any major table in the data warehouse, there are likely to be several candidate columns competing for the honor of being selected as the Primary Index.

The objective of this exercise is to identify all possible UPI and NUPI candidates for the six tables, based on the distribution demographics provided by the ELDM. Primary Index candidates, unique or non-unique may be identified based on the following guidelines:

> All unique columns or combination of columns marked "ND" (No Duplicates) are candidates for a UPI.

> The PK of the table (single or composite) is a candidate for UPI

> Any other column with Maximum Rows per Value, Maximum Rows NULL AND Typical Rows per Value, each less than 100 is a candidate for a NUPI.

Example:

TABLE 0 (EXAMPLE)

10,000,000 ROWS

	Col 1	Col 2	Col 3	Col 4	Col 5	Col 6	
PK/FK	PK, UA						
				NN, ND			
DISTINCT VALUES	10M	1.5M	200K	10M	3M	3M	
MAXIMUM ROWS/VAL	1	12	300	1	3	100K	
MAX ROWS NULL	0	5	0	0	1.5M	0	
TYPICAL ROWS/VAL	1	7	50	1	3	9K	
PI/SI	UPI	NUPI	NUPI?	UPI			

Col 1 is the PK and becomes a candidate for a UPI.

Col 2 has Maximum Rows/Val, Maximum Rows NULL and Typical Rows/Val below the threshold of 100, and so Col 2 becomes a candidate for a NUPI.

Col 3 has a high Maximum Rows/Val. Since it qualifies for a NUPI in all other respects but one, it does little harm to mark it as a NUPI (but with a question mark).

Col 4 is marked "NN/ND" (NOT NULL, NO DUPLICATES). It is therefore unique and for that reason alone, Col 4 becomes a candidate for a UPI.

Col 5 and Col 6 have very high maximum and typical values, and so do not qualify.

Implementation for Performance

EXERCISE 1

TABLE 1 (PRIME ENTITY)

1,500,000 ROWS

	Col 1	Col 2	Col 3	Col 4	Col 5	Col 6	
PK/FK	PK, UA						
DISTINCT VALUES	1.5M	1.3M	7K	5.5K	400K	15K	
MAXIMUM ROWS/VAL	1	2	400	350	3	100	
MAX ROWS NULL	0	0	0	0	500K	0	
TYPICAL ROWS/VAL	1	1	320	300	2	90	
PI/SI							

TABLE 2 (PRIME ENTITY)

150,000 ROWS

	Col 7	Col 8	Col 9	Col 10	Col 11	Col 12	
PK/FK	PK, UA						
DISTINCT VALUES	150K	1.2K	130K	12	5	3K	
MAXIMUM ROWS/VAL	1	200	2	15K	30K	60	
MAX ROWS NULL	0	0	4K	0	0	0	
TYPICAL ROWS/VAL	1	100	1	8K	20K	50	
PI/SI							

TABLE 3 (DEPENDENT)

800,000 ROWS

	Col 1	Col 13	Col 14	Col 15	Col 16	Col 17	
PK/FK	PK						
	FK	SA			NN,ND		
DISTINCT VALUES	300K	5	16K	300K	800K	600K	
MAXIMUM ROWS/VAL	3	200K	75	2	1	2	
MAX ROWS NULL	0	0	0	390K	0	150K	
TYPICAL ROWS/VAL	1	50K	50	1	1	1	
PI/SI							

EXERCISE 1 - CONTINUED

TABLE 4 (ASSOCIATIVE)

4,500,000 ROWS

	Col 1	Col 7	Col 18	Col 19	
PK/FK	PK				
	FK	FK			
DISTINCT VALUES	2M	150K	150	15K	
MAXIMUM ROWS/VAL	5	50	25K	400	
MAX ROWS NULL	0	0	0	0	
TYPICAL ROWS/VAL	3	30	19K	350	
PI/SI					

TABLE 5 (ASSOCIATIVE)

1,500,000 ROWS

	Col 1	Col 13	Col 7	Col 20	Col 21	
PK/FK		PK				
		FK	FK			
DISTINCT VALUES		1.2M	150K	9K	1.5K	
MAXIMUM ROWS/VAL		3	15	180	1.35K	
MAX ROWS NULL		0	0	0	0	
TYPICAL ROWS/VAL		1	8	170	1K	
PI/SI						

TABLE 6 (HISTORY)

12,000,000 ROWS

	Col 1	DATE	Col 4	Col 5	Col 6	
PK/FK		PK				
	FK					
DISTINCT VALUES	3M	455	N/A	N/A	N/A	
MAXIMUM ROWS/VAL	18	18K	N/A	N/A	N/A	
MAX ROWS NULL	0	0	N/A	N/A	N/A	
TYPICAL ROWS/VAL	3	17K	N/A	N/A	N/A	
PI/SI						

| 8 | Secondary Indexes and Referential Integrity |

Tables in the data warehouse tend to be used for multiple applications by multiple departments within a single organization. The Marketing Dept., for example, may need a report which lists the Customers who placed each order *(Figure 8-1)*. The Accounting Dept. may be required to identify all the orders placed by a specific customer. Sales may be interested in the total value of parts for each order, while the Warehouse might need to know what specific parts are required to fill existing orders.

```
SELECT Order_Number FROM ORDER WHERE Customer_Number = . . . ;
SELECT Customer_Number FROM ORDER WHERE Order_Number = . . . ;
```

ORDER

ORDER NUMBER	CUSTOMER NUMBER
PK	
UPI	

```
SELECT Part_Number FROM ORDER_PART WHERE Order_Number = . . . ;
SELECT Order_Number FROM ORDER_PART WHERE Part_Number = . . . ;
```

ORDER PART

ORDER NUMBER	PART NUMBER	
PK		
FK	FK	
NUPI		

Figure 8-1

Each table in the data warehouse may have one, and only one, Primary Index. Applications which access a table using the Primary Index value will enjoy the benefits of a single AMP operation. Applications which access the table by way of other columns, would be forced into a full table scan. If these were the only available options, the physical implementation team would quickly find itself in the unenviable position of deciding which applications to favor and which to prejudice. Fortunately, it does not have to be an all-or-nothing situation, and the judicious application of Unique and Non-Unique Secondary Indexes can generally provide for all applications on a more-or-less equal basis.

Secondary Indexes provide applications using an alternate access path with better performance. Secondary Indexes may be unique (USI) or non-unique (NUSI), and may be dynamically created and dropped by the user for optimum performance, according to application requirements.

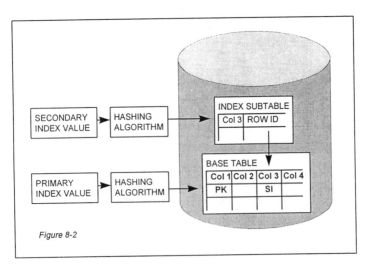

Figure 8-2

A table may have up to 64 Secondary indexes. Unlike the Primary Index, each Secondary index requires the maintenance of a separate subtable *(Figure 8-2)*, and involves additional disk storage space. Each subtable stores the base table Secondary Index Row Hash, column values and the Row IDs of the row(s) in the base table with that column value. Secondary Index subtables are automatically maintained by the RDBMS but require additional disk I/O. They cannot be accessed directly by the user, but are updated only as values in the base data tables change. Secondary Index subtables are provided with the same level of FALLBACK protection as the base table.

Unique and Non-Unique Secondary Indexes

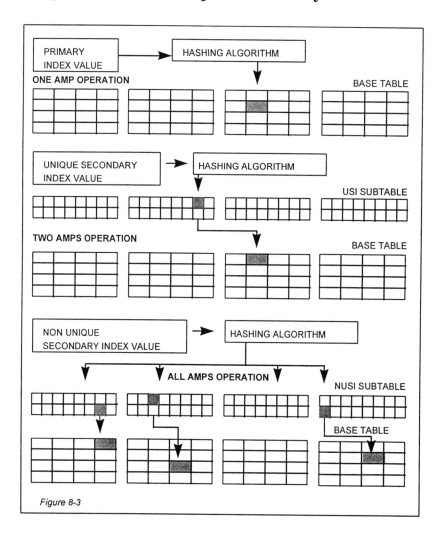

Figure 8-3

The Teradata RDBMS uses Primary and Secondary Indexes to locate rows in very different ways *(Figure 8-3)*. If it is supplied with a value for the Primary Index column in the SQL, Teradata calculates the ROW ID and locates the row directly from the Master Index and Cylinder Index.

All Secondary indexes however, require subtables. If the value of a column defined with a USI is supplied in the SQL, the hashing algorithm is used to locate the appropriate row in the USI subtable which carries the Row ID of the appropriate base table row. This Row ID is then returned to the Communications Layer, and the base table row is located using the Master Index and Cylinder Index. Location of a row using a USI subtable therefore requires the services of two (logical) AMPs and typically 2 disk I/Os.

Primary and Unique Secondary Index candidates are chosen partly on the basis of being unique or nearly unique. An SQL select based on the value of a NUSI column will generally involve multiple AMPs and will typically return a much larger number of rows. Unlike a USI subtable, which must carry one subtable row for each row in the base table, NUSI subtables normally maintain only one row per AMP per value. As a result NUSI subtables often carry a relatively small number of rows, which Teradata believes are more efficiently accessed by an all-AMPs full table scan. NUSI subtable rows contain multiple Row IDs for all the appropriate base table rows on the same AMP, which are then located in the normal fashion by reference to the AMP's Master Index and Cylinder Index.

Unique Secondary Indexes

ROW LENGTH	ROW ID		2 BYTES	SECONDARY INDEX VALUE	ROW ID BASE TABLE ROW		ROW LENGTH
	ROW HASH	UNIQUENESS VALUE			ROW HASH	UNIQUENESS VALUE	
2 BYTES	4 BYTES	4 BYTES		VARIABLE	4 BYTES	4 BYTES	2 BYTES

Figure 8-4

Figure 8-4 shows the structure of a row in a USI subtable. Like any other row in the Teradata Database, it has leading and trailing row length

fields and a Row ID composed of a 4-byte row hash of the Secondary
Index value and a 4-byte uniqueness value. The Secondary Index value
therefore becomes the Primary Index column of the subtable. Rows of a
USI subtable have only two data columns, the literal value of the
Secondary Index and the Row ID (based on the Primary Index value) of
the relevant base table row.

USI rows are distributed on Row Hash, like any other row and there is
one index subtable row for each base table row.

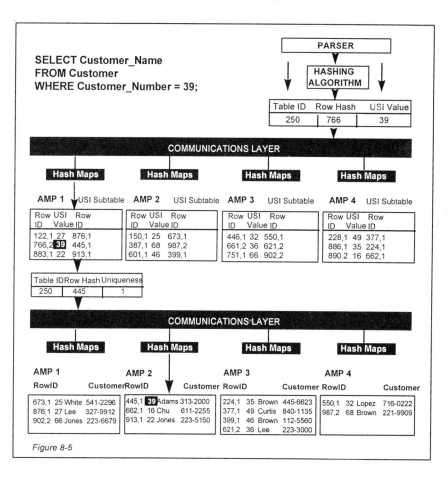

Figure 8-5

In *Figure 8-5*, the Customer Number column is defined as a Unique Secondary Index and a literal value is provided in the SQL. The 3-part message is built using the hash of the Customer Number and is sent to the Communications Layer from whence it is forwarded to the AMP responsible for the subtable row:

> The subtable row is read using the AMP's Master Index and Cylinder Index.

> The Row ID of the base table row (including the uniqueness value) is read from the subtable row.

> The base table Row ID is returned to the Communications Layer and directed, using the hash maps, to the AMP responsible for the base table row.

> Since the uniqueness value of the base table row has been provided, the row can be accessed directly using the AMP's Master Index and Cylinder Index.

Locating the base table row by Unique Secondary Index involves two AMPs and typically 2 I/Os.

Unique Indexes and Duplicate Rows

The fundamental rule of Relational Database Theory is that each row in a table must be unique. ANSI standards, on the other hand, optionally permit the storage of duplicate rows. While the Teradata Database bows to ANSI standards in "ANSI mode", it does not permit duplicate rows in its "native" mode. Enforcement of row uniqueness by the RDBMS normally involves a lengthy byte-by-byte comparison of entire rows. Each relational table must have a column, or combination of columns, designated as a Primary Key, and these values must be unique. If a table is defined with a NUPI, the need for highly expensive uniqueness checks at the full row level can be easily avoided by assigning a single or multiple-component USI on the PK columns, or by designating the column(s) as a Primary Key in the CREATE TABLE statement.

Referential Integrity

As an extended implementation of the Unique Secondary Index, the Teradata Database Version 2 optionally provides automatic referential integrity checking defined at the table and column level. In Chapter 1, we described how each table in a relational database must have a column or group of columns identified as the "Primary Key". This Primary Key must be unique, never NULL and not subject to change. Tables may also have single or multiple columns designated as "Foreign Keys". Any value in a column or columns identified as a Foreign Key must either be a valid value in the Primary Key of the same or another table, or it may be NULL. (Teradata extends this by allowing Foreign Keys to reference any unique column or combination of columns in the same, or another, table.)

If a table has a single column Primary Key, it may be identified in the CREATE table statement as a column constraint. Note that any column or columns identified as a Primary Key must also be constrained as "NOT NULL". If the identified Primary Key is also intended to be the Unique Primary Index, it may be allowed to default. For example:

```
CREATE SET TABLE Customer
    (Customer_Number          SMALLINT NOT NULL
                              PRIMARY KEY
    ,Customer_Name            VARCHAR(30)
                              NOT CASE SPECIFIC
    ,Billing_Location_Number  INTEGER
    ,Phone_Number             INTEGER);
```

Customer Number is both the Primary Key and a Unique Primary Index.

Primary Keys may also be defined at the column level:

```
CREATE SET TABLE Order_Item
    (Order_Number    INTEGER NOT NULL
    ,Item_Number     INTEGER NOT NULL
    ,Quantity        INTEGER NOT NULL
    ,Status_Code     CHAR(2)  NOT NULL
    ,PRIMARY KEY (Order_Number, Item_Number));
```

The combination of Order Number and Item Number is both PK and UPI. If the Primary Key is based on different columns than the Primary Index, both may be defined:

```
CREATE SET TABLE Order_Item
        (Order_Number      INTEGER NOT NULL
        ,Item_Number       INTEGER NOT NULL
        ,Quantity          INTEGER NOT NULL
        ,Status_Code        CHAR(2)  NOT NULL
        ,PRIMARY KEY     (Order_Number, Item_Number))
        ,PRIMARY INDEX  (Order_Number);
```

Order Number becomes a NUPI, and the combination of Order Number and Item Number is mapped to a unique secondary index.

If a unique column or combination of columns, other than the Unique Primary Index of a table, is referenced by a Foreign Key column in the same or another table, the Teradata RDBMS maintains an additional USI subtable on the column(s). In addition, for each FK column or combination of columns, which reference unique column(s) in the same or another table, Teradata creates an index subtable (FK-USI). This is similar to a USI, except that it contains only the FK value and a count of the total instances of that value occurring in the table.

While Teradata does not require that the parent table containing the PK, UPI, USI or other UNIQUE column(s) be created prior to the definition of a Foreign Key (FK) which references it, insert or update operations which attempt to insert a value into the FK column will fail if the parent table does not exist. Foreign Keys are defined at the table level.

For example:

```
CREATE SET TABLE Item
        (Item_Number        INTEGER
                            NOT NULL PRIMARY KEY
        ,Category_Number    SMALLINT
                            NOT NULL
        ,Description        VARCHAR(30) NOT NULL
                            NOT CASE SPECIFIC
```

```
,On_Hand_Quantity    INTEGER
,Daily_Rental_Amount DECIMAL (5,2) NOT NULL
,FOREIGN KEY (Category_Number)
 REFERENCES Category (Category_Number));
```

In this way no row which has an invalid value for Category Number can be inserted into the ITEM table. While it is considered an unreasonable update, the RDBMS must ensure that whenever a change occurs to the Primary Key (Category Number), the corresponding Foreign Key values for Category Number in the ITEM table remain consistent. This involves an additional read of the FK-USI in the ITEM table.

An additional option, which can be defined at either the column or table level, is the CONSTRAINT, which may be named, and is used to place value limitations on specific column values. In the following example, the Description column is defined as UNIQUE and this constraint may be provided with a unique name for data management at the domain level. Any column with a UNIQUE constraint must also be NOT NULL.

```
CREATE SET TABLE Category
        (Category_Number    SMALLINT
                            NOT NULL PRIMARY KEY
        ,Description         VARCHAR(30)
                            NOT NULL CONSTRAINT
                            Unique1 UNIQUE);
```

Non-Unique Secondary Index *(Figure 8-6)*

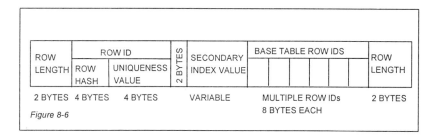

Figure 8-6

NUSI subtable rows are distributed on Row Hash, like any other row. The Row ID is calculated on the base table Secondary Index value. The NUSI subtable row differs from the USI subtable row in that it includes multiple base table Row IDs for rows on the same AMP.

The maximum size of a NUSI subtable row is 32,000 bytes, and base table Row IDs are stored in ascending order within each NUSI subtable row. A single NUSI subtable row can accommodate nearly 4,000 base table Row IDs before additional rows are required. However, multiple NUSI subtable rows are not sorted between data blocks. If multiple NUSI subtable rows exist for the same column value, all relevant subtable rows must be read every time. Maintenance of a Non-Unique Secondary Index, which contains multiple subtable rows per column value, involves additional disk I/Os and adds significantly to the cost of the transaction.

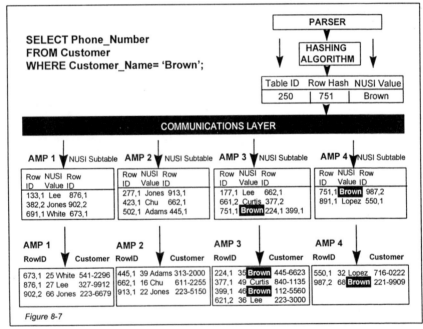

Figure 8-7

In *Figure 8-7*, Customer Number is identified as a Non-Unique Secondary Index. The 3-part message is sent to the Communications Layer and, without reference to the hash maps, is forwarded to all the

AMPs on the system. Each AMP performs a full table scan of the Secondary Index subtable, from which it determines the Row ID of each base table row with that column value. Appropriate base table rows are then accessed by Master Index and Cylinder Index and verified by the literal index value.

NUSIs are considerably less useful than Primary Indexes or USIs. The Teradata Optimizer, the Parser component responsible for ensuring that SQL instructions are executed in the most efficient manner possible may, or may not, use a NUSI depending on its selectivity. If, based on the best statistics available, the Optimizer determines that a NUSI is "weakly selective" (likely to return more than 10% of the rows in the base table), it may elect to bypass the NUSI in favor of a more efficient full table scan.

To assist it in this endeavor, the Optimizer uses statistics collected either by dynamically sampling of distribution values on one data block of one cylinder on one AMP, chosen at random, or by accessing statistics from the DD, collected as a user option. Dynamic sampling is current, often remarkably accurate, but may be seriously impacted if the data is poorly distributed amongst the AMPs. Collected statistics, on the other hand, are completely reliable when they are gathered, but they are static in nature and need to be frequently monitored to ensure they remain current. If collected statistics are available, the Optimizer will assume they are up to date and will use them, even if this subsequently results in poor performance.

In determining whether or not to use an available NUSI, the Optimizer has the capability of not only calculating the selectivity of the index for values in general, but also uses a value frequency graph to calculate the net selectivity of specific values. For example, if a NUSI has a high incidence of NULLs which are expected to return more than 10% of the base table rows, the Optimizer may choose to bypass the NUSI for SQL requests based on that particular value. On the other hand, it may choose to use the NUSI for values other than NULL, if the selectivity for that value is considered to return fewer than 10% of the rows. For that reason, a NUSI candidate should be identified as a column likely to return fewer than 10% of the rows, for the majority of distinct values, but not necessarily all.

In the production environment, to determine whether or not a NUSI is being used, the following approach is recommended:

> Create the index.
> Collect Statistics on the index (or column).
> Use EXPLAIN to see if the index is being used.

(By typing the word "EXPLAIN" on front of any SQL request, the user can cause Teradata not to fully execute an SQL request, but instead to return information about:

> The estimated cost of the query in terms of computer resources.
> A relative time estimate.
> The access method chosen by the Teradata Optimizer.

Value-Ordered NUSI

In another variation of the NUSI, in Release V2R2.1, Teradata Database announced support for the Value-Ordered NUSI. A Value-Ordered Index may be created on any single column of no more than 4 bytes in length which is defined as a numeric data type, including a non-fractional decimal. Value-Ordered NUSIs are created using the SQL "CREATE INDEX" statement with an "ORDER BY" clause, and the user has the option to specify the sort by column value or by hash.

NUSIs which are ordered by value are particularly useful for range-testing SQL constructs including:

> LESS THAN.
> GREATER THAN.
> BETWEEN, etc.

Hash-Ordered NUSIs are typically used to locate rows from a literal value supplied in the SQL. The input column value is processed by the hashing algorithm, and the result is used to locate rows with the identical hash value in the NUSI subtable. Searching a Hash-Ordered NUSI in this way is considerably more efficient than performing a full table scan of a non-ordered NUSI subtable.

"Covering" NUSIs and Aggregate Processing

If the Optimizer is able to avoid accessing the base table and resolve a query by access to a NUSI subtable alone, the index is said to be "covering". The Optimizer will always favor a "covering" NUSI where the literal value is provided in the "WHERE" clause or any other expression. It is not necessary to provide a "WHERE" clause for each individual component of a multiple column NUSI.

In the following example, the column Item Number is included in the composite NUSI, but not referenced in the select list. Despite this, the query can still be resolved from the NUSI subtable without reference to the base table and would be considered by the Optimizer for index "covering".

```
CREATE INDEX (Item_Number
            , Category_Number
            , Daily_Rental_Amount)
      ON Item;

SELECT Category_Number
     , AVG(Daily_Rental_Amount)
       FROM Item
       WHERE Item_Number > 2000
       GROUP BY Category_Number ;
```

DUAL NUSI Access

Base tables may be accessed by SQL queries which provide literal values for multiple columns, none of which is defined as a Primary or Unique Secondary Index. Where a NUSI is required on these columns, it is generally preferable to define multiple NUSIs, each on a separate column, rather than a single NUSI which spans all the columns:

```
CREATE INDEX (From_Date) ON Order;
CREATE INDEX (To_Date) ON Order;
```

SELECT Order_Number, Customer_Number
      FROM Order
      WHERE From_Date = 12/23/97
      AND To_Date = 01/02/98;

SELECT Order_Number, Customer_Number
      FROM Order
      WHERE From_Date = 12/23/97
      OR To_Date = 12/23/97;

This permits a NUSI or combination of NUSIs to be used, even if only some of the expected values are available. Even though each individual NUSI may be weakly selective, multiple weakly selective NUSIs may still be used to advantage if their aggregate selectivity is strong.

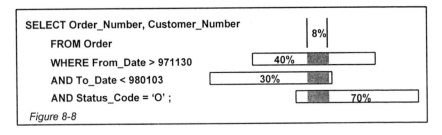

Figure 8-8

Figure 8-8 shows three weakly selective NUSIs, "From Date", "To Date" and "Status Code" which together become strongly selective and return only 8% of the rows. The aggregation of multiple weakly selective NUSIs involves a process known as "NUSI Bit Mapping".

NUSI bit mapping can only be used where the SQL operators are linked with an "AND" operative, although conditions other than equality (greater than, less than etc.) may be used. The RDBMS stores the Row IDs for all the rows selected by each NUSI, and uses a bit map to determine the Row IDs which are common to all. This procedure is considerably faster than copying, sorting, and comparing the Row ID lists, and dramatically reduces the number of base table I/Os.

In order for the Optimizer to use bit mapping:

At least two NUSI equality conditions must be specified.

The aggregate selectivity of the NUSIs must be less than 10% of the table.

While the Optimizer may choose NUSI bit mapping based on statistics derived from dynamic sampling, this is relatively rare. Collected Statistics are generally required to help the Optimizer to take full advantage of the economies of NUSI bit mapping.

Decomposable NUSIs

One of the most important, and yet perhaps least acknowledged rule of the relational database, is that columns must contain information drawn from no more than a single domain and must be decomposed to the finest level of any access. SQL constructs, such as the "LIKE" or "SUBSTR" operators generally indicate that part of the data in a column has a meaning independent of the remainder.

In *Figure 8-9*, the Column C2 initially contains an ID number composed of a sequence of alpha and numeric characters. That each component has a meaning separate and independent of the rest of the data is evidenced by the need for the following SQL:

WHERE C2 LIKE 'SAN%';

WHERE C2 LIKE 'SAN095%';

WHERE SUBSTR(C2,1,3) = 'SAN'
AND SUBSTR(C2,7,1) = 'B';

Since the data is not completely numeric, it cannot be defined as a Value Ordered Index, and the Teradata RDBMS cannot hash on a partial value. As a result, each of the above SQL constructs result in a full table scan and the NUSI on column C2 is never used.

Table A (With Decomposable Data)

	C2
	NUSI
	SAN095B6
	SAN095B9
	SAN099A1
	SFO100B2
	SFO100B6

Table A (Fully Decomposed Data)

	C2	C3	C4	C5
	NUSI	NUSI	NUSI	NUSI
	SAN	095	B	6
	SAN	095	B	9
	SAN	99	A	1
	SFO	100	B	2
	SFO	100	B	6

Figure 8-9

By decomposing the C2 value into its four constituents and defining a separate NUSI on each one, individual columns may now be accessed with an equality condition and the Optimizer may now consider the powerful option of bit-mapping:

WHERE C2 = 'SAN';

WHERE C2 = 'SAN'
AND C3 = 095;

WHERE C2='SFO'
AND C4='B';

Join Indexes

```
CREATE JOIN INDEX CustOrdIdx AS
    SELECT Customer.Customer_Number
           ,Customer_Name
           ,Order _Number
    FROM Order, LEFT JOIN Customer
    ON Order.Customer_Number = Customer.Customer_Number ;
```

ORDER

ORDER NUMBER	CUSTOMER NUMBER
PK	FK
UPI	
2002	106
2005	107
2007	107
2008	110
2011	102
2012	
2015	107

CUSTOMER

CUSTOMER NUMBER	CUSTOMER NAME
PK	FK
UPI	
102	Smith
106	Jones
107	Lee
110	Adams

JOIN INDEX   CustOrdIdx

CUSTOMER NUMBER	CUSTOMER NAME	ORDER NUMBER
FIXED PART		REPEATING PART
106	Jones	2002
107	Lee	2005
		2007
		2015
110	Adams	2008
102	Smith	2011
?	?	2012

Figure 8-10

To improve performance, and lessen the workload, when two tables are frequently joined together with an equality condition (on columns in each table with a common domain), the user has the option of creating a Join Index.

A Join Index is a subtable which stores, and dynamically maintains, the result from joining two or more tables together and avoids the need for frequent access to the base tables. A Join Index behaves more like a separate data table than an index subtable, and permits the creation of additional secondary indexes on top of the Join Index itself. However, unlike a base table, SQL cannot be used to directly select, insert, update, or delete rows from the Index. While a Join Index, like a normal index subtable, can store applicable Row IDs, these are presently unused and intended only for future development.

A Join Index subtable has two parts:

A required, "fixed part" which is unique and stored only once.

An optional "repeated part" which is populated only as needed.

In *Figure 8-9*, a JOIN INDEX is created on the CUSTOMER table and the ORDER table, based on an equality condition for the Customer Number column in each table. The OUTER JOIN on the Customer Number is used since the Customer Number is NULL for some Orders and these rows would not ordinarily be returned by a normal INNER JOIN.

Since the JOIN Index was defined with an OUTER JOIN, the following query can be resolved using the index alone without the need for access to the base table:

```
SELECT Customer_Number
       ,Customer_Name
FROM Customer;
```

Conclusion

Referential Integrity and other data constrains are automatically maintained by the RDBMS and require no additional user intervention or tuning of any kind. The Teradata Optimizer will always use Primary and Unique Secondary Indexes for access wherever possible. It will only use Non-Unique Secondary Indexes if it determines that there are more rows than data blocks and that the aggregate selectivity of the NUSIs returns fewer than 10% of the base table rows.

Multiple-column USIs are often used to avoid the excessive overhead of a duplicate row check. Composite "covering" NUSIs can substantially improve performance by avoiding access to the base tables. As a general rule however, composite NUSIs should be avoided unless the additional component(s) can be demonstrated to substantially improve the selectivity of the index. (Is the combination of City + State Code really necessary?) Multiple single-column NUSIs provide the opportunity for the Optimizer to access rows using the highly efficient bit-mapping techniques.

Secondary and Join Indexes consume disk space for their subtables and involve additional I/O for inserts, updates and deletes to base table rows. While NUSIs are often useful in decision support applications, their impact on batch maintenance and transaction processing applications should be carefully weighed. USI changes are written to the Transient Journal, while NUSI changes are journalized with the base table row.

Collected statistics help the Optimizer choose more efficient access paths, but must be constantly monitored to ensure they remain current. In addition, a periodic EXPLAIN to ensure that defined NUSIs are still being used, should be scheduled as a regular part of application maintenance. A NUSI which is maintained, but never used, becomes a highly expensive form of excess baggage.

Instructions for Exercise 2

The object of Exercise 2 is to select candidate columns for Unique and Non-Unique Secondary indexes. The exercise begins with the Primary Index candidates chosen in Exercise 1:

All Primary Index candidates are Secondary Index candidates.

Typical Rows/Value should be less than 10% of table row count for NUSIs.

A column is still a possible NUSI candidate even if it has an excessive number of rows with NULL or a single value, but otherwise the typical rows per value is small.

Example:

TABLE 0 (EXAMPLE)

10,000,000 ROWS

	Col 1	Col 2	Col 3	Col 4	Col 5	Col 6	
PK/FK	PK, UA						
				NN,ND			
DISTINCT VALUES	10M	1.5M	200K	10M	3M	3M	
MAXIMUM ROWS/VAL	1	12	300	1	3	100K	
MAX ROWS NULL	0	5	0	0	1.5M	0	
TYPICAL ROWS/VAL	1	7	50	1	3	9K	
PI/SI	UPI	NUPI	NUPI?	UPI			
	USI	NUSI	NUSI?	USI	NUSI?	NUSI?	

EXERCISE 2

1,500,000 ROWS

TABLE 1 (PRIME ENTITY)

	Col 1	Col 2	Col 3	Col 4	Col 5	Col 6	
PK/FK	PK, UA						
DISTINCT VALUES	1.5M	1.3M	7K	5.5K	400K	15K	
MAXIMUM ROWS/VAL	1	2	400	350	3	100	
MAX ROWS NULL	0	0	0	0	500K	0	
TYPICAL ROWS/VAL	1	1	320	300	2	90	
PI/SI	UPI	NUPI				NUPI	

150,000 ROWS

TABLE 2 (PRIME ENTITY)

	Col 7	Col 8	Col 9	Col 10	Col 11	Col 12	
PK/FK	PK, UA						
DISTINCT VALUES	150K	1.2K	130K	12	5	3K	
MAXIMUM ROWS/VAL	1	200	2	15K	30K	60	
MAX ROWS NULL	0	0	4K	0	0	0	
TYPICAL ROWS/VAL	1	100	1	8K	20K	50	
PI/SI	UPI	NUPI				NUPI	

800,000 ROWS

TABLE 3 (DEPENDENT)

	Col 1	Col 13	Col 14	Col 15	Col 16	Col 17	
PK/FK		PK					
	FK	SA			NN,ND		
DISTINCT VALUES	300K	5	16K	300K	800K	600K	
MAXIMUM ROWS/VAL	3	200K	75	2	1	2	
MAX ROWS NULL	0	0	0	390K	0	150K	
TYPICAL ROWS/VAL	1	50K	50	1	1	1	
PI/SI	NUPI		NUPI		UPI		

117

EXERCISE 2 - CONTINUED

TABLE 4 (ASSOCIATIVE)

4,500,000 ROWS

	Col 1	Col 7	Col 18	Col 19	
PK/FK	PK				
	FK	FK			
DISTINCT VALUES	2M	150K	150	15K	
MAXIMUM ROWS/VAL	5	50	25K	400	
MAX ROWS NULL	0	0	0	0	
TYPICAL ROWS/VAL	3	30	19K	350	
PI/SI	NUPI	NUPI			
	----UPI ----				

TABLE 5 (ASSOCIATIVE)

1,500,000 ROWS

	Col 1	Col 13	Col 7	Col 20	Col 21	
PK/FK		PK				
		FK	FK			
DISTINCT VALUES	1.2M		150K	9K	1.5K	
MAXIMUM ROWS/VAL	3		15	180	1.35K	
MAX ROWS NULL	0		0	0	0	
TYPICAL ROWS/VAL	1		8	170	1K	
PI/SI	NUPI		NUPI			
	-----UPI -----					

TABLE 6 (HISTORY)

12,000,000 ROWS

	Col 1	DATE	Col 4	Col 5	Col 6	
PK/FK	PK					
	FK					
DISTINCT VALUES	3M	455	N/A	N/A	N/A	
MAXIMUM ROWS/VAL	18	18K	N/A	N/A	N/A	
MAX ROWS NULL	0	0	N/A	N/A	N/A	
TYPICAL ROWS/VAL	3	17K	N/A	N/A	N/A	
PI/SI	NUPI					
	---UPI---					

9 | Changing Index Values

SQL is a fourth generation (4GL) computer language. Unlike all previous languages, the user is no longer required to tell the computer, step-by-step, how to execute a task. In SQL, the user issues a high-level request to select, insert, update and delete rows and the RDBMS takes care of the rest. As a result, the user becomes heavily insulated against the internal operations performed by the RDBMS, and may find it difficult to properly assess the true cost and complexity of the operation involved. Even the RDBMS cannot accurately predict the amount of elapsed time needed to fulfill a request, since it depends heavily on the mechanical efficiency of the individual hardware components of the system and the current level of other user competition for the limited system resources available.

In searching for a reliable yard-stick needed to measure and compare the relative performance costs of proposed transactions, we are logically directed towards the disk, as the performance limiting factor for the entire system. Even a simple count of the physical I/O operations needed to complete each task becomes complicated by the limited availability of shared resources and the happenstance of any particular data, or index block, being resident in memory at any specific moment in time.

While the accurate calculation of the *physical* I/Os required for a specific operation remains necessarily complex, it is comparatively simple to count *logical* disk I/Os (ignoring the possibility of data in cache) as a relative measure of transaction cost.

For the purposes of this exercise, consider:

> Join Indexes as additional tables, with the join condition as the Unique Primary Index.

> Primary Keys (which are not the Unique Primary Index) as additional USIs.

Foreign Keys as additional USIs.

Value-Ordered Indexes as NUSIs.

INSERT and DELETE operations

INSERT and DELETE OPERATIONS

	DATA ROW	EACH USI	EACH NUSI
READ BLOCK			
WRITE TRANSIENT JOURNAL			
WRITE NEW BLOCK			
WRITE CYLINDER INDEX			

Figure 9-1

In *Figure* 9-1, we can clearly see that each insert or delete of a data row involves 1 READ and 3 WRITE *logical* disk I/O operations. Any insert or delete of a data row must be reflected in any relevant Secondary Index subtables. As a result, all USI subtables of the affected base table must also be subject to the same insert or delete as the base table and bear a similar cost of 1 READ and 3 WRITE logical disk I/Os.

NUSI subtables occur on the same AMP as the base table rows to which they refer. Changes to base table rows and NUSI subtables are recorded with a single entry into the Transient Journal. Consequently, changes to NUSI subtable rows do not require a separate disk access to write the Transient Journal and their maintenance requires a total of 1 READ and only 2 WRITE logical disk I/Os.

We can, in consequence, deduce a simple formula for calculating the relative cost in logical disk I/Os for update and delete operations on a single base table row:

Total Data I/Os per row =
4 + 4 * (number of USIs) + 3 * (number of NUSIs)

Double for FALLBACK.

UPDATE Operations

The number of logical disk I/Os needed to update base tables rows is identical to the number required for insert and delete operations *(Figure 9-2)* and this update may or may not affect Secondary Index subtables.

UPDATE OPERATIONS

	DATA ROW	EACH USI	EACH NUSI
READ DATA / INDEX BLOCK	■	■	■
WRITE TRANSIENT JOURNAL	■	■	
WRITE NEW DATA / INDEX BLOCK	■	■	■
WRITE CYLINDER INDEX	■	■	■
READ NEW INDEX BLOCK		■	■
WRITE TRANSIENT JOURNAL		■	
WRITE NEW INDEX BLOCK		■	■
WRITE CYLINDER INDEX		■	■

Figure 9-2

If the column values being changed include any defined as a Secondary Index , any pre-existing Secondary Index subtable rows for that column value must be deleted and new rows, reflecting the revised value, inserted. This requires a 2 READ I/Os and 6 WRITE I/Os for each USI subtable and 2 READ I/Os and 4 WRITE I/Os for each NUSI subtable affected:

> **Total Data I/Os per row =**
> **4 + (8 * (number of USIs *changed*)) +**
> **(6 * (number of NUSIs *changed*))**
>
> **Double for FALLBACK.**

Primary Index Value UPDATE

Any change to the Primary Index value of a base table row requires the computation of a new Row ID and a relocation of the row, probably to another AMP. This will necessarily require a similar change to each Secondary Index subtable row which references the base table row. Thus, an update of the Primary Index column of a row is equivalent to:

A DELETE of the old base table row.

An INSERT of the new base table row.

A DELETE of each referencing USI row.

An INSERT of a new USI row.

A DELETE and INSERT or UPDATE of each relevant NUSI row.

Total Data I/Os per row =
8 + 8 * (number of USIs) + 6 * (number of NUSIs)
Double for FALLBACK

Referential Integrity I/O

Whenever the value of a column defined as the PK of a table is changed, the FK index of every referenced table must be read to ensure that the change does not result in orphan or "dangling" FK values. Equally if the value of a column defined as a Foreign Key is changed, the referenced PK column must be read to ensure that the new FK value remains valid.

If automatic referential integrity is implemented therefore, one or more I/Os must be added to the previously derived formulas for each change of a PK or FK value, according to the table in *(Figure 9-3)*.

Thus, where automatic referential integrity is implemented:

Total I/Os = Total Data I/Os + Total Referential I/Os

INSERT	FOR EACH PK USI	NO ADDITIONAL I/Os
	FOR EACH FK USI	1 I/O FOR REFERENCED PK TABLE
DELETE	FOR EACH PK USI	1 I/O FOR EACH REFERENCED FK
	FOR EACH FK USI	NO ADDITIONAL I/Os
UPDATE	FOR EACH PK USI CHANGED	1 I/O FOR EACH REFERENCED FK
	FOR EACH FK USI CHANGED	1 I/O FOR REFERENCED PK TABLE
PI VALUE UPDATE	FOR EACH PK USI	1 I/O FOR EACH REFERENCED FK
	FOR EACH FK USI	1 I/O FOR REFERENCED PK TABLE

Figure 9-3

Permanent Journal I/O

In addition to Unique and Non-Unique Secondary Indexes and automatic referential integrity, the user may optionally have decided to take advantage of the supplemental transaction and data protection afforded by before-image or after-image Permanent Journals (PJ). If the base table is FALLBACK, the Permanent Journal tables are also FALLBACK. If the base table is not FALLBACK-protected, the user may choose to maintain single or dual copies of the journal(s).

Whenever insert, update or delete operations are performed against the base table data rows, the changes must be reflected in the PJ Tables, not only for the data rows, but for the USI subtables as well. Changes to NUSI columns involve no additional disk I/Os.

BEFORE IMAGE	AFTER IMAGE	PJ I/O COUNT
NONE	NONE	0
NONE	SINGLE	2
SINGLE	NONE	2
SINGLE	SINGLE	4
NONE	DUAL OR FALLBACK	4
DUAL OR FALLBACK	NONE	4
SINGLE	DUAL OR FALLBACK	6
DUAL OR FALLBACK	SINGLE	6
DUAL OR FALLBACK	DUAL OR FALLBACK	8

Figure 9-4

The total number of logical disk I/Os required for each combination of PJ tables defined, is provided in *Figure 9-4*. We may therefore deduce a formula for determining the total number of logical I/Os for PJ tables as:

INSERT: Total PJ I/O = Count + (#USIS * Count)

DELETE: Total PJ I/O = Count + (#USIs * Count)

UPDATE: Total PJ I/O = Count + (#USIS changed * Count * 2)

Changes to PI columns double the counts.

Total I/O = Total Data I/O + Total Referential I/O + Total PJ I/O

Conclusion

The huge amounts of Data Cache RAM available on all Teradata supported Version 2 hardware systems ensures that the number of physical disk I/Os necessary to process write transactions against tables is a small fraction of the logical disk I/Os. Nevertheless, from the formulas derived in this Chapter, it becomes clear that the update of Primary Index column values should be avoided. Secondary Indexes and automatic Referential Integrity on *volatile* columns are very expensive, and the costs of such changes should be carefully weighed against the benefits.

Instructions for Exercise 3

Having identified all the possible Primary and Secondary Index Candidates, the remaining exercises in this series are concerned with eliminating those which fail to qualify on the basis of:

> Change Rating Statistics.
>
> Value Access Statistics.
>
> Join Access Statistics.

The objective of Exercise 3 is to eliminate remaining Primary and Secondary Index candidates, based on how often the values of a candidate column change. The Change Rating statistics were discussed in Chapter 2 and were assigned on a scale of 0 to 9, on the following basis:

> 0 = column values never change.
>
> 1 = column changes no more than once in its lifetime.
>
> 2 = column changes up to twice in its lifetime.
>
> 5 = column values change about 50% of the time.
>
> 9 = column changes with every write operation, etc.

The rules of the relational database state that columns marked "PK" must never change. Historical data columns should logically not be subject to change. Hence PK columns and historical data columns should always have a Change Rating of zero.

Data that does not normally change should have a Change Rating of 1, while update columns will always have a Change Rating of 9.

The cost of updating Primary Index columns is always excessive, and the cost of updating Secondary Indexes might be high. Primary Indexes should therefore be based on columns with very stable data values (maximum Change Rating of 2) and Change rating for Secondary Index candidates should never exceed a value of 5.

In Exercise 3 therefore, we must eliminate Primary Index candidates with a Change Rating greater than 2, and Secondary Index Candidates with a Change Rating higher than 5.

In the example below, Col 2 was eliminated as a Primary Index candidate, since it has a Change Rating greater than 2.

Example:

TABLE 0 (EXAMPLE)

10,000,000 ROWS

	Col 1	Col 2	Col 3	Col 4	Col 5	Col 6	
PK/FK	PK, UA						
				NN,ND			
DISTINCT VALUES	10M	1.5M	200K	10M	3M	3M	
MAXIMUM ROWS/VAL	1	12	300	1	3	100K	
MAX ROWS NULL	0	5	0	0	1.5M	0	
TYPICAL ROWS/VAL	1	7	50	1	3	9K	
CHANGE RATING	0	3	2	1	1	3	
PI/SI	UPI	NUPI	NUPI?	UPI			
	USI	NUSI	NUSI?	USI	NUSI?	NUSI?	

Implementation for Performance

EXERCISE 3

TABLE 1 (PRIME ENTITY)

1,500,000 ROWS

	Col 1	Col 2	Col 3	Col 4	Col 5	Col 6	
PK/FK	PK, UA						
DISTINCT VALUES	1.5M	1.3M	7K	5.5K	400K	15K	
MAXIMUM ROWS/VAL	1	2	400	350	3	100	
MAX ROWS NULL	0	0	0	0	500K	0	
TYPICAL ROWS/VAL	1	1	320	300	2	90	
CHANGE RATING	0	3	2	1	1	1	
PI/SI	UPI	NUPI				NUPI	
	USI	NUSI	NUSI	NUSI		NUSI	

TABLE 2 (PRIME ENTITY)

150,000 ROWS

	Col 7	Col 8	Col 9	Col 10	Col 11	Col 12	
PK/FK	PK, UA						
DISTINCT VALUES	150K	1.2K	130K	12	5	3K	
MAXIMUM ROWS/VAL	1	200	2	15K	30K	60	
MAX ROWS NULL	0	0	4K	0	0	0	
TYPICAL ROWS/VAL	1	100	1	8K	20K	50	
CHANGE RATING	0	0	9	1	2	0	
PI/SI	UPI	NUPI				NUPI	
	USI	NUSI	NUSI	NUSI?		NUSI	

TABLE 3 (DEPENDENT)

800,000 ROWS

	Col 1	Col 13	Col 14	Col 15	Col 16	Col 17	
PK/FK		PK					
	FK	SA			NN,ND		
DISTINCT VALUES	300K	5	16K	300K	800K	600K	
MAXIMUM ROWS/VAL	3	200K	75	2	1	2	
MAX ROWS NULL	0	0	0	390K	0	150K	
TYPICAL ROWS/VAL	1	50K	50	1	1	1	
CHANGE RATING	0	0	3	1	0	1	
PI/SI	NUPI		NUPI		UPI		
	NUSI	NUSI	NUSI	NUSI?	USI	NUSI?	
	---USI ---						

127

EXERCISE 3

TABLE 1 (PRIME ENTITY)

1,500,000 ROWS

	Col 1	Col 2	Col 3	Col 4	Col 5	Col 6	
PK/FK	PK, UA						
DISTINCT VALUES	1.5M	1.3M	7K	5.5K	400K	15K	
MAXIMUM ROWS/VAL	1	2	400	350	3	100	
MAX ROWS NULL	0	0	0	0	500K	0	
TYPICAL ROWS/VAL	1	1	320	300	2	90	
CHANGE RATING	0	3	2	1	1	1	
PI/SI	UPI	NUPI				NUPI	
	USI	NUSI	NUSI	NUSI		NUSI	

TABLE 2 (PRIME ENTITY)

150,000 ROWS

	Col 7	Col 8	Col 9	Col 10	Col 11	Col 12	
PK/FK	PK, UA						
DISTINCT VALUES	150K	1.2K	130K	12	5	3K	
MAXIMUM ROWS/VAL	1	200	2	15K	30K	60	
MAX ROWS NULL	0	0	4K	0	0	0	
TYPICAL ROWS/VAL	1	100	1	8K	20K	50	
CHANGE RATING	0	0	9	1	2	0	
PI/SI	UPI	NUPI				NUPI	
	USI	NUSI	NUSI	NUSI?		NUSI	

TABLE 3 (DEPENDENT)

800,000 ROWS

	Col 1	Col 13	Col 14	Col 15	Col 16	Col 17	
PK/FK		PK					
	FK	SA			NN,ND		
DISTINCT VALUES	300K	5	16K	300K	800K	600K	
MAXIMUM ROWS/VAL	3	200K	75	2	1	2	
MAX ROWS NULL	0	0	0	390K	0	150K	
TYPICAL ROWS/VAL	1	50K	50	1	1	1	
CHANGE RATING	0	0	3	1	0	1	
PI/SI	NUPI		NUPI		UPI		
	NUSI	NUSI	NUSI	NUSI?	USI	NUSI?	
	--- USI ---						

10	# Domains, Data Types and Indexes

There is a strong kinship between domains, a relational concept rarely implemented in a physical environment, and indexes which play no part in the logical data model. While this association might, on the face of it, appear obvious, it is nevertheless frequently misunderstood.

Domains

Each column of every table must fall within a sub-group of columns known as a "Domain". For example, the column Customer Number appears in the Customer, Location and Order tables. If the values in both columns mean the same real world person, place, thing or idea (in this case a numeric identification for a Customer), they are said to be in the same domain. Columns which fall within the same domain should have similar names. Imagine the confusion when the Sales Department refers to a customer as an "Account", the Legal Department refers to the same customer as a "Client" and the Bookkeeping also use the term "Account" to describe a page in a ledger.

A good understanding of domains can help to alleviate the confusion caused by homonyms - words which sound the same but mean different things, and synonyms - words which sound different, but mean the same thing.

Each domain must have a name, a data type and a description.

As we briefly mentioned in Chapter 1, if two columns can be logically added, subtracted or compared, they fall within the same domain.

Using *Figure 10-1* as an example:

> Location Number and Billing Location Number can be logically compared to determine whether the bill is to be sent to the same location as the shipment. These columns fall within the same domain Location Number, which is numeric.

CATEGORY

Category_Number	(1)
Description	(2)

LOCATION

Location_Number	(5)
Customer_Number	(3)
Department	(11)
Street	(12)
City	(13)
State_Code	(14)
Zip	(15)
Country_Code	(16)

USER

UserID	(21)

CUSTOMER

Customer_Number	(3)
Customer_Name	(4)
Billing_Location_Number	(5)
Phone_Number	(6)

ORDER

Customer_Number	(3)
Location_Number	(5)
From Date	(18)
To Date	(18)
Status_Code	(19)
Update Date	(18)
Update Time	(20)
User ID	(21)

ITEM

Item_Number	(7)
Category_Number	(1)
Description	(8)
On Hand Quantity	(9)
Daily Rental Amount	(10)

ORDER ITEM

Order_Number	(17)
Item_Number	(7)
Quantity	(9)
Status_Code	(19)
Update Date	(18)
Update Time	(20)
User ID	(21)

DOMAIN	DESCRIPTION	DATA TYPE
(1) Category Number	Category ID	SMALLINT
(2) Category Description	Category Description	CV 30
(3) Customer Number	Customer ID	SMALLINT
(4) Customer Name	Customer Name	CV 30
(5) Location Number	Location ID	INTEGER
(6) Phone Number	Phone Number	INTEGER
(7) Item Number	Item ID	INTEGER
(8) Item Description	Item Description	CV 30
(9) Quantity	Quantity	INTEGER
(10) US $ Amount	US $ Amount	DECIMAL(10,2)
(11) Location Department	Location Department	CV 30
(12) Street Address	Street Address	CV 30
(13) City	City	CV 25
(14) State Code	State Code	CF2
(15) Zip Code	Postal Code	INTEGER
(16) Country Code	Country Code	CF3
(17) Order Number	Order ID	INTEGER
(18) Date	Date	DATE
(19) Status Code	Status Code	CF2
(20) Time	Time	FLOAT
(21) UserID	UserID	CF3

Figure 10-1

Although both columns have identical names, to compare the "Description" column in the Category table with "Description" in the Item table makes little logical sense. These columns are therefore in different domains.

"From Date", "To Date" and "Update Date" can be logically compared to determine the how soon in advance of shipment an order was processed. Since all columns which involve calendar dates may be logically compared, they each fall into a general domain called "Date". Other general domains include "Quantity", "Time" and "US$ Amount".

Not only do domains define the logical rules of access to data in relational tables, they may also be used as the basis of an easily understandable and predictable column naming convention. Each column should be called by the underlying domain name, qualified as necessary to avoid ambiguity. Thus the columns "To Date", "From Date" and "Update Date" all have the recognizable domain name of "Date", appropriately qualified for clarity.

Indexes

Although Dr. Edgar Codd once praised the Teradata Database as the most truly relational of all relational database vendors (primarily because of Teradata's insistence upon row uniqueness in its native mode), even the Teradata RDBMS does not directly recognize the concept of domains. Like all RDBMS vendors, NCR/Teradata is more concerned with physical access to data rather than maintaining the aesthetic purity of the relational model. Teradata supports five access methods:

1. Unique Primary Index - the most efficient access method, which returns a single row and involves one AMP, typically one disk I/O and no spool file.

2. Non-Unique Primary Index - very efficient if the number of rows per value is less than 100. While NUPI access may return multiple rows, it involves one AMP, typically one disk I/O, but may require a spool file.

3. Unique Secondary Index - also an extremely efficient access method. It returns a single row, never involves a spool file but requires the services of two AMPs and typically two disk I/Os.

4. Non-Unique Secondary Index - efficient only if the number of rows accessed is a small percentage of the total data rows in the table. NUSI access is always an all-AMPs operation which requires multiple disk I/Os and may require a spool file.

5. Full Table Scan - surprisingly efficient with the Teradata Database since each data block is touched only once. FTS is an all-AMPs operation which requires one disk I/O for each data block and might require a spool file.

		COL2		
		USI	NUSI	NOT INDEXED
COL 1	UPI	COL 1	COL 1	COL 1
	NUPI	Unique index preferred even though it may require 2-AMPs	COL 1	COL 1
	USI	EITHER	COL 1	COL 1
	NUSI	COL 2	Depends on selectivity, Col 1+ Col 2, Bit Map or FTS	Depends on selectivity of index
	NOT INDEXED	COL 2	Depends on selectivity of index	FTS

Figure 10-2

The Optimizer dynamically chooses the fastest access method based on the best statistical information available. *Figure 10-2* shows the choices typically made by the Optimizer when accessing a table based on literal values provided for two different columns in the SQL. Collected Statistics help the Optimizer make good decisions.

SELECT ... WHERE Col_1 = value AND Col_2 = value;

Search by Partial Value

A relational rule states that column values must not be decomposable. In other words, if rows of a table are ever accessed by supplying a partial column value in the SQL, the data in the column is not decomposed to its finest level. For example, if the data in the Phone Number column includes the area code, and the row is *ever* accessed by the area code value alone, this indicates the column contains data from multiple domains and forces the Optimizer into a full table scan. If the area code and phone number were maintained separately, in different columns, the Optimizer will almost certainly be able to choose a more efficient access method.

Use of SQL constructs such as "LIKE", "INDEX" and "SUBSTR" therefore become a strong indication of decomposable data and should be treated with some suspicion. Data storage and display are, after all, different issues.

Numeric to Character Data Conversions

Whenever it is called upon to compare values in columns with different data types, the Teradata RDBMS will perform a data conversion of one or both columns (except byte data types) automatically and in uncomplaining fashion. Data conversion is however an expensive operation for any computer and is generally unnecessary if data types are implemented at the domain level.

FROM	TO		
	NUMERIC	DATE	CHARACTER
NUMERIC	NUMERIC	NUMERIC	NUMERIC
DATE	NUMERIC	DATE	DATE
CHARACTER	NUMERIC	DATE	CHARACTER

Figure 10-3

Operands must be of the same data type to be compared. If operand data types differ, internal conversion becomes necessary (*Figure 10-3*).

Character data is compared using the collating sequence of the user's server. Unequal length character strings are converted by right padding the shorter one with blanks. Numeric values are converted to the same underlying representation.

Considerably more expensive however is the conversion of character data to numeric. This is dramatically demonstrated by the output from two following EXPLAIN operations, which submit almost identical SQL, but result in very different performance.

ORDER

Order Number	Location Number	Customer Number	From Date	To Date	Status Code	Update Date	Update Time	User ID
UPI								
2002 2005 2007								

CHAR(10)

Figure 10-4

The ORDER table shown in *Figure 10-4* has a Primary Index of Order Number which is defined as a CHARACTER data type. In this first example, the Order Number is correctly specified in the SQL as a character literal:

EXPLAIN SELECT * FROM Order WHERE Order_Number = '2002';

Explanation

1) First, we do a single-AMP RETRIEVE step from Rents.Order by way of the unique primary index "Rents.Order_Number = '2002'" with no residual conditions. The estimated time for this step is 0.04 seconds.
=>The row is sent directly back to the user as the result of statement 1. The total estimated time is 0.04 seconds.

This is a single AMP request using the Unique Primary Index and results in a relative time estimate of .04 seconds. (The total estimated time output by the Optimizer does not necessarily reflect the true elapsed time of the query, but is used only to compare the relative performance of alternate access plans.)

The second example is identical to the first, except that the value for Order Number is quoted as numeric instead of character. Since the Primary Index of the Order table *(Figure 10-4)* is defined as a character data type, the Optimizer is forced to convert both values into a common FLOAT data type. The query gives the same result as the example above, but takes nearly *100 times as long*:

EXPLAIN
SELECT * FROM Order WHERE Order_Number = 2002;

Explanation

1) First, we lock Rents.Order for read.
2) Next, we do an all-AMPs RETRIEVE step from Rents.Order by way of an all-rows scan with a condition of ("Rents.Order. Order_Number (FLOAT, FORMAT '-9.99999999999999E-999'))= (2002)') into Spool 1, which is built locally on the AMPs. The size of Spool 1 is estimated to be 2,218 rows. The estimated time for this step is 3.93 seconds.
3) Finally, we send out an END TRANSACTION step to all AMPs involved in processing the request.
=>The contents of Spool 1 are sent back to the user as the result of statement 1.
The total estimated time is 3.93 seconds.

The reason for this major difference in performance lies in the inability of the Optimizer to reliably predict the form of the valid character literal from a given numeric value. For example, the following character literals all evaluate to the numeric value of 2002:

> '2002'
> '02002'
> '002002'
> '+02002'
> '2002.0' etc.

This particular problem can be easily avoided, performance improved and valuable disk space saved, if columns containing numeric character data are defined as numeric data types and are strictly controlled at the domain level. Different data types for the same numeric value do not produce the same result from the hashing algorithm. For example:

> The Row Hash of 99 (BYTEINT)
>> is NOT equal to the Row Hash of 99 (SMALLINT).
>> is NOT equal to the Row Hash of 99 (INTEGER).
>> is NOT equal to the Row Hash of 99 (DECIMAL).
>> is NOT equal to the Row Hash of 99 (FLOAT).
>> is NOT equal to the...   , etc.

To avoid unnecessary data conversions, columns which belong in the same domain throughout the data warehouse, should be defined with an identical data type.

Conclusion

All data conversions are expensive, some more so than others. However with proper control of data types at the domain level, and by ensuring that columns only contain data from a single domain, most costly conversions and many full table scans can be avoided. After all, if the system is required to perform an excessive number of data conversions or full table scans, it is a clear indication that the concept of domains is not well understood.

11 | Sizing the Data Warehouse

One of the most important functions of the physical implementation team is to ensure that the physical hardware of the data warehouse system has enough capacity, not only to support current needs, but sufficient for at least the next two years. The major portion of any data warehouse application involves the storage of historical data. History is probably unique in that it is available in virtually unlimited supply. Each day more and more becomes available, and the greater the sample, the more accurate the results. Success tends to feed upon itself, and it is inevitable that, when the supply of historical data exceeds the physical capacity of the system to store it, the Sales and Marketing Departments will resist all efforts to archive outdated information, and opt instead for expanding the disk capacity.

In addition to the raw data stored, the RDBMS requires a certain amount of space for row and table overhead. Calculating the disk capacity used to store a table on a pre-existing system, including the overhead, requires little more than a simple SQL query of the Data Dictionary, which can then be adjusted by the anticipated rate of growth:

```
SELECT SUM(CurrentPerm)
       FROM DBC.TableSize
       WHERE DatabaseName = 'Rents'
       AND TableName = 'Order';
```

In the absence of this current information, the physical implementation team needs to be familiar with the exact nature of the RDBMS overhead in order to make a reasonably precise projection.

Data Rows

Data rows are variable in length and may accommodate up to 32,000 bytes of raw data. Columns in a data row are not necessarily stored in the order specified in the CREATE TABLE statement, although this has no effect on the default order of output.

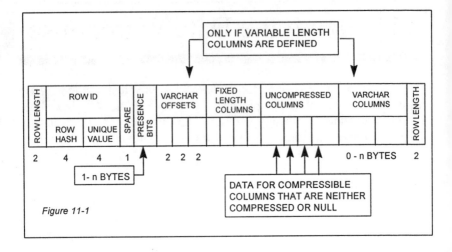

Figure 11-1

As *Figure 11-1* shows, the fixed-length columns are stored first in the data row, followed by uncompressed columns and columns defined with variable length data. In addition to the leading and trailing row length fields and the Row ID, each data row has:

> One spare byte (for future use).
> At least one byte of presence bits.
> Multiple two-byte offset fields (for each column of variable length data + 1).

Presence Bits

Presence bits are contained within a data row in order to "flag" columns which are NULL (contain no data), and columns which are compressed to NULL (COMPRESSIBLE) based on a single, constant value defined in the SQL CREATE TABLE statement.

While the RDBMS requires no disk space to record the value of columns which are NULL, each NULLABLE column requires a presence bit to indicate whether it is, in fact NULL. If a column is both NULLABLE and COMPRESSIBLE, two presence bits are required. Presence bits are always written to the byte boundary and by default, each row carries one byte, which permits eight presence bits at no additional overhead. If more are required, the RDBMS expands the row by whole bytes to accommodate them. The bit settings are as follows:

NULLABLE

One bit for every NULLABLE column *(Figure 11-2)*.

1 = Corresponding column value is present.

0 = Corresponding column value is NULL.

COMPRESSIBLE

Valid only for fixed length columns.

One bit for each COMPRESSIBLE column *(Figure 11-2)*.

1 = Non Compress value is present.

0 = Column has been compressed.

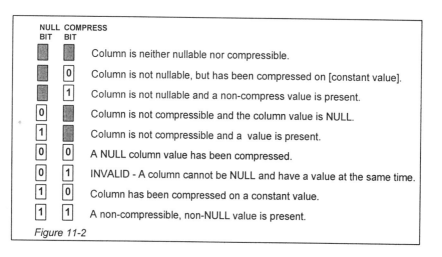

Figure 11-2

NULL and COMPRESS

All fixed length columns in a table may be compressed to NULL value (NULLABLE), unless expressly defined as "NOT NULL". In addition, NULLABLE columns may be compressed to zero bytes based on one specific value. In the example below:

```
CREATE TABLE Location
(Location_Number    INTEGER
,Street              CHAR(30) NOT NULL
,City                CHAR(30) COMPRESS  'Los Angeles'
,State_Code          CHAR(2)
. . . . . . ;
```

"Street" is fixed length, but may not carry a NULL value.

"City" is NULLABLE and may be compressed to zero bytes if it carries the (frequently occurring) value of "Los Angeles".

"State Code" may be compressed to zero bytes if it is NULL.

While Unique Primary Index columns may contain a single NULL, and a Non-Unique Primary Index column may contain multiple NULLs (treated as if NULLs were a value), the Primary KEY is not permitted to be NULL. Hence Primary Key columns, and all columns marked "NN" (NO NULLS) in the logical data model, should be declared as "NOT NULL" in the CREATE TABLE statement.

The default for all columns is NULLABLE and NOT COMPRESSIBLE, and in order for the RDBMS to locate compressible data, it must compute its location in the row. Compression saves disk space but costs computational overhead. While the additional overhead is generally small, the COMPRESS option should only be used where at least 20% of the rows qualify, and where the NULL column values are seldom subject to change. Despite this, adding a new column to a table requires the RDBMS to expand each and every pre-existing row in the table, if the new column is defined as "NOT NULL", or if there are no spare presence bits available in the row to accommodate it. Equally dropping a previously populated column from a table is likely to involve a complete re-write of every row in the table.

Variable Column Offsets

The Offset Array records the starting location of each column defined with a variable-length data type. The length of each column is determined by subtracting its starting location from the starting location of the next column. Definition of variable length columns requires one additional 2 byte offset field, which points to the last byte of the final variable length column.

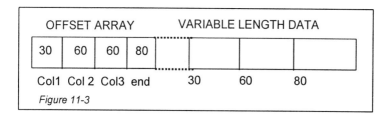

Figure 11-3

Data Types

In computing the length of a row, it is important to make the calculation based, not on the length of the output, but rather on the internal disk storage requirements. While the printed output of an integer value may be up to 11 bytes in length, the Teradata Database requires only 4 bytes of internal storage. Even the largest number likely to be encountered in the "real" universe can be stored in 8 bytes as a FLOAT data type.

Figure 11-4 lists the data types supported by Teradata with the disk storage length for each.

DATA TYPE	RANGE OF VALUES FROM	TO	STORAGE LENGTH
BYTEINT	-128	+127	1 byte whole number
SMALLINT	-32,768	+32,767	2 byte whole number
INTEGER	-2,147,438,648	+2,147,483,647	4 byte whole number
DECIMAL(m,n) NUMERIC(m,n)	Maximum 18 significant digits		1-2 digits = 1 byte 3-4 digits = 2 bytes 5-9 digits = 4 bytes 10 -15 digits = 8 bytes
REAL DOUBLE PRECISION FLOAT(n) FLOAT	IEE Floating Point Same as FLOAT.		A value in sign/ magnitude form. Exponent from *E-308 to E+307* *8-bytes*
DATE	Special type of INTEGER		4 Bytes FORMAT YYMMDD
CHAR(n)	Fixed length character		
VARCHAR(n)	Variable length character		
LONG VARCHAR	Variable length character		Maximum 32,000 bytes
BYTE	Fixed length binary		
VARBYTE	Variable length binary		
GRAPHIC	Fixed length 2-byte graphic		
VARGRAPHIC	Variable length 2-byte graphic		

Figure 11-4

Calculating Row Size

Figure 11-5 provides a useful form for determining row size and, as an example of its use, calculates the number of bytes needed to store a single row of the LOCATION table. For variable length columns the row size should include the *maximum* number of bytes needed, rather than the average.

LOCATION

LOCATION NUMBER	CUSTOMER NUMBER	DEPARTMENT	STREET	CITY	STATE CODE	ZIP	COUNTRY CODE
PK,SA	FK		NN	NN			NN
INT	SMALLINT	CV30	CV30	CV25	CF2	INT	CF3

TABLE NAME *LOCATION*

VARIABLE DATA DETAIL

VARCHAR / VARBYTE

COLUMN NAME	TYPE	MAX	AVG
Department	CV	30	10
Street	CV	30	25
City	CV	25	20

VARGRAPHIC

COLUMN NAME	TYPE	MAX (*2)	AVG (*2)
	SUM (a) =		55

DATA TYPE	NUMBER OF COLS	SIZING FACTOR	TOTAL
BYTEINT		1 =	
SMALLINT	1	2 =	2
INTEGER	2	4 =	8
DATE		4 =	
FLOAT		8 =	
DEC 1-2		1 =	
3-4		2 =	
5-9		4 =	
10-18		8 =	
CHAR(n)		SUM (n)	5
BYTE (m)		SUM (m)	
GRAPHIC ___ *2 (o)		SUM (o)	
Variable		SUM (a)	55
	LOGICAL SIZE		
	OVERHEAD	=	14
VARIABLE COLUMNS (3 * 2)			6
FINAL VARCHAR OFFSET			2
_3_ COMPRESS COLS			
___ NULLABLE COLS			
_3_ / 8 (Quotient only)			0
	PHYSICAL SIZE		92

SUM (a) = SUM of the AVERAGE number of bytes expected for variable length columns
Figure 11-5

Tables

The Teradata Database supports a number of options which result in variable length rows and variable length data blocks:

> COMPRESS.
> VARCHAR.
> LONG VARCHAR.
> VARBYTE.
> VARGRAPHIC.

While these features provide maximum flexibility, they also make accurate space estimation for tables and their indexes more difficult.

In addition to its data rows, each table has a subtable known as a "Table Header", which contains one row per AMP. Table Headers are written to the sector boundary, and hence must be at least 512 bytes in length but seldom more than 1024.

The Table Header *(Figure 11-6)* contains all the information needed by the RDBMS including:

> Database and table names.
>
> The Database ID.
>
> Creation Date and Permanent Journal
> options.
>
> Primary and Secondary Index descriptors.
>
> Utility locks for the FastLoad and Archive/Recovery
> utilities.
>
> Base table column information, etc.

STANDARD ROW HEADER	
LENGTH, ROW ID, PRESENCE/ SPARE BYTES	
FIELD 2 OFFSET	
FIELD 3 OFFSET	
FIELD 4 OFFSET	
FIELD 5 OFFSET	
FIELD 6 OFFSET	
FIELD 7 OFFSET	
FIELD 8 OFFSET	
FIELD 9 OFFSET	
FINAL OFFSET	
DATABASE AND TABLE NAMES	F I E L D 1
DATABASE ID	
OTHER INTERNAL INFO. CREATION DATE, PROTECTION, TYPE OF JOURNALING, JOURNAL ID STRUCT VERSION ETC.	
INDEX DESCRIPTORS 36 BYTES * #INDEXES PLUS 20 BYTES PER INDEX COLUMN	F 2
ALWAYS NULL	3
FASTLOAD & RESTORE INFORMATION USUALLY NULL	F 4
BASE COLUMN INFO. COUNT OF COLUMNS, LOCATION OF FIRST FIXED FIELD, NUMBER OF PRESENCE BITS, ETC. 24 BYTES	F I E L D 5
COLUMN INFORMATION FOR EACH COLUMN 20 BYTES / COL + COMPRESS VALUE DATA TYPE OFFSET WITHIN ROW. NULLABLE/NOT NULLABLE. COMPRESS/NO COMPRESS PRESENCE BIT LOCATION ETC.	
RESTARTABLE SORT INFO USUALLY NULL	F 6
ALWAYS NULL	7
ALWAYS NULL	8
ALWAYS NULL	9
STANDARD ROW TRAILER LENGTH	

Figure 11-6

145

Unless the table has Large Rows or Oversize Rows, the typical block size for Teradata Version 2 systems is calculated by:

Maximum Block Size / 2 + (512 or 1024)

The maximum block size is user tunable, but if it is set at the maximum length of 32K (64 sectors), the system will attempt to maintain a typical block size of between 33 and 34 sectors (16,896 - 17,408 bytes).

Once the row size has been calculated (as in *Figure 11-5*), and the typical block size derived from the computation above, the size of the data table can now be ascertained using the following formulae:

(BlockSize - 16) / (RowSize + 12) = RowsPerBlock (rounded down)

RowCount / RowsPerBlock = Blocks (rounded up)

NumAmps * 512 = Header

(Blocks * TypicalBlockSize) + Header = NO FALLBACK

(Blocks * TypicalBlockSize) * 2 + Header = FALLBACK

PARAMETERS:

> 16 = (Block Header) + (Block Trailer)
> 12 = Pointer Array
> 512 = Minimum header size
> BlockSize = Bytes per block
> NumAmps = Number of AMPs in the system
> RowCount = Number of table rows expected
> RowSize = Physical row size

Unique Secondary Indexes

Each Unique Secondary Index subtable *(Figure 11-7)* has one row for each base table row.

ROW LENGTH	THIS ROW'S ROW ID		2 BYTES	SECONDARY INDEX VALUE	BASE TABLE ROW ID		ROW LENGTH
	ROW HASH	UNIQUENESS VALUE			ROW HASH	UNIQUENESS VALUE	
2 BYTES	4 BYTES	4 BYTES		VARIABLE	4 BYTES	4 BYTES	2 BYTES

Figure 11-7

Size = ((Row count) * (Index Value size + 25))

Where 25 = Block Headers and Trailers
+ Row Headers and Trailers
+ This row's Row ID
+ Spare byte
+ Presence bytes
+ Base table ROW ID

Double this figure for FALLBACK.

Non-Unique Secondary Indexes

The NUSI subtable has at least one index row per AMP for each distinct index value which occurs in the base table rows of that AMP:

Size = (Row count) * 8
+ ((#distinct values)
**   * (Index value size + 17)**
**   * MIN((#AMPS) ,(Rows per value)))**

Where MIN(___, ___) means the smaller of the two values.

Double this figure for FALLBACK.

For example, if there are more typical rows per value than AMPs, every AMP is likely to have at least one row for every value and each AMP will probably have a subtable row for every value. This often indicates a weakly selective index.

If the number of AMPs on the system is greater than the typical number of rows per value, some AMPs will not have a subtable row for every value, and the NUSI will probably be more strongly selective.

Spool

When sizing tables, the physical implementation team must also be keenly aware of the space requirements for spool. Maximum spool needs vary with the table size, the frequency of use, and whether it is used primarily for transaction processing or decision support. Larger systems (with a greater number of AMPs) need greater amounts of both PERM and spool than smaller systems (with fewer AMPs), to maintain an identical volume of data. Since the Teradata RDBMS requires free cylinders for spool, and the disk space is evenly divided amongst the AMPs, larger systems will also require more free cylinders for spool in order to duplicate tables on each AMP for Product Joins (Chapter 15).

Conclusion

In order to correctly estimate the disk space needed for a database, the calculation must include:

   Tables (double for FALLBACK).

   Secondary Indexes (double for FALLBACK).

   Permanent Journals (double for DUAL or FALLBACK).

   Spool space

Due to the variable size of columns, rows, and data blocks, deriving space estimates using the formulae provided is time-consuming and inexact. A less labor-intensive and more accurate way of sizing a production database or table is to rely instead on empirical sizing. For example, in order to estimate the space required by an Secondary Index subtable:

1. Load a known percentage (at least 10%) of rows onto the system.

2. Query the Data Dictionary through the DBC.TableSize view:

   SELECT SUM(CurrentPerm)
       FROM DBC.TableSize
       WHERE DatabaseName = 'Rents'
       AND TableName = 'Customer';

   Sum(CurrentPerm)
       219,136, 690

3. Create a Secondary Index:

   CREATE INDEX (Customer_Name) ON Customer;

4. Query the Data Dictionary through DBC.TableSize:

   SELECT SUM(CurrentPerm)
       FROM DBC.TableSize
       WHERE DatabaseName = 'Rents'
       AND TableName = 'Customer';

   Sum(CurrentPerm)
       264,192,420

5. Repeat steps 3 and 4 as necessary.

6. Subtract the results to compute individual index sizes.

7. Multiply the results to determine the production size.

.

Results obtained using empirical sizing are 100% exact for the sample tested - the larger the sample, the more accurate the result. Whatever method is selected however, one thing is certain. It is far, far better to recognize the true scope of potential disk space problems during the physical design stage, than to suddenly encounter them in the production environment.

12	The Parser

It is all too easy to forget, as we casually mouse-click on an object, run an item over a scanner or issue a high level computer command in the plain English of SQL, that it was not too long ago that to make a computer do anything, an engineer had to sit patiently, laboriously coding each machine instruction in ones and zeros, bit by bit, byte by byte. While the principles of the hardware have not changed much - machine instructions are still coded in ones and zeros - it is ingenious software which effectively masks the complexities, and allows us to perform elaborate tasks with effortless ease.

If the AMPs contain the raw power of the Teradata Database, the SQL Parser is its brain. It is the Parser, for example which:

Accepts a request from the user.

Determines whether past experience, with previous requests, can be used to save valuable processing time.

Ensures that the command is well understood.

Discovers the source of the data.

Checks the user's permission to make the request.

Considers multiple ways of performing the task and selects the most efficient.

Generates machine code.

Applies execution-time variables if appropriate.

Issues processing instructions to the AMPs.

Moreover, it is the Parser which performs all these tasks simultaneously for up to a hundred users at a time, in the tiny fractions of a second, incomprehensible in the real-time world.

Data Parcels

In *Figure 12-1*, the channel or network connection between the user's host computer and the Teradata Database is pictured as a conveyor belt which provides communications between the user's server, or host, to a specific Teradata Parsing Engine (PE). Multiple or single SQL requests destined for the Teradata Database are packaged by the host-resident Traffic Director Program (TDP) or Micro-TDP and transmitted across the channel or network as a series of request parcels, in plain English text.

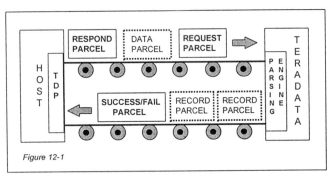

Figure 12-1

If the SQL is constructed with a "USING" clause, which involves the substitution of execution-time variables, the request parcel may be followed by one or more parcels which contain the literal data values (data parcels). Finally each SQL request is followed by a "respond" parcel which contains the size of the user's response buffer. A respond parcel may however be sent on its own, as a continuation request for additional data from a previous SQL request.

Having received and processed the in-coming messages, the Teradata Parser responds to each individual SQL request with a "success" parcel, which may be followed by additional parcels containing the requested records, or a "failure parcel".

The Parcels

A request parcel must contain at least one SQL statement, but may contain more as a multiple-statement request. Each request parcel may be a transaction by itself (default), or may be one parcel of a multiple-request transaction. In either event, a request parcel becomes the parsing unit.

The request parcel may be followed by one or more data parcels if a USING clause was explicitly declared in BTEQ. For example:

```
USING    CustNo  SMALLINT
         , CName  CHAR(20)
         , CPhone INTEGER
EXEC NewCustomer
         (:CustNo, :CName, :CPhone);
```

Teradata utilities such as BulkLoad, TPump and the COBOL, C and PL/I Preprocessors, automatically provide a USING clause. Others, such as FastLoad, MultiLoad and FastExport do not use the SQL protocol. Detailed information about the use and performance characteristics of BulkLoad, FastLoad, MultiLoad and FastExport are available in "The Teradata Database - Application and Archive/Recovery Utilities", by the same author.

The SQL Parser

Figure 12-2 provides a broad overview of function of each component of the SQL Parser from the time an SQL request is received to the final output of machine-readable AMP instructions (AMP steps).

Some of the memory in each Teradata PE is reserved for Software Cache, which is used to retain processing steps and/or data from previous requests, which might be effectively used to avoid the overhead of regenerating and fetching the same information for recurring similar requests.

For incoming requests which are already in cache, the Parser retrieves previously generated AMP steps to bypass the Syntaxer, Resolver, Optimizer and Generator modules. If no information is available in cache, the SQL is forwarded to the Syntaxer.

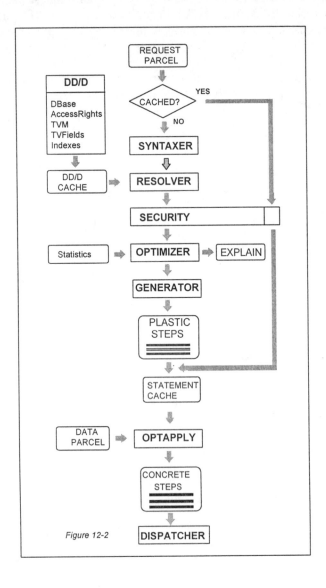

Figure 12-2

The Statement Cache

While the Parser is unable to predict the future, it is capable of determining the kind of transactions which are likely to be repetitive. SQL requests which include a USING clause for example, are most likely to be generated by a data maintenance or "batch" operation, and are highly likely to be repeated. The Statement cache *(Figure 12-3)* is therefore used to selectively store the SQL text and "plastic steps" (AMP steps before the data parcel is bound in), generated in respect of previous requests. SQL requests with hard-coded literal values, or with execution-time variables but without a USING clause, are not immediately cached. Some requests, particularly those which contain literal values for non-indexed columns are considered unlikely to be repeated, and are never cached. Other in-coming SQL requests, which include execution-time variables, but without a USING clause, are hashed and the hash value is stored in a test area of the Statement cache, which can hold up to 200 entries.

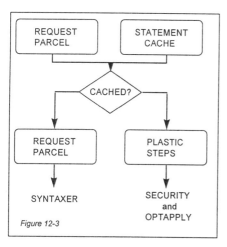

Figure 12-3

(Any amount of data, long or short, can be input to the hashing algorithm.) Since the algorithm rarely produces synonyms, a simple comparison of the hash of non-cached incoming SQL statements with the values in the test area is generally sufficient to identify repetitive requests not cached on the first occasion. AMP steps generated in respect of requests for which a matching hash value is located in the test area, are then committed to cache.

One of the more interesting features of the Teradata standard "work-horse" utility, BTEQ (Basic Teradata SQL) lies in its ability to measure the actual elapsed time required to execute multiple, single-session SQL transactions running in a "batch" environment. If the elapsed time of the first execution of a cached transaction is compared to the elapsed time for subsequent similar requests, directed to the same PE, the effect of the Statement Cache can be clearly seen.

Cached steps may be shared by multiple sessions and users within a single Parsing Engine. Cache maintenance is automatic, completely transparent to the user and is maintained in least-recently-used sequence.

Unlike AMPs, Parsing Engines have no direct access to disk storage facilities. Consequently they must rely on a "buddy" AMP for software, maintenance and temporary storage of lesser-used, but not yet obsolete, cache. Each PE is assigned to a single "buddy" AMP and no AMP can be a "buddy" to more than one PE. As a result, a Teradata system cannot be configured with more PEs than AMPs.

While the Optimizer often relies heavily on available statistics to decide between various execution plans, SQL queries which access data using UPIs, USIs and some Nested Joins are demographically independent, and are specifically marked when placed into cache. As a safeguard to ensure that the cache remains current and that execution plans remain efficient, the system purges unmarked entries every four hours.

DDL requests, which change the structure of a database, table, view or macro, are never cached. They result in a "Spoiling" message, which is broadcast to all PEs on the system to inform them that cached statistics and plans, which refer to the restructured object, are no longer valid and must be re-collected.

For an incoming request which is already in cache, the Parser retrieves the plastic steps and is thereby able to send the request directly to OPTAPPLY and bypass the overhead of the SYNTAXER, RESOLVER, OPTIMIZER and GENERATOR modules. If no information is available in cache, the SQL is forwarded to the SYNTAXER.

The SYNTAXER

The SYNTAXER checks the SQL syntax of an incoming request. If errors are discovered, a "failure" parcel is issued and the user is informed without delay. If no errors are found, the SYNTAXER

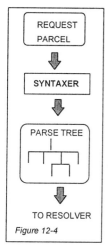

Figure 12-4

produces an initial Parse Tree and passes it to the RESOLVER *(Figure 12-4)*. The Parse Tree might fancifully be imagined as a Christmas Tree, attractively decorated with the individual components and clauses of the SQL request.

While the SYNTAXER module is extremely efficient, it is not surprising that larger request parcels take longer to process. Using macros to reduce parcel size can sometimes result in dramatic improvements in performance.

The RESOLVER

Database and user names must be unique within the Teradata system but table, view and macro names need only be unique within a database or user. However, each database/user, table, view and macro is assigned a globally unique numeric ID, which is maintained in the Data Dictionary (DD). Similarly, each column and each index is assigned a numeric ID, unique within the table.

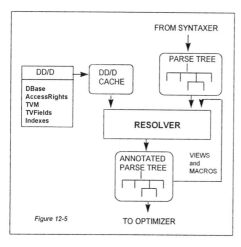

Figure 12-5

To avoid the need for frequent access to the disk of the "buddy" AMP for DD information, the most recently used SQL names, numeric IDs and statistical information are maintained in memory (DD Cache) *(Figure 12-5)*. SQL statements that alter currently cached values generate "spoiling" messages which are relayed to every PE on the system. On receipt of a "spoiling" message, each PE drops the relevant entries from cache. In any event, the DD cache is purged on each PE every four hours sequentially to avoid temporary "hot spots". Purging the cache forces the Parser to re-optimize all current requests.

The RESOLVER first interrogates the DD Cache, before disturbing its "buddy" AMP, to verify logical names and convert them to unique IDs, meaningful to the system. As it does so, the RESOLVER replaces all view and macro names with their underlying text. While the Teradata RDBMS permits the nesting of views and macros to eight levels deep, any such nesting involves a substantial increase in the workload of the RESOLVER. Finally the RESOLVER annotates the Parse Tree with unique object IDs and statistical information and passes the Annotated Parse Tree to the Security module.

The SECURITY Module

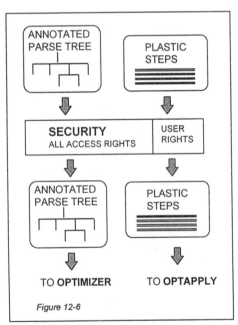

Figure 12-6

Although the US Government has yet to authorize specific benchmark tests, the Teradata Database is believed to be amongst the few RDBMS vendors who qualify, in all known respects, for the "C-2" security rating - the highest in the industry for all existing relational databases. Any user who wishes to access the Teradata system must first successfully negotiate several different levels of security both on the host and within the Teradata Database itself.

For example, a user wishing to access data on the Teradata Database must:

Be authorized to access Teradata from a specific host.

Log on to the Teradata Database with a valid User ID and password.

Have been specifically granted the rights to access the specific data object.

This authority emanates from the System Administrator and permissions may be granted, changed or revoked dynamically. Moreover, SQL optimizations in the Statement cache are not restricted to the user who submitted the original request. For those reasons, each execution of an SQL request, whether or not the steps are taken from cache, must be subject to security check.

For each request *(Figure 12-6)*, the SECURITY module is required to verify the user's permission to access the referenced databases, tables, views or macros listed in the SQL. The initial parsing of a request requires a more detailed examination of the rights and privileges, not only pertaining to user, but also the entire ownership hierarchy of referenced views and macros. (A full and complete explanation of Access Rights is provided in Chapter 17 of "The Teradata Database - SQL".)

Having satisfied the requirements of the SECURITY module, the Annotated Parse Tree received from the RESOLVER is passed on to the OPTIMIZER, or the plastic steps retrieved from the Statement Cache are forwarded to OPTAPPLY.

The OPTIMIZER

The Teradata Database is unique amongst contemporary parallel-processing RDBMS vendors, in that its OPTIMIZER has had nearly two decades to mature and refine without major changes in its logical architecture. As a result of this long evolution, the Teradata

OPTIMIZER is seen by many as having acquired something akin to "artificial intelligence." Like any intelligence however, it relies heavily on the quality of input information and can be easily misled by poor advice.

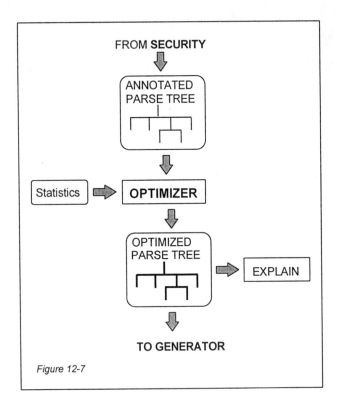

Figure 12-7

To choose between alternative execution plans for the fulfillment of an SQL request, the OPTIMIZER requires accurate statistics, which it gathers in one of two ways:

Dynamic Sampling.

Collected Statistics.

As mentioned in Chapter 8, Dynamic Sampling is up-to-date, but depends for accuracy on the assumed evenness of data distribution, while Collected Statistics are accurate when gathered, but require frequent maintenance to ensure they remain current.

As apart of the optimization process:

Data Definition Language (DDL) and Data Control Language (DCL) statements in the Annotated Parse Tree are replaced by Data Manipulation Language (DML) changes to the Data Dictionary.

DML statements are evaluated for possible access paths, such as:

Available indexes referenced in the WHERE clause.

Possible join plans from the WHERE clause.

Full Table Scans.

In selecting the most efficient execution plan for a request, the OPTIMIZER does not look at every possibility, but chooses from among several of the more likely candidates. As it does so, it considers whether or not the eventual outcome of the query will be changed if intermediate steps are allowed to execute in parallel, and determines whether the performance can be enhanced if the results from one step can be safely used to eliminate duplicate processing for another (Common Steps).

Having selected what it believes to be the most efficient execution plan, the OPTIMIZER collapses the Parse Tree to reflect the chosen plan *(Figure 12-7)*. If the SQL statement is prefaced with the word "EXPLAIN", the collapsed Parse Tree is passed to the EXPLAIN module and the steps are summarized, described in plain English text and returned to the user. Otherwise the collapsed Parse Tree becomes input for the GENERATOR.

The GENERATOR

The GENERATOR *(Figure 12-8)*, is responsible for converting the collapsed Parse Tree (which does not yet contain data parcels from the USING clause) into the series of machine-readable instructions known as "plastic steps".

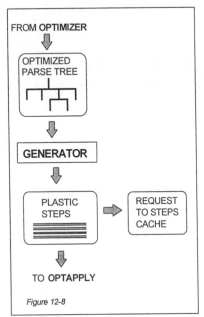

FROM **OPTIMIZER**

OPTIMIZED PARSE TREE

GENERATOR

PLASTIC STEPS

REQUEST TO STEPS CACHE

TO **OPTAPPLY**

Figure 12-8

In Teradata Version 2, it does so in one of two ways:

1. By retrieving previously compiled machine code segments from the Data Dictionary.

2. By preparing and compiling new code segments in anticipation of identical repetitive queries, if it calculates that performance will be significantly enhanced by doing so.

Plastic Steps are then stored in the Statement Cache and passed to OPTAPPLY.

OPTAPPLY and DISPATCHER

The function of the OPTAPPLY module *(Figure 12-9)* is to bind any data parcel generated by the SQL USING clause into the plastic steps, producing "concrete" steps, which are then passed to the DISPATCHER for transmission across the Communications Layer to the AMPs.

Since the binding of the data parcel occurs late in the parsing sequence, the Teradata Database is said to support a "late-binding parser". It is because of the late binding parser, that the phenomenal savings in processing cycles afforded by the Statement cache, become possible and the EXPLAIN can be used to describe a typical, rather than data-specific, execution plan.

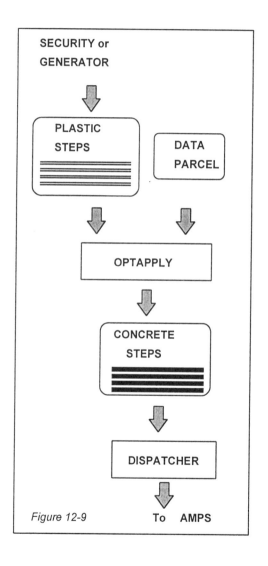

SECURITY or
GENERATOR

PLASTIC
STEPS

DATA
PARCEL

OPTAPPLY

CONCRETE
STEPS

DISPATCHER

To   AMPS

Figure 12-9

Conclusion

Since no other RDBMS vendor has the benefit of Teradata's long experience in the world of parallel-processing data warehouse, the optimizer modules of other RDBMS vendors tend to be considerably less sophisticated. As a result, other vendors tend to pass responsibility for the design, coding, compilation and storage of efficient execution plans directly to the user. This is always a time-consuming and expensive procedure. Data in a data warehouse is moreover notoriously volatile and, like collected statistics, pre-compiled plans quickly become outdated and inevitably fall victim to other, higher priority, tasks. As a result the effectiveness of the plans tend to erode and effect is quickly seen in the deterioration of system performance.

In contrast, the OPTIMIZER of the Teradata Database stands firmly on its own. It is sophisticated enough to produce reasonably efficient execution plans for the most complex queries, providing that Primary and Secondary Indexes are chosen wisely. Teradata's OPTIMIZER is however only as good as the statistics it has available. As we shall explore in the next chapter, most of the time dynamic sampling is sufficient to deliver reliable statistics and result in highly efficient plans. Occasionally the user may be required to collect and regularly maintain statistics for a more aggressive optimization. However, the optional collection and occasional refreshing of statistics is considerably more agreeable and less onerous as task than the required periodic redesign, re-coding, re-compiling and re-implementation of new execution plans which become necessary to supplement the less efficient and less reliable optimizers provided by alternative RDBMS vendors.

13	Statistics

According to the well known quote from President Harry Truman, "There are liars, damned liars and statisticians". If it were capable of rational thought, the Teradata Optimizer might well be forgiven for sharing this view since it can be easily misled, and perhaps unjustly criticized, for making the occasional poor choice of execution plans as a result of poor statistics.

The Optimizer needs accurate table and column demographics to decide on the most efficient execution plan. It must determine, for example:

> The number of rows in the table.
>
> Whether or not the column is indexed.
>
> Whether the index is unique or non-unique.
>
> The number of distinct values in the column.
>
> The number of rows per value, etc.

It acquires these statistics in one of two ways:

> By Collected Statistics.
>
> By Dynamic AMP Sampling.

Like its users, the Optimizer lives in a world of constant compromise between the amount of time needed to do the job properly and the time available to do it. In an ideal world, there would be sufficient time for users to regularly collect and refresh statistics on every table, column and index used to access the data. In the "real world", which demands a sub-second response, there is never enough time. While the Optimizer may enjoy the luxury of Collected Statistics when they are available, it must largely forage on its own when they are not. As a result, while there is nothing to technically prevent the Optimizer from dynamically collecting complete statistical information about every column and index used to access the data, time constraints force it to make reasonable assumptions and risk short cuts, which are believed to produce reasonably accurate results, most of the time.

Dynamic (Random) AMP Sampling

If Collected Statistics are not available in the Data Dictionary, the Optimizer dynamically collects table, column and index statistics by choosing an AMP for dynamic data sampling. The AMP is chosen at random using the current session number as a "seed". This prevents a single AMP from being overloaded with data sampling requests. If additional data samples are needed later, the Optimizer increments the random number and chooses a new AMP.

The Dynamic Data Sampling process involves seven distinct steps:

1. Select a random AMP based on the Session number.
2. Read its Master Index.
3. Count the cylinders with data for this table.
4. Select one cylinder and read its Cylinder Index.
5. Count the data blocks for this table, on this cylinder.
6. Read one data block for this table and count its rows.
7. Calculate the approximate number of rows in the table:

Total Rows =
　　(Number of Rows in this Data Block)
　* 　**(Number of Data Blocks in the sampled Cylinder)**
　* 　**(Number of Cylinders with data for this table on this AMP)**
　* 　**(Number of AMPs in this configuration)**

Secondary Index demographics are collected concurrently in a similar fashion.

While Dynamic Data Sampling is 100% current and produces reliable results most of the time, it makes the broad assumptions that the table has enough rows and is sufficiently well distributed that any AMP (chosen at random) becomes fully representative of all. Random Samples are less complete than Collected Statistics, and any imbalance in the sample may mislead the optimizer into a poor choice of execution plan and perhaps result in disappointing performance.

Collected Statistics

Collected Statistics often improve the performance of complex queries and joins, and the Optimizer relies on them for access plans which involve aggressive procedures, such as NUSI bit mapping. Statistics may be collected either at the column or secondary index level *(Figure 13-1)*, although since Secondary Indexes tend to be created and dropped to favor specific applications, the column level is preferred.

```
{ COLLECT }  STATISTICS [ ON ] tablename    [ COLUMN columnname                              ]
{ DROP    }                                  [ INDEX ( columnname [ . . . , columnname ] )   ]

COLLECTING STATISTICS

COLLECT STATISTICS ON Order COLUMN Location_Number;
COLLECT STATISTICS ON Order INDEX Customer_Number;

REFRESHING STATISTICS
COLLECT STATISTICS ON Order;
```

Figure 13-1

If the table being accessed is large and rows are evenly distributed amongst all the AMPs on the system, Collected Statistics may produce results which are no different from those achieved by Dynamic AMP Sampling. In this event, the collecting of statistics involves substantial additional workload for no particular advantage.

Whenever Collected Statistics are available, the Optimizer is obliged to honor them in preference to Dynamic AMP Sampling, and will assume they are both current and accurate. If it can be demonstrated, using the EXPLAIN facility described in the next chapter, that Collected Statistics result in better performance, the additional workload may prove worthwhile. If conversely, the decision is made to stay with Dynamic

AMP Sampling, the user should plan to revisit the situation at a later date.

Collected Statistics are stored in the Data Dictionary and are unaffected by a reconfiguration of the AMP processors. While Collected Statistics may be more complete than those produced by Dynamic AMP Sampling, they may quickly become obsolete and misleading as the demographics of the tables change. Any decision to take advantage of Collected Statistics therefore also implies a commitment to refresh them whenever five to ten percent of the rows in the table change.

COLLECT STATISTICS is a DDL statement which requires a full table scan for each column. It also places a lengthy WRITE lock on two important DD tables, DBC.TVFIELDS or DBC.INDEXES, which effectively prevents the parsing of all new requests against the data table. For these reasons, the collection of statistics should be assigned to the after-hours data maintenance window, and should be avoided during production hours.

Statistics for a column or index reside in a (logical) frequency distribution chart of 20 intervals *(Figure 13-2)*. Each interval represents about 5% of the table's rows. For each interval the system records:

The most frequent value in the interval.

The number of rows with the most frequent value.

The number of other values.

The number of rows with other values.

The maximum data value within the interval.

An additional summary of information, collected globally for the whole table includes:

The most frequent value for the column or index.

The number of rows with the most frequent value.

The number of other values for the column or index.

The number of rows with other values.

The minimum data value for the column or index.

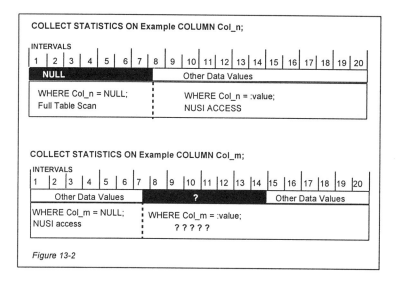

Figure 13-2

In the first example in *Figure 13-2*, if the value specified in the SQL request to access rows is "NULL", the Optimizer can quickly determine that this value is likely to return considerably more than 10% of the rows (seven intervals in the frequency distribution chart). For this particular query, the Optimizer will elect to by-pass the NUSI in favor of a full table scan. For values other than NULL however, it will most likely elect to use the NUSI for access.

Similarly, in the second example, the Optimizer might resort to a full table scan for specific values which are expected to return more than 10% of the rows and yet use the NUSI for more strongly selective values. This why columns which are generally strongly selective, but include one or perhaps two values which, though weakly selective, are still considered as valid NUSI candidates.

"Soft" vs. "Hard" Parameters

In testing whether or not to collect statistics or rely instead on Dynamic AMP Sampling, it is important to remember that the EXPLAIN outlines the Optimizer's access plan with respect to the precise values in the SQL statement being optimized. For example, the following macro does not include a USING clause, but has an execution-time parameter (:CustNo):

CREATE MACRO SelectCustomer (CustNo SMALLINT)
AS (SELECT * FROM Customer
WHERE Customer_Number = :CustNo ;) ;

This is followed by a request to EXPLAIN the EXEC (Execute) for the specific value of 1002:

EXPLAIN EXEC SelectCustomer (1002) ;

This creates a request parcel, but no data parcel, and the parameter value of 1002 is treated as a hard-coded literal value. As a result the Optimizer access plan described in the EXPLAIN will be based on the (hard) specific Customer Number value of 1002, and may not, in consequence, be truly representative of other values encountered in the production environment. In order to produce a more generalized plan for all values of Customer Number, the EXEC statement should be provided a USING clause:

EXPLAIN USING (CustNo SMALLINT)
EXEC SelectCustomer (1002) ;

The addition of the USING clause creates both a request parcel and a data parcel. Because the Teradata Database has a "late-binding" Parser, the data parcel is not applied to the plastic steps until after the Optimizer has generated its plan. In developing its plan therefore, the Optimizer is obliged to analyze statistics for all the (soft) values of Customer Number, and not just the specific value of 1002. The result is an execution plan which more accurately reflects the production environment.

Viewing Statistics

```
HELP STATISTICS Order ;

Date        Time       Unique Values    Column Names
98/09/01    09:10:11          1,989     Location_Number
98/09/01    09:11:20          1,307     Customer_Number

HELP INDEX Order ;

BTEQ SCRIPT:

Set SideTitles ON;
Set FoldLine ON;
LOGON Classics, Class;
HELP INDEX Chr;
* *   Help information returned. 2 rows.
*** Time was 15.37 seconds.
Unique?                          Y
Primary // or // Secondary?      P
Column Names                     Order Number
Index Id                         1
Approximate Count                1 1,986
Unique?                          N
Primary // or // Secondary?      S
Column Names                     Customer_Number
Index Id                         4
Approximate Count                1,308
```
Figure 13-3

Collected Statistics are maintained in the Data Dictionary in "internal DBC format", and cannot be read or directly adjusted by the user other than by loading data in tables. The HELP STATISTICS statement *(Figure 13-3)* will however return the date and time statistics were last collected, the count (used by the Optimizer) of distinct values, and the relevant column names. HELP INDEX will provide an approximate count of distinct values for indexed columns.

Conclusion

To assist the Optimizer in formulating efficient execution plans, as a general rule, statistics should be collected on:

> All non-unique indexes.
> The UPI of tables with fewer than 1,000 rows per AMP.
> Any non-indexed column used for select or join operations.
> Data Constraints.

If the Optimizer has collected statistics available, it will tend to be more aggressive in developing plans. While an aggressive plan is designed to offer a significant performance advantage, an aggressive plan based on stale statistics might well have the reverse effect. The OPTIMIZER is considerably more conservative when it must rely on Dynamic AMP Sampling.

Unlike other RDBMS vendors, the Teradata Database provides few options for user tuning of tables and applications, since it needs little or none. Because of its unique ability to perform well even with a massive logical data model implemented in fully third normal form, Teradata's Optimizer has frequently been described as the best in the industry, and continues to improve with each new software release.

Even with good statistics however, Teradata's Optimizer is, on very rare occasions, still capable of error. Using an earlier version of the software, a user collected statistics for a table and was more than content with the performance of the query. As the table grew by 10%, the user refreshed the statistics, which seemed to cross an unanticipated internal threshold in the Optimizer (which has since been fixed), and caused it to choose a less favorable plan. While the user was provided with no facility for directly influencing the Optimizer into reverting back to the former plan, it was nevertheless achieved by temporarily dropping 10% of the rows, re-collecting statistics on the lesser table size, and allowing them to become stale. In this way, the Optimizer was indirectly influenced to revert to the former acceptable access plan, and the customer was happy with the result. While maintaining stale statistics is not a recommended tuning option, it did, on this one occasion, prove to be very effective.

14 The EXPLAIN

One of the more daunting assignments which inevitably confronts a typical high school student is to paraphrase a lengthy passage of prose into a few well chosen sentences that effectively preserve the essence and style of the original. The undertaking is relatively arduous since it requires the construction of precise, concise and unambiguous sentences using a high level of vocabulary, completely free of the irrelevances and circumlocutions which characterize everyday communications. As difficult as this kind of task may be for people, it is much more so for a calculating device as primitive as a modern binary computer. Yet this is what the Teradata EXPLAIN facility is asked to do, many times a day, almost every day of the year.

EXPLAIN may be used on any SQL statement, except EXPLAIN itself. It translates the output of the Optimizer (the Collapsed Parse Tree) into somewhat stylized but plain English. Once the results are returned to the user, the execution plan is discarded, AMP steps are not generated and no changes whatever are made to the data referenced in the SQL.

While it may be tempting to assume that any EXPLAIN text is somehow binding on future optimizations of similar queries, there is no such guarantee. Output from the EXPLAIN simply describes what the Optimizer would have done on this occasion, had the SQL query been allowed to complete. For demographically independent plans, Primary Index requests, full table scans, etc., an EXPLAIN of one incidence of a query may reasonably be accepted as typical of another. However, if the execution plan was chosen on the basis of Collected Statistics or Dynamic Sampling, any difference in input might lead to a different result. Despite this, Teradata's EXPLAIN facility provides a superb way to learn about the system and SQL, and deserves to be consistently used to analyze joins, as well as long-running and complex queries.

Like any tool, the EXPLAIN must be properly used. Frequently the more gregarious students may invite the Instructor to comment on the output from an EXPAIN, and in response to the obvious question, will frequently reply, "I don't know what my SQL is trying to do. I just wanted to see what happens". Somewhat amused, the Instructor then feels obliged to make the "ought-to-be-obvious" observation that, "You have to know what the SQL request is supposed to do, before trying to EXPLAIN it".

Although most text output by the EXPAIN is simple and relatively understandable, it is highly specialized in function, and therefore requires an equally specialized lexicon of terms:

(Last Use)...
Indicates that this is the last time a referenced spool file is needed and that the space will be released back to the system after completion of the current step.

with no residual conditions
All applicable conditions specified in the SQL "WHERE" clause(s) have been applied to the rows, and there are no remaining conditions to be satisfied.

ENDTRANSACTION...
Transaction locks are released, and changes to data are committed.

eliminating duplicate rows ..
Performing a DISTINCT operation to eliminate duplicate records from the output. (While duplicate rows may be forbidden in tables, there is no such restriction for output records).

by way of the sort key in spool field1
The rows to be sorted are written to spool, with the sort data values appended as an additional field (Field 1) to the beginning of each record. Field 1 then becomes a "tag" by which the records can be sorted. The "tag" is, of course, discarded in the response to the user.

we do an ABORT test...
A "True/False" test of the existence or value of an object, the failure of which results in an ABORT or ROLLBACK of the entire transaction.

we do a SMS (set manipulation step)...
Combining rows using a UNION, MINUS, or INTERSECT operator.

we do a BMSMS
The RDBMS performs a Bit Map Set Manipulation step, using a bit map to handle two or more weakly selective NUSIs linked by an "AND" condition in the SQL "WHERE" clause.

which is redistributed by hash code to all AMPs.
Redistributing data rows amongst all the AMPs by hashing on a value other than a Primary Index in preparation for a join. Redistribution of rows logically requires no additional disk space.

which is duplicated on all AMPs.
Making a complete copy of the entire table or spool file on every AMP in the system, in preparation for a join. (If a table has 1MB of data and there are 100 AMPs on the system, duplicating the data will require 100MB of space.)

We execute the following steps in parallel.
The following, indented and renumbered steps may be executed in any order without prejudice to the final result. Depending on the distribution of the data and the total number of AMPs on the system, the steps may be executed on different AMPs in parallel. In computing final elapsed time, steps designated as parallel are assumed to execute in the same time-frame.

Format of the EXPLAIN

The following SQL request is an example of a demographically independent query, in which the Optimizer has no choice but to choose a full table scan of the CUSTOMER table:

EXPLAIN SELECT * FROM Customer;

<u>**Explanation**</u>

1) First, we lock a distinct RENTS. "psuedo table" for read on a RowHash to prevent global deadlock for RENTS.Customer.

2) Next, we do an all-AMPs RETRIEVE step from RENTS.Customer by way of an all-rows scan with no residual conditions into Spool 1, which is built locally on the AMPs. The size of Spool 1 is estimated to be 24 rows. The estimated time for this step is 0.09 seconds.

3) Finally, we send out an END TRANSACTION step to all AMPs involved in processing the request. The contents of Spool 1 are sent back to the user as the result of statement 1. The total estimated time is 0.09 seconds.

IN OTHER WORDS ...

The RDBMS puts a READ lock on the CUSTOMER table to prevent any other users from writing to this object while the request is being processed.

Since there is no "WHERE" clause (no residual conditions) in the SQL, each AMP puts all of its rows from the Customer table into a temporary spool file called "Spool 1". Each AMP has its own portion of Spool 1, and the total number of rows on *all* the AMPs is estimated to be 24 rows. This operation takes 0.09 seconds. The contents of Spool 1 is then sent back to the user. The total time required for the complete operation is 0.09 seconds (less than 1/10th of a second).

Spool size estimates are global (based on the total number of rows on all AMPs). Timings do not necessarily represent a true estimate of elapsed time, but are issued by the Optimizer based, in part, on a calculation of logical disk I/Os. While the timings represent a useful measurement for comparing the relative cost of alternate Optimizer execution plans, they are not intended to be taken at face value.

EXPLAIN of a DDL

Data Definition Language SQL statements which are used to create, drop and alter users, databases, tables, views and macros represent another class of demographically independent optimizations. Since the Optimizer has no choice of action with regard to DDL statements, there is little sense in requesting an EXPLAIN of a DDL statement, other than for purely educational purposes. The following CREATE TABLE, and the resulting EXPLAIN output, are therefore presented simply as an another example of EXPLAIN terminology:

```
EXPLAIN CREATE TABLE Customer
        (Customer_Number       SMALLINT
        ,Customer_Name         VARCHAR(35)
        ,Billing_Location_Number INTEGER
        ,Phone_Number          INTEGER)
        UNIQUE PRIMARY INDEX (Customer_Number);
```

Explanation

1) First, we lock RENTS.Customer for exclusive use.

2) Next, we lock DBC.TVFields for write on a RowHash, we lock DBC.Indexes for write on a RowHash, we lock DBC.AccessRights for write on a RowHash, we lock DBC.TVM for write on a RowHash, and we lock DBC.DBase for write on a RowHash.

3) We execute the following steps in parallel.

    1) We do a single-AMP ABORT test from DBC.DBase by way of the unique primary index.

    2) We do a single-AMP ABORT test from DBC.TVM by way of the unique primary index with no residual conditions.

    3) We do a single-AMP UPDATE from DBC.DBase by way of the unique primary index with no residual conditions.

    4) We do an INSERT into DBC.TVFields.

    5) We do an INSERT into DBC.TVFields.

    6) We do an INSERT into DBC.TVFields.

    7) We do an INSERT into DBC.TVFields.

    8) We do an INSERT into DBC.Indexes.

    9) We do an INSERT into DBC.TVM.

    10) We do an INSERT into DBC.AccessRights.

    11) We do an INSERT into DBC.AccessRights.

12) We do an INSERT into DBC.AccessRights.
13) We do an INSERT into DBC.AccessRights.
14) We do an INSERT into DBC.AccessRights.
15) We do an INSERT into DBC.AccessRights.
16) We do an INSERT into DBC.AccessRights.
17) We do an INSERT into DBC.AccessRights.

4) We create the table header.

5) Finally, we send out an END TRANSACTION step to all AMPs involved in processing the request.

No rows are returned to the user as the result of statement 1.

IN OTHER WORDS...

Steps 1 and 2 first place an exclusive lock on the DD table "NEXT", which protects the new object ID for the table being created, before placing row hash write locks on various other DD tables affected by the CREATE TABLE operation.

The next 17 steps are performed in parallel and include:

An existence test on the parent database.

A non-existence test on the table name.

An update of DBC.Dbase to reset accumulator fields (of interest primarily to the RDBMS).

An insert into DBC.TVFields for each column.

An insert into DBC.Indexes for the Primary Index.

An insert into DBC.TVM for the Table ID and name.

The insert of seven access rights into the DD.AccessRights table which represent privileges automatically accruing to the creator of the table.

Finally, the table header is created, locks are released and the user is notified of successful completion.

Step Diagrams

The standardized format of the EXPLAIN output and the consistent numbering of steps and sub-steps permit the easy conversion of EXPLAIN output text into helpful step diagrams. For example, the following SQL selects customer details for each order by performing a JOIN between the ORDER and CUSTOMER tables based on matching values in the Customer Number domain *(Figure 14-1):*

```
SELECT Order_Number
        ,Order.Customer_Number
        ,Customer_Name
FROM   Order, Customer
WHERE Order.Customer_Number =
        Customer.Customer_Number;
```

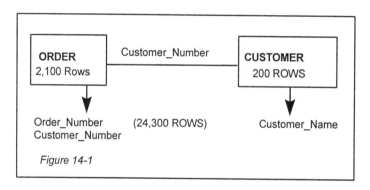

Figure 14-1

Explanation

1) First, we lock RENTS.Customer for read, and we lock RENTS. Order for read.

2) Next, we execute the following steps in parallel.

    1)   We do an all-AMPs RETRIEVE step from RENTS. Customer by way of an all-rows scan with no residual conditions into Spool 2, which is duplicated on all AMPs. Then we do a SORT to order Spool 2 by row hash. The size of Spool 2 is estimated to be 1,728 rows. The estimated time for this step is 5.40 seconds.

2) We do an all-AMPs RETRIEVE step from RENTS.Order by way of a RowHash match scan with no residual conditions into Spool 3, which is built locally on the AMPs. Then we do a SORT to order Spool 3 by row hash. The size of Spool 3 is estimated to be 2096 rows. The estimated time for this step is 2.86 seconds.

3) We do an all-AMPs JOIN step from Spool 2 (Last Use) by way of an all-rows scan, which is joined to Spool 3 (Last Use). Spool 2 and Spool 3 are joined using a merge join, with a join condition of ("Spool3.Customer_Number = Spool2.Customer_Number"). The result goes into Spool 1, which is built locally on the AMPs. The size of Spool 1 is estimated to be 24,300 rows. The estimated time for this step is 12.43 seconds.

4) Finally, we send out an END TRANSACTION step to all AMPs involved in processing the request.

⇨   The contents of Spool 1 are sent back to the user as the result of statement 1. The total estimated time is 17.84 seconds.

IN OTHER WORDS . . .

The RDBMS begins by placing READ locks on the CUSTOMER table and the ORDER table.

It then performs a full table scan of the CUSTOMER table, puts the results in Spool 2 and sends a complete copy of Spool 2 to every AMP on the system. Thus each AMP has a complete copy of the CUSTOMER table in Spool 2, with the rows sorted ascending by the Row Hash of the Primary Index, Customer Number. The total number of rows in Spool 2 for all of the AMPs is estimated at 1,728.

At the same time (in parallel), each AMP builds a new copy of its rows from the ORDER table in Spool 3. The rows in Spool 3 are identical to those of the ORDER table, except that Spool 3 now has a Primary Index of Customer Number (the join condition) and each row has a new Row ID. Each AMP then sends all of the rows in Spool 3 to the Communications Layer which redistributes them based on the hash maps and the new Row ID. Thus, each AMP now has its portion of 2,096 rows of the ORDER table in Spool 3 sorted ascending by the Row Hash of Customer Number.

With rows in Spool 2 and Spool 3 both sorted by the Row Hash of Customer Number, it now becomes a relatively simple matter for each AMP to determine the common Row IDs and verify matched rows using the literal values of Customer Number. The required data from the 24,300 matching rows are then consigned to Spool 1, which is merged into a coherent stream over the Communications Layer and returned to the user. The entire process is awarded a time estimate of 17.84 seconds (far longer than the actual operation is expected to take).

In Figure 14-2, which is drawn from the EXPLAIN above, the numbered sequential steps are depicted in vertical fashion, while parallel steps are horizontal.

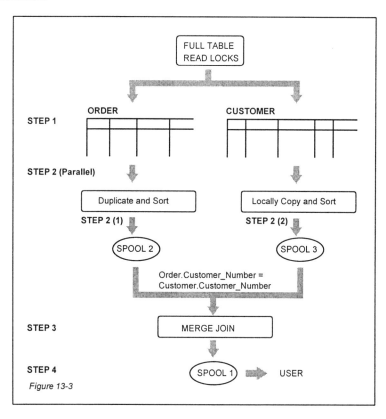

Figure 13-3

Parallel and Common Steps

In the EXPLAIN example above, Step 2 (1) has an estimated timing of 5.40 seconds and Step 2 (2) of 2.80 seconds. Since these sub-steps are designated as parallel steps, the Optimizer assumes they will be executed in parallel, and only considers the largest value when evaluating the estimated time. In its ability to recognize the potential of parallel steps, the Optimizer is able to dramatically improve the performance of a query.

In addition to parallel steps, the Optimizer is also able to save expensive processing cycles by recognizing when results derived from one part of the plan, can be effectively re-used in another. These are known as "Common Steps".

For example, consider the following SQL which produces a list of valid Order Number and Part Number combinations from the ORDER and ORDER ITEM tables, and identifies Order Numbers from the ORDER table for which no parts have been ordered:

```
SELECT      Order.Order_Number
            ,Item_Number (CHAR(11))
FROM        Order, Order_Item
            WHERE Order.Order._Number =
            Order_Item.Order_Number
AND         Order.Order_Number IN
      ( SELECT Order_Number
            FROM Order_Item )        UNION
SELECT      Order.Order_Number
            ,'INVALID ORDER'
FROM        Order, Order_Item
            WHERE Order.Order._Number =
            Order_Item.Order_Number
AND         Order.Order_Number NOT IN
      ( SELECT Order_Number
            FROM Order_Item );
```

The EXPLAIN output from the above query has been used to prepare the step diagram in *Figure 14-3*:

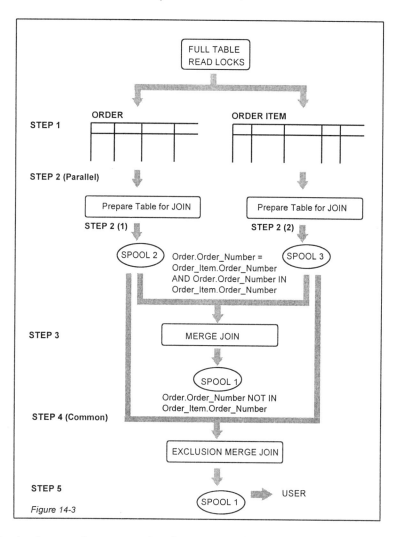

Figure 14-3

As in the previous example, the rows to be joined are first placed in local AMP Spools 2 and Spool 3. Records with Row IDs common to both Spool 2 and Spool 3 are verified and placed in Spool 1. In the same way that Spool 2 and Spool 3 were used to determine the Order Number values common to both files, the same Spool files can be also used (in an EXCLUSION join), to determine the Order Numbers which appear in Spool 2 but not in Spool 3. AMP steps which re-use the results of one part of a query to qualify another are known as "Common Steps".

Referential Integrity

Automatic referential integrity (FK to PK relationships) built in to the system using the Primary Key and Foreign Key options of the SQL CREATE TABLE statement is an expensive luxury. The price must be paid every time a change is made to the designated columns, whether or not it is really necessary. Consider the case, for example, where the Customer Number in the ORDER table is designated in the SQL as a Foreign Key. Since customers are rarely expected to know their Customer Number, customers calling in are first identified by Phone Number and the Customer Number is then passed without interruption to the ORDER table. Even though there is no realistic possibility of error, the Customer Number inserted into the ORDER table must still be subjected to a referential integrity check.

With a clever use of its macro facility, the Teradata Database provides an effective low-cost alternative which frequently allows multiple data and referential integrity checks only as specifically required, for the *total* elapsed time of a single disk I/O. The NEWORDER macro, presented below, performs two sample data integrity checks and two referential integrity checks before committing a new insert to the ORDER table.

```
REPLACE MACRO NewOrder
        ( OrdNo INTEGER
        , LocNo INTEGER
        , CustNo SMALLINT
        , FromDate DATE
        , ToDate DATE )
        AS  (
        ROLLBACK 'Invalid From Date'
        WHERE :FromDate < DATE;

        ROLLBACK 'Invalid To Date'
        WHERE :ToDate < DATE + 1;
```

```
ROLLBACK 'Invalid Customer Number'
WHERE :CustNo NOT IN
(SELECT Customer_Number
        FROM Customer
        WHERE Customer_Number = :CustNo);

ROLLBACK 'Invalid Location Number'
WHERE :LocNo NOT IN
(SELECT Location_Number
        FROM Location
        WHERE Location_Number = :LocNo);

INSERT INTO Order
    VALUES (
        :OrdNo
    , :LocNo
    , :CustNo
    , :FromDate
    , :ToDate
    , :'O'
    , DATE
    , TIME
    , USER ); ) ;
```

Integrity of input data is checked first, since these require no access to disk and no additional activity, other than to return an error message, in the event of failure:

```
ROLLBACK 'Invalid From Date'
WHERE :FromDate < DATE;

ROLLBACK 'Invalid To Date'
WHERE :ToDate < DATE + 1;
```

Total cost so far: zero elapsed disk I/Os.

There is no practical limit as to the number of data integrity checks which can be performed effortlessly and almost cost-free in this way.

Once the input data values have been verified, the next step is to check
the FK to PK relationships:

> **ROLLBACK 'Invalid Customer Number'**
> **WHERE :CustNo NOT IN**
> **(SELECT Customer_Number**
> **FROM Customer**
> **WHERE Customer_Number = :CustNo);**

> **ROLLBACK 'Invalid Location Number'**
> **WHERE :LocNo NOT IN**
> **(SELECT Location_Number**
> **FROM Location**
> **WHERE Location_Number = :LocNo);**

Total cost so far: (probably) one elapsed disk I/O.

By definition, a Primary Key in one table is used to validate a Foreign
Key in the same or another table. The overwhelming preponderance of
the tables in any database are minor entities, which invariably have a
Primary Index based on the Primary Key. At the same time, since
PK/FK relationships imply heavy access, it is rare for the PK tables
involved in a PK/FK relationship to have a Primary Index based on
anything but the Primary Key. We may therefore safely assume that, for
upwards of 99% of the time, the PK involved in a PK/FK relationship is
also the Primary Index of the validation table. Despite this, it might
appear that even a simple referential integrity check might involve a full
table scan:

> **ROLLBACK 'Invalid Customer Number'**
> **WHERE :CustNo NOT IN**
> **(SELECT Customer_Number**
> **FROM Customer);**

However, the addition of a simple WHERE clause which resolves an
execution-time variable to an input value of the macro, is sufficient to
change an all-AMPs full table scan requiring multiple disk I/Os, to a one
AMP, single I/O, Primary Index select:

```
ROLLBACK 'Invalid Customer Number'
        WHERE :CustNo NOT IN
        (SELECT Customer_Number
        FROM Customer
        WHERE Customer_Number = :CustNo);
```

Teradata systems with fewer than 8 AMPs are rare, and is equally rare for a single transaction to require more than a small number of referential integrity (RI) checks. Depending on the number of RI checks required and the number of AMPs available, we may reasonably assume that the RI checks and the final insert can execute in parallel for the total elapsed time of one disk I/O:

```
EXPLAIN EXEC NewOrder (2020, 1900,1007,980930,981031);
```

Explanation
1) We do an ABORT test with a condition of ("980930 < 980901")
2) We do an ABORT test with a condition of ("981031 < 980902")
3) We execute the following steps in parallel.

> 1) We do a single-AMP ABORT test from RENTS.Location by way of the unique primary index "RENTS.Location. Location_Number = 1900" with no residual conditions. The size is estimated to be 1 rows. The estimated time for this step is 0.07 seconds.
>
> 2) We do a single-AMP ABORT test from RENTS.Customer by way of the unique
>
> primary index "RENTS.Customer.Customer_Number = 1007" with no residual conditions. The size is estimated to be 1 rows. The estimated time for this step is 0.07 seconds.
>
> 3) We do an INSERT into RENTS.Order.

4) Finally we send out an END TRANSACTION step to all AMPs involved in processing the request.
No rows are returned to the user as the result of statement 1.
No rows are returned to the user as the result of statement 2.
No rows are returned to the user as the result of statement 3.
No rows are returned to the user as the result of statement 4.
No rows are returned to the user as the result of statement 5.
No rows are returned to the user as the result of statement 6.

Conclusion

With its ability to summarize many pages of complex OPTIMIZER access plans into a few paragraphs of plain but precise English text, the Teradata EXPLAIN facility is perhaps the most useful tool for Data Designers, Administrators, and Users provided by any RDBMS vendor. Along with a simple-to-produce step diagram, the EXPLAIN output should be an essential component of all design reviews and formal system documentation. In its ability to expose inefficiencies in query structures and joins, the EXPLAIN becomes a formidable adversary of poor performance, but only if the data redistribution and duplication techniques it describes are well understood.

15 | JOIN Processing

The more tables a relational database has the greater the opportunity to join them together in ever new and creative ways, to turn masses of raw data into rich mines of useful intelligence. No RDBMS, currently available, is more efficient at joining large numbers of tables together by unleashing the awesome power of parallel processing than the Teradata Database. Because Teradata performs complex joins without the need for painstaking preparation or tuning, no other RDBMS is as quick to respond to the unpremeditated demands for high levels of instant, up-to-date information needed by users to compete in a rapidly changing market place.

The Teradata Database can join between 2 and 64 tables together in a single SQL statement. It does so as a series of 2 table joins, by matching columns of the same domain in each table, and combining the qualifying rows from both tables as if they were a single data record *(Figure 15-1)*.

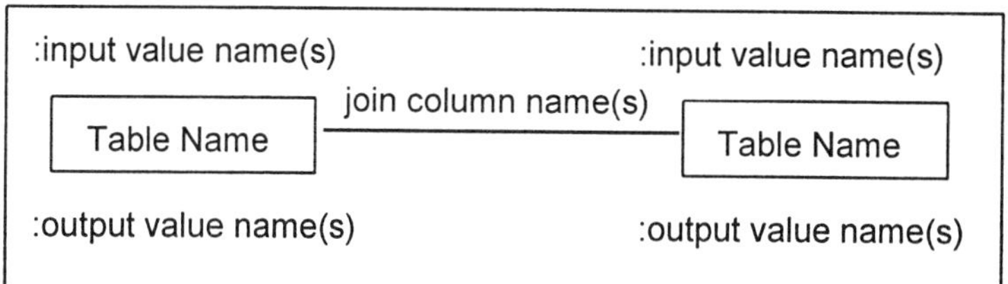

:input value name(s)   :input value name(s)

join column name(s)

| Table Name | | Table Name |

:output value name(s)   :output value name(s)

Figure 15-1

In the following example *(Figure 15-2)*, rows from the ORDER table and the CUSTOMER table joined together to form a single record, which includes the Order Number, the Customer Number and the Customer Name for rows in both tables which have a similar value in the Customer Number column.

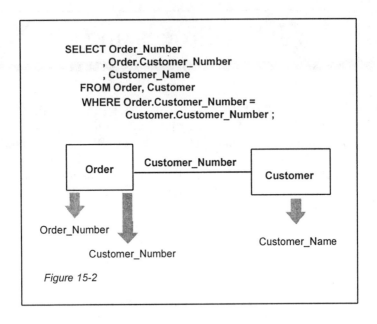

```
SELECT Order_Number
     , Order.Customer_Number
     , Customer_Name
FROM Order, Customer
WHERE Order.Customer_Number =
      Customer.Customer_Number ;
```

Figure 15-2

In order to determine whether or not two values are equal, a computer must move both values into adjacent registers of the same CPU and compare them left-to-right, byte-by-byte. For Teradata, this means that 2 rows to be joined must occur on the same AMP. If rows are being joined are based on a common Primary Index value, and have identical data types, they will already occur on the same AMP and the join becomes a simple matter of comparison, with all AMPs working in parallel. If the tables are being joined on column values other than a common Primary Index, the RDBMS must ensure that one or both rows are moved, in spool, to a common AMP before the join can commence. (Join processing never moves or changes the original table rows in any way.)

In developing its execution plan, the Optimizer may choose between six major types of join using available indexes, Collected Statistics, and/or Dynamic AMP Sampling:

> Join Index
> Nested Join
> Row ID Join

Product Join.
Merge Join
Exclusion Join.

Output from the EXPLAIN clearly indicates the particular join strategy adopted.

Multiple Table Joins

All multiple table joins are reduced to a series of two-table joins *(Figure 15-3)*, and the Optimizer attempts to determine the most efficient join order based on the best available statistics. Collected Statistics help the Optimizer in making a wise choice.

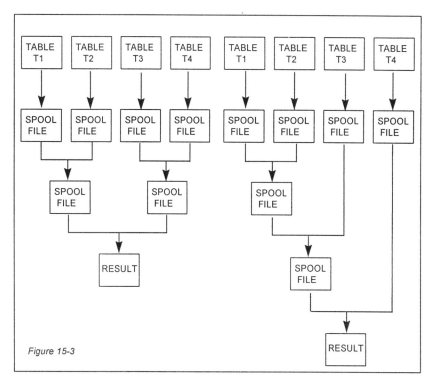

Figure 15-3

Row Distribution in Preparation for a Join

The examples in *Figure 15-4*, describe three main redistribution strategies.

1

SELECT . . .
FROM Table1, Table2
WHERE Table1.Col1 = Table2.Col1;

No redistribution needed

TABLE1		
Col1	Col2	Col3
PI		

TABLE2		
Col1	Col2	Col3
PI		

2

SELECT . . .
FROM Table1, Table2
WHERE Table1.Col1 = Table2.Col2;

Redistribute Table2 rows on Col2

TABLE1		
Col1	Col2	Col3
PI		

TABLE2		
Col1	Col2	Col3
PI		

SPOOL

Col1	Col2	Col3
	PI	

3

SELECT . . .
FROM Table1, Table2
WHERE Table1.Col2 = Table2.Col3;

Redistribute Table1 rows on Col2
Redistribute Table2 rows on Col3

TABLE1		
Col1	Col2	Col3
PI		

TABLE2		
Col1	Col2	Col3
PI		

SPOOL

Col1	Col2	Col3
	PI	

SPOOL

Col1	Col2	Col3
		PI

Figure 15-4

Once again, rows must be on the same AMP to be joined. In Example 1, the join of Table1 and Table2 is based on the Primary Index columns of each table. Since rows of both tables are already distributed based on the hash of the Primary Index value, rows with a common PI value will already be located on the same AMP.

In Example 2, the tables are being joined based on common values in Table1.Col1 (the Primary Index), and Table2.Col2, a column other than the Primary Index. Since Table1 is already distributed based on the join condition (Col1), the Optimizer chooses to build a copy of Table2 in spool with a new Primary Index of Col2 and redistribute those rows over the Communications Layer. Rows of both tables, with equal join columns, will now be located on the same AMP, and the join may now proceed.

Tables, in the third example, are required to be joined on columns in the same domain, neither of which is defined as the Primary Index. In this event, the Optimizer must commit rows of both tables to temporary spool, with a new Primary Index based on the join column, and redistribute the rows of both tables over the Communications Layer.

Join Conditions

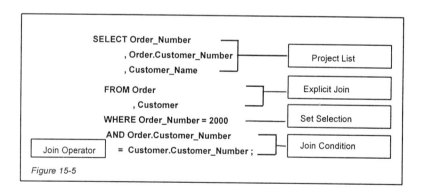

Figure 15-5

A two table join condition must always reference two table names or aliases, and one or more column names in each table *(Figure 15-5)*. For a join of "n" tables, there must always be at least "n-1" join conditions which must reference each and every table or alias involved in the join.

If join conditions are not based on equality, or fail to recognize every table involved, the result will be a partial or full Cartesian Product Join which, if unintended, may result in massive volumes of useless response data.

The Join Index

A Join Index might be likened to Pre-Join (a temporary table used for joins which is created as a result of a previous join between two tables). If the complete join operation involves just the tables and columns involved in the join index, the Optimizer will treat it as "covering" index and will avoid accessing the base tables. Since the Join Index is dynamically maintained by the RDBMS no data redistribution, duplication or comparisons are required, and data is returned as if from a single table. If the join operation involves columns or rows from tables not featured in the Join Index, the Optimizer treats the Index as a normal data table for consideration in developing the most efficient access plan.

The Nested Join

The Nested Join is a special join case, since it is the only join that does not necessarily use all of the AMPs. The join is "nested" since it uses two "nested" indexes to access rows. The Nested Join is, in consequence, the most efficient type of join, in terms of system resources, and becomes the best choice for OLTP applications.

To choose a Nested Join *(Figure 15-6)*, the Optimizer must have:

An equality value for a unique index (UPI or USI) on Table 1:

(Order_Number = 2005)

A join on a column of that single row to any Primary Index, Unique , or (rarely) a Non-Unique Secondary Index on Table 2:

(Order.Customer_Number = CustomerCustomer_Number)

```
SELECT  Order_Number
         ,Customer.Name
    FROM Order, Customer
    WHERE
    Order_Number = 2005
    AND Order.Customer_Number
        = Customer.Customer_Number;
```

ORDER

ORDER NUMBER	CUSTOMER NUMBER
PK	FK
UPI	
2002	106
2005	107
2007	107
2008	110
2011	102
2012	110
2014	107
2015	107

CUSTOMER

CUSTOMER NUMBER	CUSTOMER NAME
PK	FK
UPI	
102	Smith
106	Jones
107	Lee
110	Adams

Figure 15-6

The Nested Join always returns a small number of rows. In the example above, the RDBMS retrieves the single row from the ORDER table and hashes on the join column value (Customer_Number) to the matching column in the CUSTOMER table.

Figure 15-7 provides an interesting case of how a costly full table scan of a table with a decomposable NUPI can be converted into an inexpensive Nested Join.

The PART table has a NUPI, which represents data from multiple domains in a single column, defined on Part Type. As a result, each of the following SQL constructs causes a full table scan of the PART table:

```
SELECT * FROM Part
WHERE Part_Type  LIKE 'ACC%';
```

```
SELECT * FROM Part
WHERE Part_Type LIKE '_ _ _ 345%';

SELECT * FROM Part
WHERE Part_Type LIKE '%C';
```

PART THOUSANDS OF ROWS		PART TYPE LESS THAN 100 ROWS
PART NUMBER	PART TYPE	PART TYPE
PK,SA		PK
	NUPI	UPI
11	ACC345C	ACC345C
12	ACC345C	ACC345L
13	ACC345L	ACC460C
14	ACC345L	ACN460C
15	ACC460C	ACX200B
16	ACN460C	
17	ACX200B	
18	ACX200B	

Figure 15-7

Creating a composite NUPI will not help, and creating a Primary Index on a partial column value of Part Type will result in poor distribution and disappointing performance for some applications. The PART TYPE table is a distinct list of all Part Types and is a minor entity. It contains fewer rows and columns than the PART table and requires fewer data blocks for storage. However, by redesigning the SQL as a join, the Optimizer has the opportunity to perform a full table scan of the smaller PART TYPE table, followed by a Nested Join to the larger PART table:

```
SELECT      Part_Number
          , Part_Type
FROM        Part_Type, Part
WHERE       Part_Type.Part_Type LIKE'_ _ _'345%'
AND         Part_Type.Part_Type= Part.Part_Type;
```

The Row ID Join

The Row ID Join is a variation of the Nested Join. It requires the input of a literal value which is used to pre-select a small number of rows from one table. Column values from these selected rows are then used in an equality join with a Secondary Index of the other table involved in the join. For example:

```
SELECT  Column1, Column2, Column3
   FROM TableA, TableB
   WHERE Table1.Column4 = 20              (NUPI)
   AND TableA.Column3=TableB.Column5;     (NUSI)
```

The qualifying rows from TableA are duplicated on all the AMPs.

The values from Column3 are used to read the Row IDs from the NUSI subtable for Column5.

The Row IDs are placed into spool and sorted by Row ID.

Rows are retrieved by Row ID and returned to the user.

The Row ID join is particularly efficient, since it does not involve a presort of the rows in preparation for the join.

The Product Join

The Product Join compares every qualifying row of one table to all the qualifying rows of the other. It owes its name to the fact that the total number of value comparisons it is required to make is equal to the *product* of the number of participating rows in each table. The large number of internal compares *(Figure 15-8)* can become costly, where there are more rows than AMP memory can hold at any one time.

Despite its undeserved reputation as the join of last resort, the product Join is often preferred by the Optimizer where one of the tables has only a small number of rows participating in the join.

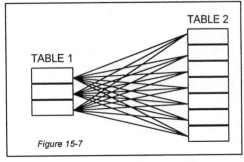

Figure 15-7

The Product Join is the most general form of join and, apart from the Nested and Row ID joins, is the only plan which does not require a pre-sort of the rows. Rather, it identifies the table with the smallest amount of data participating in the join (small table), and duplicates the qualifying rows, in spool, on all the AMPs in the system. Thus, if the "small table" of a Product Join has 50 rows, each AMP will have all 50 rows, and this ensures that rows with common join values can be matched on the same AMP.

The Merge Join

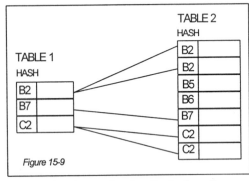

Figure 15-9

The Merge Join is more efficient than a Product Join, since it requires significantly fewer value comparisons *(Figure 15-9)*.

Unlike the Product Join, the Merge Join is required to read blocks from both tables only once. For this reason, it is the plan most frequently chosen by the Optimizer for an equality join condition.

In a Merge Join, the RDBMS first identifies the table with the smallest number of rows participating in the join. If necessary, it then:

Puts qualifying data of one or both tables into spool(s).

Moves the spool rows to AMPs based on the join column hash.

Sorts the spool rows into join column hash sequence.

The Exclusion Join

Exclusion Joins are used to return rows which do not have a match of the join condition. Exclusion Joins generally result from SQL "NOT IN" subqueries and "MINUS" operations. They are similar to regular joins in that the Optimizer first determines the rows which match on the join condition and then returns the remainder.

Exclusion joins on NULLABLE columns use a three-value logic (equal, not equal and unknown). In order to avoid rows from both tables which are simply NULL in the join column, either:

> Define columns used for "NOT IN" join conditions as NOT NULL on the CREATE TABLE, or

> Qualify the join as:

> **"WHERE Tablename.ColumnName IS NOT NULL".**

Join Strategies

The net cost of joins rises in direct proportion to the number of rows that must be moved, and sorted, and plans for the same tables may change as the demographics change.

In *Figure 15-10*, the tables are being joined based on Vendor Number, the common Primary Index column of both tables. Thus, the rows are already distributed on the join condition, and rows from both tables with matching Vendor Numbers are located on the same AMPs. No further redistribution is required.

```
SELECT . . .
  FROM Vendor, Vendor_Category
  WHERE Vendor.Vendor_Number
  = Vendor.Category.Vendor_Number;
```

VENDOR

VENDOR NUMBER	VENDOR NAME
PK,UPI	
130	INTEL
213	SEAGATE
190	TOSHIBA
180	TEAC

VENDOR CATEGORY

VENDOR NUMBER	CATEGORY NUMBER
PK	
FK,NUPI	FK
130	100
213	200
180	200
180	400
180	300
190	200
190	100
190	400

VENDOR rows hash distributed on Vendor Number (UPI)

AMP 1	AMP 2	AMP 3	AMP 4
213 SEAGATE	180 TEAC	130 INTEL	190 TOSHIBA

VENDOR CATEGORY Category rows hash distributed on Vendor_Number (NUPI)

AMP 1	AMP 2	AMP 3	AMP 4
213 200	180 200 180 400 180 300	130 100	190 200 190 100 190 400

Figure 15-10

Rows to not have to be in sorted for a Product Join. The smaller table is duplicated on all the AMPs *(Figure 15-11)*. While creating a complete copy of one of the tables on all AMPs ensures that rows with matching values for the join column(s) are located on the same AMP, it might require a significant investment in temporary spool space.

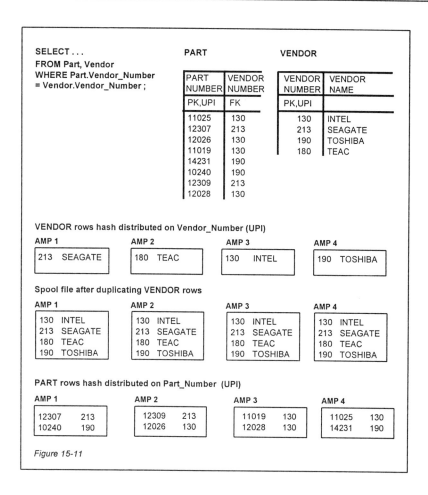

Figure 15-11

Alternatively, in order to perform a Merge Join, the rows must be presorted in join column row hash sequence. There are three main distribution strategies for the Merge Join:

    1. DO NOTHING if the tables are being joined based on matching Primary Index values.

2. **REDISTRIBUTE** one or both sides (depending on the Primary Indexes used in the join), and **SORT** on join column row hash.

3. **DUPLICATE** the smaller table on all AMPs, and **SORT** on join column row hash. **LOCALLY BUILD** a spool copy of the larger table and **SORT** on join column row hash.

Redistribute

```
SELECT . . .
FROM Part, Vendor
WHERE Part.Vendor_Number
= Vendor.Vendor_Number ;
```

PART

PART NUMBER	VENDOR NUMBER
PK,UPI	FK
11025	130
12307	213
12026	130
11019	130
14231	190
10240	190
12309	213
12028	130

VENDOR

VENDOR NUMBER	VENDOR NAME
PK,UPI	
130	INTEL
213	SEAGATE
190	TOSHIBA
180	TEAC

PART rows hash distributed on Part_Number (UPI)

AMP 1		AMP 2		AMP 3		AMP 4	
12307	213	12309	213	11019	130	11025	130
10240	190	12026	130	12028	130	14231	180

Spool file after redistribution on PART.Vendor_Number

AMP 1		AMP 2		AMP 3		AMP 4	
12307	213	14231	180	11019	130	10240	190
12309	213			12026	130		
				12028	130		
				11025	130		

VENDOR rows hash-distributed on Vendor_Number (UPI)

AMP 1		AMP 2		AMP 3		AMP 4	
213	SEAGATE	180	TEAC	130	INTEL	190	TOSHIBA

Figure 15-12

In the example provided as *Figure 15-12*, the Optimizer builds a complete copy of the rows from the PART table in spool, with a Primary Index based on the join column, Vendor Number. These rows are then redistributed over the Communications Layer.

Rows for the VENDOR table have already been distributed amongst the AMPs based on the row hash of the Primary Index column, Vendor Number, and so rows from both tables with matching values for Vendor Number will now be located on the same AMP.

Duplicate and Build

This row redistribution technique *(Figure 15-13)* is similar to the duplication of the small table on all AMPs used for the Product Join, except that it may involve committing both tables to spool and sorting the rows. The Optimizer first calculates which of the tables is the small table (the table with the smallest amount of data involved in the join). It will then decide whether it is less expensive to duplicate this table on all AMPs or to hash-redistribute the rows individually. The final choice is then made based on the cost of sorting one or both tables compared to the cost of the additional comparisons needed for the Product Join.

Limiting the Rows to be Joined

Selecting rows, based on a WHERE clause is considerably less arduous for the RDBMS than performing join operations, and the Optimizer is careful to ensure that column projection and row selection precede any join. The following SQL is used to join the ITEM and REPAIR tables *(Figure 15-14)*, based on the common domain value of Repair Number:

```
SELECT ...
  FROM Item, Repair
  WHERE Item.Repair_Number = Repair.Repair_Number ;
```

The user is clearly requesting a complete list of all the items which are currently undergoing repair. All 10 million rows from the ITEM table participate in the join. 500,000 rows have matching Repair Number column values and are returned.

SELECT . . .
FROM Part, Vendor
WHERE Part.Vendor_Number
= Vendor.Vendor_Number ;

PART

PART NUMBER	VENDOR NUMBER
PK,UPI	FK
11025	130
12307	213
12026	130
11019	130
14231	190
10240	190
12309	213
12028	130

VENDOR

VENDOR NUMBER	VENDOR NAME
PK,UPI	
130	INTEL
213	SEAGATE
190	TOSHIBA
180	TEAC

PART rows hash distributed on Part_Number (UPI)

AMP 1		AMP 2		AMP 3		AMP 4	
12307	213	12309	213	11019	130	11025	130
10240	190	12026	130	12028	130	14231	180

Spool file after redistribution on PART.Vendor_Number

AMP 1		AMP 2		AMP 3		AMP 4	
12307	213	14231	180	11019	130	10240	190
12309	213			12026	130		
				12028	130		
				11025	130		

VENDOR rows hash-distributed on Vendor_Number (UPI)

AMP 1		AMP 2	AMP 3		AMP 4	
213	SEAGATE	180 TEAC	130	INTEL	190	TOSHIBA

Figure 15-13

In examining the demographics of the ITEM table more closely however, it becomes apparent that more than 9.5 million of the values in the Repair Number column are NULL. (Only 500,000 items are undergoing repair at any one time.) If columns with NULL value are first excluded in the WHERE clause, the Optimizer need only consider the 500,000 rows which are not NULL:

> **SELECT ... FROM Item, Repair**
> **WHERE Item.Repair_Number = Repair.Repair_Number**
> **AND Item.Repair_Number IS NOT NULL;**

ITEM				REPAIR		
10,000,000 ROWS	ITEM NUMBER	REPAIR NUMBER		**10,000,000 ROWS**	REPAIR NUMBER	
PK/FK	PK, SA			PK/FK	PK, SA	
DISTINCT VALUES	10M	5000		DISTINCT VALUES	5000	
MAXIMUM ROWS/VAL	1	200		MAXIMUM ROWS/VAL	1	
MAX ROWS NULL	0	9.5M		MAX ROWS NULL	0	
TYPICAL ROWS/VAL	1	150		TYPICAL ROWS/VAL	1	
PI/SI	UPI			PI/SI	UPI	

Figure 15-14

In this event, a rudimentary understanding of the nature of the query, the demographics of the table and the addition of a simple WHERE clause results in a major improvement in performance.

Conclusion

With the response data in spool on each AMP, the final stage of the join process involves the merge of records from all AMPs into a single coherent stream. It is at this stage that the differences between one RDBMS vendor and another become apparent.

All major vendors of relational data warehouse have, by now, adopted some form or variation of the Symmetric Multi-Processing (SMP) architecture as their standard hardware platform for parallel-processing. Those with no proprietary interface between multiple SMP units become effectively limited by the resources available in a standard SMP unit. As a result they find no alternative but to accumulate the individual results of all the processor units in a single processor unit, where the response data can be effectively merged into a single file for delivery to the user *(Figure 15-15, Example 1)*. One processor therefore becomes extremely busy (HOT), while the remainder stand idle. This built-in processing imbalance in the system has the net effect of severely limiting the growth potential of the RDBMS to that of one or perhaps two SMP units, and becomes an insurmountable upper level constraint on the performance capabilities of the RDBMS.

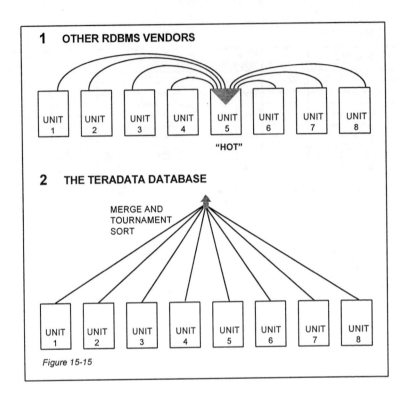

Figure 15-15

The Teradata Database, on the other hand, was designed from its moment of conception to function in a fully parallel environment with hundreds or even thousands of inter-communicating processors. It is, in consequence no stranger to the need to merge huge volumes of data from multiple AMPs into a single answer set *(Figure 15-15 Example 2)* without prejudice to any single processor. With its powerful Communications Layer, Teradata is able to merge the parallel results from hundreds of SMP units and thousands of AMPs into a single smooth, but fast-flowing, sequential data stream. While data redistribution techniques are important to the Teradata Database, they mean little unless they are ultimately supported by the awesome merge capabilities of the Bynet.

16 | JOIN Analysis

Armed with a good knowledge of the redistribution techniques of the Teradata Database (Chapter 15), and fortified by the experience gained in Chapter 14, we are now ready to confront and master the EXPLAIN at its most formidable - the analysis of complex queries and joins. Perhaps we have over-estimated the challenge. Perhaps we have under-estimated the skill and genius of the Teradata design engineers. Either way, we shall be prudent and make a cautious approach by beginning with the Join Index.

The Join Index

The following SQL creates a Join Index on the CUSTOMER and ORDER tables, and requests an EXPLAIN of a simple row select:

```
CREATE JOIN INDEX  AS CustOrdInd
    SELECT Customer.Customer_Number
          ,Customer_Name
          ,Order _Number
    FROM Order, LEFT JOIN Customer
    ON Order.Customer_Number =
        Customer.Customer_Number ;

EXPLAIN SELECT Customer.Customer_Number
              , Customer_Name
              , Order_Number
    FROM Customer, Order
    WHERE Customer.Customer_Number =
            Order.Customer_Number;
```

Explanation

1) First, we lock a distinct RENTS. "pseudo table" for read on a RowHash to prevent global deadlock for RENTS.CustOrdInd.

2) Next, we lock RENTS. CustOrdInd for read.

3) We do an all-AMPs RETRIEVE step from *join index* table RENTS.CustOrdInd by way of an all-rows scan with no residual conditions into Spool 1 which is built locally on the AMPs. The input table will not be cached in memory, but it is eligible for synchronized scanning. The result spool file will not be cached in memory. The size of Spool 1 is estimated to be 1,000,000 rows. The estimated time for this step is 4 minutes and 27 seconds.

Finally, we send out an END TRANSACTION step to all AMPs involved in processing the request.

Since the Join Index is sufficient to "cover" the request, there is no data redistribution between AMPs, and 1 million rows are returned to the user with no need to access the base table rows.

The Nested Join

Nested Joins can usually execute in parallel and therefore become the join plan of choice for transaction processing applications. In the following example a single row is selected from the RENTS.ORDER table by supplying the Unique Primary Index value of 2005 for Order Number. The Customer Number is read from this row and is used to select a single row from the CUSTOMER table using the Unique Primary Index. The Nested Join therefore requires the services of only two AMPs, which leaves the remainder free to work on other tasks.

```
SELECT Order_Number
       ,Customer_Name
FROM Order, Customer
WHERE Order_Number = 2005
AND Order.Customer_Number =
       Customer.Customer_Number;
```

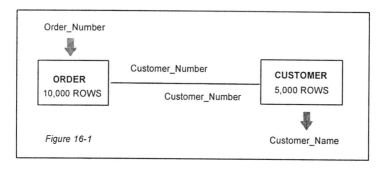

Figure 16-1

Explanation

1) First, we do a single-AMP JOIN step from RENTS.Order by way of the unique primary index "RENTS.Order.Order_Number 2005 " with no residual conditions which is joined to RENTS.Customer by way of the unique primary index "RENTS.Customer.Customer_Number = RENTS.Order.Customer_Number".

RENTS.Order and RENTS. Customer are joined using a *nested join.* The result goes into Spool 1 which is built locally on that AMP. The size of Spool 1 is estimated to be 1 rows. The estimated time for this step is 0.10 seconds.

->The contents of Spool 1 are sent back to the user as the result of statement 1. The total estimated time is 0.10 seconds.

The join is clearly identified in the EXPLAIN as a Nested Join. (Italics in the EXPLAIN text are the author's.) Since only a single row is returned from this Nested Join, the spool file referenced as "Spool 1" occupies a 32K memory buffer and does not require additional disk I/O.

The MERGE Join

We will consider two examples of the Merge Join:

1. With matching Primary Indexes.

2. Involving redistribution of rows.

1. Matching Primary Indexes *(Figure 16-2)*

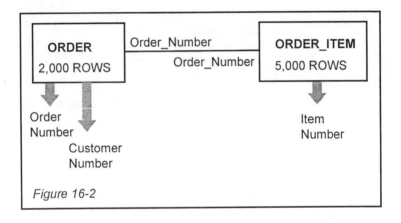

Figure 16-2

SELECT Order.Order_Number,
,Customer_Number
,Item_Number
FROM Order, Order_Item
WHERE Order.Order_Number
= Order_Item.Order_Number ;

Explanation

1) First, we lock RENTS.Order for read, and we lock RENTS. Order_Item for read.

2) Next, we do an all-AMPs JOIN step from RENTS.Order by way of a RowHash match scan with no residual conditions, which is joined to RENTS.Order_Item. RENTS.Order and RENTS.Order_Item are joined using a *merge join*, with a join condition of ("RENTS.Order. Order_Number = RENTS.Order_Item.Order_Number"). The result goes into Spool 1, which is built locally on the AMPs. The size of Spool 1 is estimated to be 4,960 rows. The estimated time for this step is 28.67 seconds.

3) Finally, we send out an END TRANSACTION step to all AMPs involved in processing the request. The contents of Spool 1 are sent back to the user as the result of statement 1. The total estimated time is 28.67 seconds.

Since both the ORDER and ORDER_ITEM tables have a Primary Index on the common column of Order Number, and this is the join condition, rows with matching values for Order Number are already located on the same AMP, and no further row distribution or sorting is required. The size of Spool 1 (4,960 rows), represents a genuine estimate of the total number of rows globally on all the AMPs. The timing of 28.67 seconds is a figure of merit only, and the actual response time will be considerably shorter.

2. Redistribution of Rows *(Figure 16-3)*

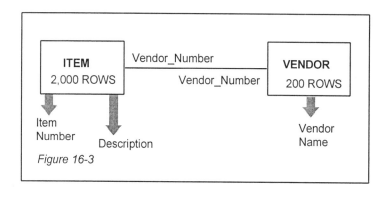

Figure 16-3

```
SELECT Item_Number
     , Description
     , Vendor_Name
FROM Item, Vendor
WHERE Item.Vendor_Number
    =  Vendor.Vendor_Number;
```

Explanation
1) First, we lock RENTS.Vendor for read, and we lock RENTS.Item for read.
2) Next, we execute the following steps in *parallel.*

1) We do an all-AMPs RETRIEVE step from RENTS.Vendor by way of an all-rows scan with no residual conditions into Spool 2, which is *duplicated on all AMPs*. Then we do a SORT to order Spool 2 by row hash. The size of Spool 2 is estimated to be 1,728 rows. The estimated time for this step is 5.40 seconds.

2) We do an all-AMPs RETRIEVE step from RENTS.Item by way of a RowHash match scan with no residual conditions into Spool 3, which is *built locally* on the AMPs. Then we do a SORT to order Spool 3 by row hash. The size of Spool 3 is estimated to be 2096 rows. The estimated time for this step is 2.86 seconds.

3) We do an all-AMPs JOIN step from Spool 2 (Last Use) by way of an all-rows scan, which is joined to Spool 3 (Last Use). Spool 2 and Spool 3 are joined using a *merge join*, with a join condition of ("Spool3.Vendor_Number = Spool2.Vendor_Number"). The result goes into Spool 1, which is built locally on the AMPs. The size of Spool 1 is estimated to be 24,300 rows. The estimated time for this step is 12.43 seconds.

4) Finally, we send out an END TRANSACTION step to all AMPs involved in processing the request.

-> The contents of Spool 1 are sent back to the user as the result of statement 1. The total estimated time is 17.84 seconds.

Since this EXPLAIN is somewhat more complex than those presented earlier in this chapter, a step diagram is needed to clarify the procedure. Examples of Step Diagrams were presented in Chapter 14.

In the EXPLAIN above, there are four distinct steps which should be presented in vertical fashion. Step 2 has two sub-steps which execute in parallel, and are therefore drawn side-by-side. The completed diagram, (*Figure 16-4*) includes spool sizes and relative time estimates.

Along with the EXPLAIN text itself, a Step Diagram should be regarded as an integral part of ongoing application documentation. Addition of the estimated row counts and relative times may prove helpful in identifying major changes in the execution plan as the tables mature.

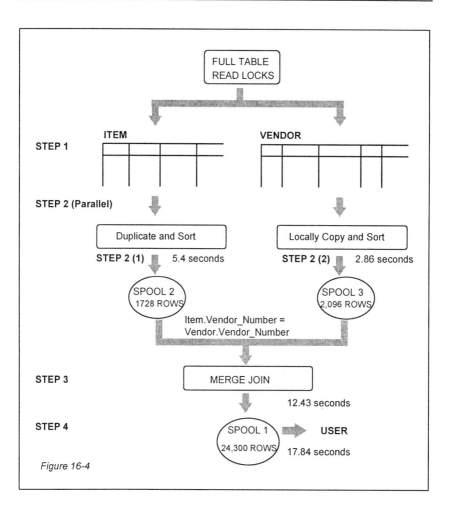

Figure 16-4

The Product Join

Any non-equality join condition or instance of multiple join conditions separated by the "OR" condition will always result in a Product Join. The following example *(Figure 16-5)* requests a complete list of all store employees AND managers:

```
SELECT Store_Name
     , Last_Name
     , First_Name
FROM Employee, Store
WHERE Employee.Store_Number
     = Store.Store_Number
OR Employee.Employee_Number
     = Store.Manager_Employee_Number;
```

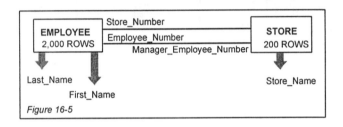

Figure 16-5

Explanation

1) First, we lock RENTS. Store for read, and we lock RENTS. Employee for read.

2) Next, we do an all-AMPs RETRIEVE step from RENTS.Store by way of an all-rows scan with no residual conditions into Spool 2, which is *duplicated on all AMPs*. The size of Spool 2 is estimated to be 1,728 rows. The estimated time for this step is 3.73 seconds.

3) We do an all-AMPs JOIN step from Spool 2 (Last Use) by way of an all-rows scan, which is joined to RENTS.Employee. RENTS.Employee and Spool 2 are joined using a *product join*, with a join condition of ("Spool 2 Manager_Employee_Number = RENTS.Employee.Employee_Number) OR (Spool2.Store_Number = RENTS.Employee.Store_Number)"). The result goes into Spool 1, which is built locally on the AMPs. The size of Spool 1 is estimated to be 3,496 rows. The estimated time for this step is 4 minutes and 35 seconds.

4) Finally, we send out an END TRANSACTION step to all AMPs involved in processing the request.

-> The contents of Spool 1 are sent back to the user as the result of statement 1. The total estimated time is *4 minutes and 39 seconds*.

Since the "OR" condition in the SQL forced the Optimizer to choose a Product Join, this query required 400,000 comparisons. On a 16 AMP system, each AMP must therefore perform about 25,000 comparisons, and the query has a high relative time estimate of 4 minutes, 39 seconds as a result.

A better solution, which replaces the "OR" condition by the simple expedient of a "UNION" delivers the same result, but permits the Optimizer to choose a more efficient Merge Join:

```
SELECT Store_Name
     , Last_Name
     , First_Name
  FROM Employee, Store
  WHERE Employee.Store_Number
      = Store.Store_Number
UNION
SELECT Store_Name
     , Last_Name
     , First_Name
  FROM Employee, Store
  WHERE Employee.Employee_Number
      = Store.Manager_Employee_Number;
```

Explanation
1) First, we lock RENTS. Store for read, and we lock RENTS. Employee for read.
2) Next, we execute the following steps in parallel.

> 1) We do an all-AMPs RETRIEVE step from RENTS.Store by way of an all-rows scan with no residual conditions into Spool 2, which is *duplicated an all AMPs*. Then we do a SORT to order Spool 2 by row hash. The size of Spool 2 is estimated to be 1,664 rows. The estimated time for this step is 4.31 seconds.
>
> 2) We do an all-AMPs RETRIEVE step from RENTS.Employee by way of a RowHash match scan with no residual conditions into Spool 3, which is *built locally* on the AMPs. Then we do a SORT to order Spool 3 by row hash.

The size of Spool 3 is estimated to be 1,936 rows. The estimated time for this step is 2.69 seconds.

3)We execute the following steps in parallel.

1) We do an all-AMPs JOIN step from Spool 2 (Last Use) by way of an all-rows scan, which is joined to Spool 3 (Last Use). Spool 2 and Spool 3 are joined using a *merge join*, with a join condition of ("Spool3.Store_Number = Spool2.Store Number"). The result goes into Spool 1, which is redistributed by hash code to all AMPs. The size of Spool 1 is estimated to be 1,936 rows. The estimated time, for this step is 10.30 seconds.

2) We do an all-AMPs RETRIEVE step from RENTS.Store by way of an all-rows scan with no residual conditions into Spool 4, which is redistributed by hash code to all AMPs. Then we do a SORT to order Spool 4 by row hash. The size of Spool 4 is estimated to be 208 rows. The estimated time for this step is 0.97 seconds.

4) We do an all-AMPs JOIN step from RENTS.Employee by way of an all-rows scan with no residual conditions, which is joined to Spool 4 (Last Use). RENTS.Employee and Spool 4 are joined using a merge join, with a join condition of ("RENTS.Employee.Employee_Number = Spool4. Manager_Employee_Number"). The result goes into Spool 1, which is redistributed by hash code to all AMPs. Then we do a SORT to order Spool 1 by the sort key in spool field 1 *eliminating duplicate rows*. The size of Spool 1 is estimated to be 208 rows. The estimated time for this step is 1.36 seconds.

5) Finally, we send out an END TRANSACTION step to all AMPs involved in processing the request

->The contents of Spool 1 are sent back to the user as the result of statement 1. The total estimated time is *15.97 seconds*.

The result is 17 times faster than the Product Join.

The CARTESIAN Product Join

A Cartesian Join is an unconstrained Product Join which matches each row of one table with all the rows of the other. This generally results in large volumes of meaningless output and typically becomes a heavy consumer of system resources. While Cartesian Product Joins rarely have any practical business use, they are supported by the Teradata Database primarily for ANSI compatibility.

The number of rows returned by a full Cartesian Join is the product of the number of rows in each participating table. Thus, if one table has a modest 100,000 rows, and the other is only slightly larger with 500,000 rows, a full Cartesian Product will return 50 *BILLION* rows. Fortunately, such a transaction aborts if, and when, the limit of the user's spool space allocation is reached.

Cartesian Product Joins are usually the result of error and often deliver huge volumes of meaningless output, if:

> The SQL WHERE clause is missing.
> Join conditions are not based on equality.
> There are too few join conditions.
> A referenced table is not named in any join condition.
> Table aliases are incorrectly used.

The exaggerated example of a Cartesian Product Join *(Figure 16-6)* was encountered by the author at an actual customer site. The names have been changed to protect the innocent:

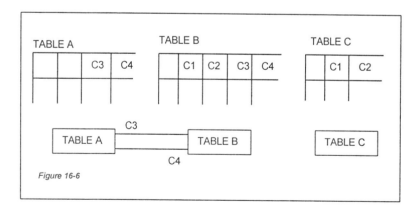

Figure 16-6

```
EXPLAIN
LOCKING A FOR ACCESS
UPDATE B SET C1 = C.C1, C2 = C.C2
    WHERE A.C3= B.C3
    AND    A.C4= B.C4;
```

While this update join involves three tables and has two join conditions, Table C is not referenced and a Cartesian product results. It is also worth noting that the user had requested an ACCESS lock for an update transaction which, as we shall discuss in Chapter 19, would cause the updates to execute in serial, rather than parallel, fashion. The following EXPLAIN was captured with an earlier release of Teradata software:

Explanation

1) First, we lock DB.A for access, we lock DB.B for read, we lock DB.C for read, we lock DB.B for write, and we lock DB.B for write.

2) Next, we execute the following steps in parallel.

    1) We do an all-AMPs JOIN step from DB.B by way of an all-rows scan with no residual conditions, which is joined to DB.A . DB.B and DB.A are joined using a merge join, with a join condition of ("(DB.A.C4 = DB.B.C4) AND (DB.A.C3 = DB.B.C3)") . The result goes into Spool 2, which is built locally on the AMPs. The size of Spool 2 is estimated to be 11,310,160 rows. The estimated time for this step is 3 hours and 46 minutes.

    2) We do an all-AMPs RETRIEVE step from DB.C by way of an all-rows scan with no residual conditions into Spool 3, which is duplicated on all AMPs. The size of Spool 3 is estimated to be 1,881,696,000 rows. The estimated time for this step is 111 hours and 40 minutes.

3) We execute the following steps in parallel.

    1) We do an all-AMPs JOIN step from Spool 2 (Last Use) by way of an all-rows scan, which is joined to Spool 3 (Last Use). Spool 2 and Spool 3 are joined using a product join. The result goes into Spool 1, which is redistributed by hash code to all AMPS. Then we do a SORT to order Spool 1 by row hash. The size of Spool 1 is estimated to be 532,057,070,784,000 rows. The estimated time for this step is 23,856,078 hours and 47 minutes.

2) We do an all-AMPs JOIN step from DB.B by way of an all-rows scan with no residual conditions, which is joined to DB.A. DB.B and DB.A are joined using a merge join, with a join condition of "(DB.A C4 = DB.B.C4) AND (DB.A.C3 = DB.B.C3)") . The result goes into Spool 5, which is duplicated on all AMPs. The size of Spool 5 is estimated to be 452,406,400 rows. The estimated time for this step is 108 hours and 24 minutes.

3) We do an all-AMPs RETRIEVE step from DB.C by way of an all-rows scan with no residual conditions into Spool 6, which is built locally on the AMPs. The size of Spool6 is estimated to be 47,042,400 rows. The estimated time for this step is 5 hours and 46 minutes.

4) We execute the following steps in parallel.

1) We do an all-AMPs JOIN step from Spool 5 (Last Use) by way of an all-rows scan, which is joined to Spool 6 (Last Use). Spool 5 and Spool 6 are joined using a product join. The result goes into Spool 4, which is redistributed by hash code to all AMPS. Then we do a SORT to order Spool 4 by row hash. The size of Spool 4 is estimated to be **532,057,070,784,000 rows**. The estimated time for this step is **24,166,946 hours and 31 minutes.**

2) We do a MERGE DELETE into DB.B from Spool 1 (Last Use).

5) We do a MERGE into DB.B from Spool 4 (Last Use).

6) FINALLY, we send out an END TRANSACTION step to all AMPs involved in processing the request..

→ No rows are returned to the user as a result of statement 1.

Even though the actual elapsed performance time might be confidently expected to be a small fraction of the relative time value output by the EXPLAIN, 24 million hours might seem excessive.

Spool Requirements for Joins

Other than for the Nested Join, which typically requires no spool at all, any user permitted to submit multiple table joins should always be allocated sufficient spool space to replicate all the data involved in the join. For Product Joins, Merge or Exclusion Joins which involve the

of one complete table on all the AMPs, the amount of spool needed can quickly over-extend the total capacity of the system.

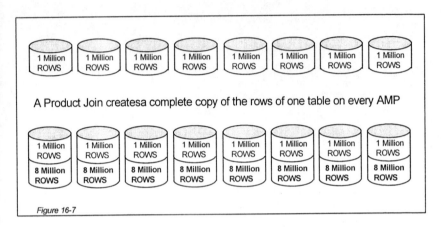

A Product Join createsa complete copy of the rows of one table on every AMP

Figure 16-7

If a table with one million rows on each AMP is duplicated on an 8-AMP system, each AMP must be capable of storing 8 million rows in spool *(Figure 16-7)*. For this reason it becomes highly important to limit the amount of data involved in a join, wherever possible, by means of a WHERE clause in the SQL, and ensure that the Optimizer is provided with the accurate and up-to-date statistics needed to produce the most efficient and least expensive join plan.

Conclusion

Inefficient joins result from poor physical design choices:

> Lack of indexes.
>
> Inappropriate indexes.
>
> Stale or missing Collected Statistics.
>
> Inefficient SQL code.

The Optimizer bases join planning on;

> Primary and Secondary Indexes.

> Estimated number of rows in each table or subtable.

> Estimated ratio of table rows per index value.

Collected statistics may improve join performance.

The most efficient joins are based on matching Primary Indexes. Collecting statistics on small tables, Non-Unique Primary Indexes or other join columns might help the Optimizer in formulating the most effective access plans for other types of joins.

Poor SQL coding can degrade performance on a good database design, and no amount of clever SQL can compensate for a poor database design. Even if the database is currently performing well, it is wise to remember that data demographics change over time, and this might eventually influence the Optimizer to make a compensatory change in its execution plans. It therefore becomes an administrator's most urgent duty to regularly revisit all index choices and re-collect out-dated statistics, at regular intervals, to ensure the system continues to deliver optimum performance.

Compared to other major vendors of RDBMS, the on-going performance maintenance required by the Teradata Database is minimal. Re-collecting statistics at regular intervals is not arduous, and analysis of EXPLAIN output using step diagrams can be an entertaining pastime.

Since the output of Teradata's EXPLAIN facility is extremely regular in form and has changed but little throughout its long history, there is perhaps an opportunity for an enterprising devotee of Microsoft Visual Basic or Visual C++ to build a useful utility which accepts EXPLAIN output as a simple text file, analyzes it and produces automated, fully documented step diagrams.

17	Final Index Choice

Having completed our study of the factors and data redistribution techniques which influence Teradata Optimizer in its choice of join plan, we are finally ready to apply the Value and Join Access statistics, derived from the Application Analysis process (Chapter 2), to the final choice of Primary and Secondary Indexes needed for optimum data distribution and application performance.

The final group of statistics which influence the choice of Primary and Secondary Indexes is:

Value Access Statistics.

Join Access Statistics.

Value Access

A column is included in the Value Access statistics each time its value is compared to a literal value provided in the SQL. For example:

WHERE colname = hardcoded_value *(literal value)*

WHERE colname = :value *(execution-time variable)*

There are two main statistics collected for Value Access:

VALUE ACC FREQ	How often annually all known transactions access rows from the table by supplying a literal value for this column. For example, a Value Access Frequency of 52 indicates that the application executes on a weekly basis,

and implies a maintenance task. A value of 10K suggests the application runs many times per day and indicates transaction-type processing.

VALUE ACC ROWS * FREQ — How many rows are accessed annually by supplying a literal value for this column across all transactions.

Join Access

While join conditions always occur in the SQL "WHERE" clause, not all SQL "WHERE" clauses are join conditions. For example the following WHERE clause does not represent a join condition, but merely provides a filter for the number of rows which must be joined:

WHERE Table1.ColumnName > 2000

Indexes or columns used for Join Access are those which appear in the SQL with an equality comparison to the value of another column in the same, or another table. For example:

WHERE Table1.ColumnName = Table2.ColumnName

Join statistics collected as a part of the Application Analysis procedure also fall into two categories:

JOIN ACC FREQ — How often annually all known transactions access rows from this table by an equality join based on a comparison of this column value to another column in a similar domain of the same, or another, table.

JOIN ACC ROWS * FREQ — How many rows are accessed annually by a join from the same, or another table, on this column across all transactions.

Instructions for Exercise 4

In this exercise, we shall begin the final index selection process, by first eliminating *NUSI candidates:*

> With zero Value and/or low Join statistics.

> Where candidate columns are accessed only for data maintenance operations:

> **(VAL ACC FREQ < 1K and   JOIN ACC FREQ < 1K):**

Example:

TABLE 0 (EXAMPLE)

10,000,000 ROWS

	Col 1	Col 2	Col 3	Col 4	Col 5	Col 6	
PK/FK	PK, UA						
				NN,ND			
VALUE ACC FREQ	100K	0	0	0	0	0	
VALUE ACC R*F	100K	0	0	0	0	0	
JOIN ACC FREQ	12M	0	0	0	0	0	
JOIN ACC R*F	12M	0	0	0	0	0	
DISTINCT VALUES	10M	1.5M	200K	10M	3M	3M	
MAXIMUM ROWS/VAL	1	12	300	1	3	100K	
MAX ROWS NULL	0	5	0	0	1.5M	0	
TYPICAL ROWS/VAL	1	7	50	1	3	9K	
CHANGE RATING	0	3	2	1	1	3	
PI/SI	UPI	~~NUPI~~	NUPI?	UPI			
	USI	~~NUSI~~	~~NUSI?~~	USI	~~NUSI?~~	~~NUSI?~~	

EXERCISE 4

TABLE 1 (PRIME ENTITY)

1,500,000 ROWS

	Col 1	Col 2	Col 3	Col 4	Col 5	Col 6	
PK/FK	PK, UA						
VALUE ACC FREQ	100K	0	0	0	0	0	
VALUE ACC R*F	100K	0	0	0	0	0	
JOIN ACC FREQ	12M	0	0	0	0	0	
JOIN ACC R*F	12M	0	0	0	0	0	
DISTINCT VALUES	1.5M	1.3M	7K	5.5K	400K	15K	
MAXIMUM ROWS/VAL	1	2	400	350	3	100	
MAX ROWS NULL	0	0	0	0	500K	0	
TYPICAL ROWS/VAL	1	1	320	300	2	90	
CHANGE RATING	0	3	2	1	1	1	
PI/SI	UPI	~~NUPI~~				NUPI	
	USI	NUSI	NUSI	NUSI		NUSI	

TABLE 2 (PRIME ENTITY)

150,000 ROWS

	Col 7	Col 8	Col 9	Col 10	Col 11	Col 12	
PK/FK	PK, UA						
VALUE ACC FREQ	0	360	12	12	4	0	
VALUE ACC R*F	0	54K	48K	96K	80K	0	
JOIN ACC FREQ	100M	0	0	0	0	0	
JOIN ACC R*F	100M	0	0	0	0	0	
DISTINCT VALUES	150K	1.2K	130K	12	5	3K	
MAXIMUM ROWS/VAL	1	200	2	15K	30K	60	
MAX ROWS NULL	0	0	4K	0	0	0	
TYPICAL ROWS/VAL	1	100	1	8K	20K	50	
CHANGE RATING	0	0	9	1	2	0	
PI/SI	UPI	NUPI				NUPI	
	USI	NUSI	~~NUSI~~	NUSI?		NUSI	

TABLE 3 (DEPENDENT)

800,000 ROWS

	Col 1	Col 13	Col 14	Col 15	Col 16	Col 17	
PK/FK		PK					
	FK	SA			NN,ND		
VALUE ACC FREQ	0	0	0	0	0	0	
VALUE ACC R*F	0	0	0	0	0	0	
JOIN ACC FREQ	700K	0	0	0	0	0	
JOIN ACC R*F	1M	0	0	0	0	0	
DISTINCT VALUES	300K	5	16K	300K	800K	600K	
MAXIMUM ROWS/VAL	3	200K	75	2	1	2	
MAX ROWS NULL	0	0	0	390K	0	150K	
TYPICAL ROWS/VAL	1	50K	50	1	1	1	
CHANGE RATING	0	0	3	1	0	1	
PI/SI	NUPI		~~NUPI~~		UPI		
	NUSI	NUSI	NUSI	NUSI?	USI	NUSI?	
	---USI ---						

EXERCISE 4 (CONTINUED)

TABLE 4 (ASSOCIATIVE)

4,500,000 ROWS

	Col 1	Col 7	Col 18	Col 19	
PK/FK		PK			
	FK	FK			
VALUE ACC FREQ	150	0	0	0	
VALUE ACC R*F	700K	0	0	0	
JOIN ACC FREQ	0	8M	0	0	
JOIN ACC R*F	0	400M	0	0	
DISTINCT VALUES	2M	150K	150	15K	
MAXIMUM ROWS/VAL	5	50	25K	400	
MAX ROWS NULL	0	0	0	0	
TYPICAL ROWS/VAL	3	30	19K	350	
CHANGE RATING	0	0	0	0	
PI/SI	NUPI	NUPI			
	NUSI	NUSI	NUSI	NUSI	
		-UPI/USI -			

TABLE 5 (ASSOCIATIVE)

1,500,000 ROWS

	Col 1	Col 13	Col 7	Col 20	Col 21	
PK/FK		PK				
		FK	FK			
VALUE ACC FREQ	0	0	0	0		
VALUE ACC R*F	0	0	0	0		
JOIN ACC FREQ	10M		25K	0	0	
JOIN ACC R*F	12M		200K	0	0	
DISTINCT VALUES	1.2M		150K	9K	1.5K	
MAXIMUM ROWS/VAL	3		15	180	1.35K	
MAX ROWS NULL	0		0	0	0	
TYPICAL ROWS/VAL	1		8	170	1K	
CHANGE RATING	0		0	0	0	
PI/SI	NUPI		NUPI			
	NUSI		NUSI	NUSI	NUSI	
		-----USI -----				

TABLE 6 (HISTORY)

12,000,000 ROWS

	Col 1	DATE	Col 4	Col 5	Col 6	
PK/FK		PK				
	FK					
VALUE ACC FREQ	15M	0	0	0	0	
VALUE ACC R*F	70M	0	0	0	0	
JOIN ACC FREQ	300	0	0	0	0	
JOIN ACC R*F	2 B	0	0	0	0	
DISTINCT VALUES	3M	455	N/A	N/A	N/A	
MAXIMUM ROWS/VAL	18	18K	N/A	N/A	N/A	
MAX ROWS NULL	0	0	N/A	N/A	N/A	
TYPICAL ROWS/VAL	3	17K	N/A	N/A	N/A	
CHANGE RATING	0	0	0	0	0	
PI/SI	NUPI					
	NUSI	NUSI				
		-UPI/USI -				

Instructions for Exercise 5

The sample tables show the remaining index candidates from Exercise 4 with non-qualifying NUSI candidates deleted. At this point we are now able to make the final choice of indexes, based on the following guidelines:

> Choose *ONE* Primary Index (UPI or NUPI) using Join Access Demographics.

> If one competing PI candidate has Value Access demographics equal to the Join Access of another, give precedence to the Join.

> If a PI candidate shows little or no Value or Join access, it is unsuitable as a Primary Index.

> Do not carry identical Primary and Secondary Indexes on the same columns.

Example:

TABLE 0 (EXAMPLE)

10,000,000 ROWS

	Col 1	Col 2	Col 3	Col 4	Col 5	Col 6	
PK/FK	PK, UA						
				NN,ND			
VALUE ACC FREQ	100K	0	0	0	0	0	
VALUE ACC R*F	100K	0	0	0	0	0	
JOIN ACC FREQ	12M	0	0	0	0	0	
JOIN ACC R*F	12M	0	0	0	0	0	
DISTINCT VALUES	10M	1.5M	200K	10M	3M	3M	
MAXIMUM ROWS/VAL	1	12	300	1	3	100K	
MAX ROWS NULL	0	5	0	0	1.5M	0	
TYPICAL ROWS/VAL	1	7	50	1	3	9K	
CHANGE RATING	0	3	2	1	1	3	
PI/SI	UPI		~~NUPI?~~	~~USI~~			
	~~USI~~			USI			

In the example, Col 1 shows frequent access both by value and by join, while no other candidate shows any. Since Col 1 is unique, it is therefore chosen as a Unique Primary Index. This eliminates all other Primary Index Candidates, along with the USI candidate on Col 1. The USI is retained on Col 4, not for reasons of access, but merely to enforce its uniqueness. Final Index Choices are provided on pages 232 and 233.

EXERCISE 5

TABLE 1 (PRIME ENTITY)

1,500,000 ROWS

	Col 1	Col 2	Col 3	Col 4	Col 5	Col 6	
PK/FK	PK, UA						
VALUE ACC FREQ	100K	0	0	0	0	0	
VALUE ACC R*F	100K	0	0	0	0	0	
JOIN ACC FREQ	12M	0	0	0	0	0	
JOIN ACC R*F	12M	0	0	0	0	0	
DISTINCT VALUES	1.5M	1.3M	7K	5.5K	400K	15K	
MAXIMUM ROWS/VAL	1	2	400	350	3	100	
MAX ROWS NULL	0	0	0	0	500K	0	
TYPICAL ROWS/VAL	1	1	320	300	2	90	
CHANGE RATING	0	3	2	1	1	1	
PI/SI	UPI					NUPI	
	USI						

TABLE 2 (PRIME ENTITY)

150,000 ROWS

	Col 7	Col 8	Col 9	Col 10	Col 11	Col 12	
PK/FK	PK, UA						
VALUE ACC FREQ	0	360	12	12	4	0	
VALUE ACC R*F	0	54K	48K	96K	80K	0	
JOIN ACC FREQ	100M	0	0	0	0	0	
JOIN ACC R*F	100M	0	0	0	0	0	
DISTINCT VALUES	150K	1.2K	130K	12	5	3K	
MAXIMUM ROWS/VAL	1	200	2	15K	30K	60	
MAX ROWS NULL	0	0	4K	0	0	0	
TYPICAL ROWS/VAL	1	100	1	8K	20K	50	
CHANGE RATING	0	0	9	1	2	0	
PI/SI	UPI	NUPI				NUPI	
	USI						

TABLE 3 (DEPENDENT)

800,000 ROWS

	Col 1	Col 13	Col 14	Col 15	Col 16	Col 17	
PK/FK		PK					
	FK	SA			NN,ND		
VALUE ACC FREQ	0	0	0	0	0	0	
VALUE ACC R*F	0	0	0	0	0	0	
JOIN ACC FREQ	700K	0	0	0	0	0	
JOIN ACC R*F	1M	0	0	0	0	0	
DISTINCT VALUES	300K	5	16K	300K	800K	600K	
MAXIMUM ROWS/VAL	3	200K	75	2	1	2	
MAX ROWS NULL	0	0	0	390K	0	150K	
TYPICAL ROWS/VAL	1	50K	50	1	1	1	
CHANGE RATING	0	0	3	1	0	1	
PI/SI	NUPI				UPI		
					USI		
	---USI ---						

EXERCISE 5 (CONTINUED)

TABLE 4 (ASSOCIATIVE)
4,500,000 ROWS

	Col 1	Col 7	Col 18	Col 19	
PK/FK	PK				
	FK	FK			
VALUE ACC FREQ	150	0	0	0	
VALUE ACC R*F	700K	0	0	0	
JOIN ACC FREQ	0	8M	0	0	
JOIN ACC R*F	0	400M	0	0	
DISTINCT VALUES	2M	150K	150	15K	
MAXIMUM ROWS/VAL	5	50	25K	400	
MAX ROWS NULL	0	0	0	0	
TYPICAL ROWS/VAL	3	30	19K	350	
CHANGE RATING	0	0	0	0	
PI/SI	NUPI	NUPI			

-UPI/USI -

TABLE 5 (ASSOCIATIVE)
1,500,000 ROWS

	Col 1	Col 13	Col 7	Col 20	Col 21	
PK/FK	PK					
	FK		FK			
VALUE ACC FREQ	0		0	0	0	
VALUE ACC R*F	0		0	0	0	
JOIN ACC FREQ	10M		25K	0	0	
JOIN ACC R*F	12M		200K	0	0	
DISTINCT VALUES	1.2M		150K	9K	1.5K	
MAXIMUM ROWS/VAL	3		15	180	1.35K	
MAX ROWS NULL	0		0	0	0	
TYPICAL ROWS/VAL	1		8	170	1K	
CHANGE RATING	0		0	0	0	
PI/SI	NUPI		NUPI			

-----USI -----

TABLE 6 (HISTORY)
12,000,000 ROWS

	Col 1	DATE	Col 4	Col 5	Col 6	
PK/FK	PK					
	FK					
VALUE ACC FREQ	15M	0	0	0	0	
VALUE ACC R*F	70M	0	0	0	0	
JOIN ACC FREQ	300	0	0	0	0	
JOIN ACC R*F	2 B	0	0	0	0	
DISTINCT VALUES	3M	455	N/A	N/A	N/A	
MAXIMUM ROWS/VAL	18	18K	N/A	N/A	N/A	
MAX ROWS NULL	0	0	N/A	N/A	N/A	
TYPICAL ROWS/VAL	3	17K	N/A	N/A	N/A	
CHANGE RATING	0	0	0	0	0	
PI/SI	NUPI					
	NUSI					

-UPI/USI -

Exercise 5
Final Index Choices

EXERCISE 5 - FINAL CHOICE

TABLE 1 (PRIME ENTITY)

1,500,000 ROWS

	Col 1	Col 2	Col 3	Col 4	Col 5	Col 6	
PK/FK	PK, UA						
VALUE ACC FREQ	100K	0	0	0	0	0	
VALUE ACC R*F	100K	0	0	0	0	0	
JOIN ACC FREQ	12M	0	0	0	0	0	
JOIN ACC R*F	12M	0	0	0	0	0	
DISTINCT VALUES	1.5M	1.3M	7K	5.5K	400K	15K	
MAXIMUM ROWS/VAL	1	2	400	350	3	100	
MAX ROWS NULL	0	0	0	0	500K	0	
TYPICAL ROWS/VAL	1	1	320	300	2	90	
CHANGE RATING	0	3	2	1	1	1	
PI/SI	UPI						

TABLE 2 (PRIME ENTITY)

150,000 ROWS

	Col 7	Col 8	Col 9	Col 10	Col 11	Col 12	
PK/FK	PK, UA						
VALUE ACC FREQ	0	360	12	12	4	0	
VALUE ACC R*F	0	54K	48K	96K	80K	0	
JOIN ACC FREQ	100M	0	0	0	0	0	
JOIN ACC R*F	100M	0	0	0	0	0	
DISTINCT VALUES	150K	1.2K	130K	12	5	3K	
MAXIMUM ROWS/VAL	1	200	2	15K	30K	60	
MAX ROWS NULL	0	0	4K	0	0	0	
TYPICAL ROWS/VAL	1	100	1	8K	20K	50	
CHANGE RATING	0	0	9	1	2	0	
PI/SI	UPI						

TABLE 3 (DEPENDENT)

800,000 ROWS

	Col 1	Col 13	Col 14	Col 15	Col 16	Col 17	
PK/FK		PK					
	FK	SA			NN,ND		
VALUE ACC FREQ	0	0	0	0	0	0	
VALUE ACC R*F	0	0	0	0	0	0	
JOIN ACC FREQ	700K	0	0	0	0	0	
JOIN ACC R*F	1M	0	0	0	0	0	
DISTINCT VALUES	300K	5	16K	300K	800K	600K	
MAXIMUM ROWS/VAL	3	200K	75	2	1	2	
MAX ROWS NULL	0	0	0	390K	0	150K	
TYPICAL ROWS/VAL	1	50K	50	1	1	1	
CHANGE RATING	0	0	3	1	0	1	
PI/SI	NUPI						
	---USI ---				USI		

EXERCISE 5 - FINAL CHOICE (CONTINUED)

TABLE 4 (ASSOCIATIVE)

4,500,000 ROWS

	Col 1	Col 7	Col 18	Col 19	
PK/FK	PK				
	FK	FK			
VALUE ACC FREQ	150	0	0	0	
VALUE ACC R*F	700K	0	0	0	
JOIN ACC FREQ	0	8M	0	0	
JOIN ACC R*F	0	400M	0	0	
DISTINCT VALUES	2M	150K	150	15K	
MAXIMUM ROWS/VAL	5	50	25K	400	
MAX ROWS NULL	0	0	0	0	
TYPICAL ROWS/VAL	3	30	19K	350	
CHANGE RATING	0	0	0	0	
PI/SI		NUPI			

-USI -

TABLE 5 (ASSOCIATIVE)

1,500,000 ROWS

	Col 1	Col 13	Col 7	Col 20	Col 21	
PK/FK	PK					
	FK		FK			
VALUE ACC FREQ	0	0	0	0	
VALUE ACC R*F	0	0	0	0	
JOIN ACC FREQ	10M	25K	0	0	
JOIN ACC R*F	12M	200K	0	0	
DISTINCT VALUES	1.2M	150K	9K	1.5K	
MAXIMUM ROWS/VAL	3	15	180	1.35K	
MAX ROWS NULL	0	0	0	0	
TYPICAL ROWS/VAL	1	8	170	1K	
CHANGE RATING	0	0	0	0	
PI/SI	NUPI				

-----USI -----

TABLE 6 (HISTORY)

12,000,000 ROWS

	Col 1	DATE	Col 4	Col 5	Col 6	
PK/FK	PK					
	FK					
VALUE ACC FREQ	15M	0	0	0	0	
VALUE ACC R*F	70M	0	0	0	0	
JOIN ACC FREQ	300	0	0	0	0	
JOIN ACC R*F	2 B	0	0	0	0	
DISTINCT VALUES	3M	455	N/A	N/A	N/A	
MAXIMUM ROWS/VAL	18	18K	N/A	N/A	N/A	
MAX ROWS NULL	0	0	N/A	N/A	N/A	
TYPICAL ROWS/VAL	3	17K	N/A	N/A	N/A	
CHANGE RATING	0	0	0	0	0	
PI/SI	NUPI					

-USI -(OPTIONAL)

Explanation of Exercise 5 (Final Choice)

Table 1 (Prime Entity)

Col 1 was chosen as the UPI since it is the only column used for value or join access. This eliminates all other Primary Index candidates and makes the Unique Secondary Index on Col 1 no longer necessary.

Table 2 (Prime Entity)

The significant amount of join access for Col 7 renders it the best choice of PI. This eliminates all other PI candidates and makes the USI on Col 7 no longer necessary.

Table 3 (Dependent)

A dependent table always has a multiple component Primary Key, of which all but one component is designated as a Foreign Key. The single FK column component of Table 3 identifies it as a first level dependency table. Since Col 1 is used for access and Col 13 is not, Col 1 becomes a NUPI. To maintain the integrity of the Primary Key however, the USI is maintained on the joint values of Col 1 and Col 13. Additionally, since Col 16 has data constraints of "NN" (Not NULL) and "ND" (No Duplicates), the USI is also retained to ensure uniqueness of the column values.

Table 4 (Associative)

This Associative table is used to model a many-to-many relationship between the entities with Col 1 and Col 7 as their respective Primary Keys. Both columns are used for access or join, but never both at the same time. Since the table can have only one Primary Index, Col 7 is chosen as a NUPI by virtue of the heavy (transaction-type) join access. The Unique Secondary Index on Col 1 and Col 7 is however retained to protect the integrity of the Primary Key.

Table 5 (Associative)

Like Table 4, Table 5 models a many-to-many- relationship between the tables referenced by the FK columns of its Primary Key. Since one FK is already composite, this indicates that Table 5 models a relationship between an already existing relationship and an entity. In this case, both foreign key components, (Col 1 + Col 13), and Col 7 are used for join access, and so precedence is given to the larger of the two. Col 1 and Col 13 therefore become the composite NUPI, at the sacrifice of Col 7, since Col 7 is non-unique and NUSIs are seldom used in joins.

Table 6 (History)

As a History Table (or Time Relation) which models, in effect, a many-to-many relationship between an attribute and a point in time, Table 6 has a composite Primary Key of the attribute (Col 1), and a point in time (date). History tables are very rarely accessed by anything other than the attribute value, and it comes as little surprise that Col 1 qualifies as a NUPI. History tables are usually the largest tables in the data warehouse by a wide margin. They are typically used for decision support and are generally subject to frequent large-scale insert operations. Moreover historical information is often captured with sufficient regularity that the integrity of the PK is unlikely to be compromised. A USI on the Primary Key does nothing to improve access, inhibits inserts and is therefore frequently avoided for history tables.

Review of Primary and Secondary Index Guidelines

	UNIQUE	NON-UNIQUE
VALUE ACCESS	ONE AMP, ONE ROW	1 AMP, ONE OR MORE ROWS
JOIN ACCESS	NESTED JOINS MERGE JOINS EXCLUSION JOINS	NESTED JOINS MERGE JOINS EXCLUSION JOINS
DISTINCT VALUES	GREATER THAN #AMPS EQUALS ROW COUNT	GREATER THAN #AMPS LESS THAN ROW COUNT COLLECT STATISTICS
MAX ROWS/VALUE	ONE	LESS THAN 100
MAX ROWS NULL	ONE	LESS THAN 100
TYPICAL ROWS/VALUE	ONE	LESS THAN MAX.
CHANGE RATING	0, 1, 2	0, 1, 2

Figure 17-2

In order for a column or group of columns to be initially chosen as a Primary Index candidate *(Figure 17-2)*, it must be one of the following:

Unique.

The Primary Key.

Any single column with Maximum Rows/Value and Typical Rows/Value less than 100.

To be finally chosen as the one and only Primary Index for the table, the candidate must have:

A Change Rating of 2 or less (the lower, the better).

Significant Value Access statistics and/or

High Join Access statistics (with precedence given to Join Access).

In order for a column or group of columns to be chosen as a Unique or Non-Unique Secondary Index candidate *(Figure 17-3)*, it must also be a valid Unique or Non-Unique Primary Index candidate.

	UNIQUE	NON-UNIQUE
VALUE ACCESS	ONE AMP, ONE ROW	1 AMP, ONE OR MORE ROWS
JOIN ACCESS	NESTED JOINS MERGE JOINS EXCLUSION JOINS	NESTED JOINS MERGE JOINS EXCLUSION JOINS
DISTINCT VALUES	GREATER THAN #AMPS EQUALS ROW COUNT	GREATER THAN #AMPS LESS THAN ROW COUNT COLLECT STATISTICS
MAX ROWS/VALUE	ONE	LESS THAN 100
MAX ROWS NULL	ONE	LESS THAN 100
TYPICAL ROWS/VALUE	ONE	LESS THAN MAX.
CHANGE RATING	0, 1, 2	0, 1, 2

Figure 17-2

Columns, which are likely to return fewer than 10% of the rows in a table and have a Change Rating no higher than 5, also qualify as NUSI candidates. A column remains a NUSI candidate even if it has an excessive number of rows with NULL, or a single specific value, if the typical number of rows per value is otherwise small, since the Optimizer decides whether or not to use the index based on the specific column value. Since they are seldom useful for data maintenance, NUSI candidates with zero value access, low JOIN ACCESS FREQUENCY values, or those whose usefulness remains in any doubt, may then be eliminated.

Once the optimum choice of Primary Index has been determined, based on Value and Join Access statistics, the remaining Primary and overlapping Secondary Index candidates may be eliminated from further consideration. Unique Secondary Index candidates which still survive, are used primarily to maintain the integrity of the Primary Key for tables with a Non-Unique Primary Index, and the uniqueness of other columns marked "ND".

Instructions for Exercise 6

In this, the final exercise in the series, students have the opportunity of testing their index selection skills, from start to finish, with three tables from the RENTS database. Unlike the previous exercises, table and column names are provided. However students are urged to make index decisions based on the statistics alone since table names and column names can be misleading. To review the procedure described in Exercises 1 through 5:

1. Choose Primary Index candidates.

2. Choose Secondary Index candidates.

3. Eliminate Primary Index candidates with a Change Rating greater than 2 and Secondary Index candidates with a Change Rating greater than 5.

4. Eliminate Non-Unique Secondary Index candidates:

   With zero Value and Join statistics or where candidate columns are accessed only for data maintenance operations:

   (VAL ACC FREQ < 1K and   JOIN ACC FREQ < 1K)

5. Select best choice of Primary Index based on Value Access and Join Access statistics, eliminate all other Primary and overlapping Secondary Index candidates.

The suggested solutions follow.

EXERCISE 6

ORDER

10,000 ROWS	ORDER NUMBER	LOCATION NUMBER	CUSTOMER NUMBER	UPDATE DATE	UPDATE TIME	STATUS CODE
PK/FK	PK, SA	FK,NN	FK,NN	SA,NN	SA,NN	SA,NN
VALUE ACC FREQ	10K	0	0	0	0	0
VALUE ACC R*F	10K	0	0	0	0	0
JOIN ACC FREQ	0	200K	30K	0	0	0
JOIN ACC R*F	0	200K	30K	0	0	0
DISTINCT VALUES	20K	8K	7K	70	2K	10
MAXIMUM ROWS/VAL	1	10	10	10	3	6K
MAX ROWS NULL	0	0	0	0	0	0
TYPICAL ROWS/VAL	1	1	320	3	1	2K
CHANGE RATING	0	2	1	9	9	9
PI/SI						

LOCATION

8,000 ROWS	LOCATION NUMBER	CUSTOMER NUMBER	STREET	CITY	STATE CODE	ZIP CODE
PK/FK	PK, SA	FK,NN	NN	NN		
VALUE ACC FREQ	125K	100	0	4	12	0
VALUE ACC R*F	125K	250	0	20K	100K	0
JOIN ACC FREQ	250K	12	0	0	0	0
JOIN ACC R*F	250K	70K	0	0	0	0
DISTINCT VALUES	8K	5K	8K	6K	45	6K
MAXIMUM ROWS/VAL	1	10	1	4	500	4
MAX ROWS NULL	0	0	0	0	1K	1K
TYPICAL ROWS/VAL	1	2	1	1	100	1
CHANGE RATING	0	0	1	0	0	0
PI/SI						

DELIVERY

10,000 ROWS	DELIVERY NUMBER	OPEN DATE	FROM LOC NBR	TO LOC NBR	UPDATE DATE	USER ID
PK/FK	PK, SA		FK, NN	FK, NN	SA, NN	SA, NN
VALUE ACC FREQ	250K	260	0	104	0	0
VALUE ACC R*F	250K	30K	0	450	0	0
JOIN ACC FREQ	0	0	12K	250K	0	0
JOIN ACC R*F	0	0	1.5M	750K	0	0
DISTINCT VALUES	10K	70	20	8K	70	20
MAXIMUM ROWS/VAL	1	100	5K	20	100	1.6K
MAX ROWS NULL	0	0	0	0	0	0
TYPICAL ROWS/VAL	1	50	200	3	50	600
CHANGE RATING	0	0	1	1	9	9
PI/SI						

EXERCISE 6 - FINAL CHOICE

ORDER

10,000 ROWS	ORDER NUMBER	LOCATION NUMBER	CUSTOMER NUMBER	UPDATE DATE	UPDATE TIME	STATUS CODE
PK/FK	PK, SA	FK,NN	FK,NN	SA,NN	SA,NN	SA,NN
VALUE ACC FREQ	10K	0	0	0	0	0
VALUE ACC R*F	10K	0	0	0	0	0
JOIN ACC FREQ	0	200K	30K	0	0	0
JOIN ACC R*F	0	200K	30K	0	0	0
DISTINCT VALUES	20K	8K	7K	70	2K	10
MAXIMUM ROWS/VAL	1	10	10	10	3	6K
MAX ROWS NULL	0	0	0	0	0	0
TYPICAL ROWS/VAL	1	1	320	3	1	2K
CHANGE RATING	0	2	1	9	9	9
PI/SI	USI	NUPI				

LOCATION

8,000 ROWS	LOCATION NUMBER	CUSTOMER NUMBER	STREET	CITY	STATE CODE	ZIP CODE
PK/FK	PK, SA	FK,NN	NN	NN		
VALUE ACC FREQ	125K	100	0	4	12	0
VALUE ACC R*F	125K	250	0	20K	100K	0
JOIN ACC FREQ	250K	12	0	0	0	0
JOIN ACC R*F	250K	70K	0	0	0	0
DISTINCT VALUES	8K	5K	8K	6K	45	6K
MAXIMUM ROWS/VAL	1	10	1	4	500	4
MAX ROWS NULL	0	0	0	0	1K	1K
TYPICAL ROWS/VAL	1	2	1	1	100	1
CHANGE RATING	0	0	1	0	0	0
PI/SI	UPI					

DELIVERY

10,000 ROWS	DELIVERY NUMBER	OPEN DATE	FROM LOC NBR	TO LOC NBR	UPDATE DATE	USER ID
PK/FK	PK, SA		FK, NN	FK, NN	SA, NN	SA, NN
VALUE ACC FREQ	250K	260	0	104	0	0
VALUE ACC R*F	250K	30K	0	450	0	0
JOIN ACC FREQ	0	0	12K	250K	0	0
JOIN ACC R*F	0	0	1.5M	750K	0	0
DISTINCT VALUES	10K	70	20	8K	70	20
MAXIMUM ROWS/VAL	1	100	5K	20	100	1.6K
MAX ROWS NULL	0	0	0	0	0	0
TYPICAL ROWS/VAL	1	50	200	3	50	600
CHANGE RATING	0	0	1	1	9	9
PI/SI	USI			NUPI		

Explanation of Exercise 6 (Final Choice)

ORDER Table

The major access to this table is Location Number, with a Join Access R*F value of 200K, compared to Order Number which has Value Access R*F of only 10K and Customer Number with a Join Access R*F of 30K. Location Number is not unique, but has low Maximum, Typical and Change Rating statistics. Location Number is therefore chosen as a Non-Unique Primary Index, with Order Number as a Unique Secondary Index.

LOCATION Table

The high Value and Join Access statistics substantiates the choice of "Location Number" for a Unique Primary Index.

DELIVERY Table

On the basis of Join Access alone, the "From Location Number" column seems like a clear winner for Primary Index. However it has a small number of Distinct Values, a high Maximum Rows per Value and an excessive Typical Rows per Value which renders it unsuitable.

The next candidate in line for Primary Index consideration is the "To Location Number" column with Join Access R*F of 750K, compared to "Delivery Number", with Value Access R*F of only 250K. Since its Maximum, Typical and Change Rating demographics all fall within recommended guidelines, "To Location Number" is selected as the Non-Unique Primary Index, and "Delivery Number" remains as a Unique Secondary Index.

Conclusion

While the results of the first five exercises may have been, to some degree, predictable by the "SWAG" method of choosing indexes (Chapter 1), the results of Exercise 6 were not. Unlike the SWAG method, the statistics derived from the Application Analysis process provide full and complete justification for all index choices even if table demographics are subsequently discovered to have changed over time. Remember that Success has many parents but Failure is an orphan. While the Teradata Database can usually deliver good performance, even in the most adverse conditions, it can never be fully "aware" of the intricacies of the user's business. For that, it must rely on the user.

18	Denormalization and Sub-Entities

The American Heritage Dictionary defines the word, "tempting" as, "alluring, enticing or seductive". Each of these synonyms implies that temptation is seldom associated with good works, but rather with less commendable actions. As a result, those with insufficient resistance to the evils of temptation might eventually be called upon to pay an appropriate price for their ill-considered indulgence. So it is with the temptation to denormalize the logical data model for performance gain. While denormalization of a data model is unlikely to be considered a moral mischief, a price will, sooner or later, need to be paid for failure to resist its allure, enticement or seduction.

Denormalization might dramatically improve the performance of some applications, but it is equally likely to constrain others. Any form of denormalization usually:

> Reduces data flexibility.

> Introduces the potential for data anomalies.

> Increases programming cost and complexity.

> Makes new applications more difficult to implement.

Many of the costs of denormalization can be mitigated however, if consideration of such performance techniques is delayed until after completion of the Logical Data Model, when all of the potentially damaging side effects can be readily identified and the costs can be accurately assessed. Some of the more common performance-enhancing denormalization techniques which often prove highly effective in the "real world" production environment include:

Repeating Column Groups.

Temporary Tables.

Pre-Joins.

Derived Data.

Summary Tables.

Multiple Primary Indexes.

Sub Entities.

Rules of Normalization

The three rules of normalization were discussed at length in Chapter 1. Normalization is a technique for placing non-key attributes in tables to:

Minimize redundancy.

Provide optimum flexibility.

Eliminate update anomalies.

Briefly stated, the rules are as follows:

Rule 1 Attributes describe the PK column and must not repeat within a table. If all the non-key attributes in a table conform to this rule, the table is said to be in "First Normal Form" (1NF).

Rule 2 For a multiple-column Primary Key, all attributes must describe all the columns in the PK, and not just some. If a table obeys the first rule and does not offend the second, it is said to be in "Second Normal Form" (2NF).

Rule 3 Non-key attributes must describe only the Primary Key and not other non-PK columns. Tables which comply with all three rules are said to be in "Third Normal Form" (3NF).

Repeating Column Groups

THIRD NORMAL FORM

EMPLOYEE_SALES_HISTORY

EMPLOYEE NUMBER	SALES DATE	SALES AMOUNT
PK,SA		
FK		
1009	970731	11056
1009	970831	12350
1009	970930	14300
1009	971031	17900
1009	971131	13201
1009	971231	10025

VIOLATION OF FIRST NORMAL FORM

EMPLOYEE_SALES_HISTORY

EMPLOYEE NUMBER	SALES FOR THE LAST SIX MONTHS					
	SALES	SALES	SALES	SALES	SALES	SALES
PK,SA						
1010	11056	12350	14300	17900	13201	10025

Figure 18-1

Repeating Column Groups is a popular and widely-used technique. In the example in *Figure 18-1*, a report must be generated to compare and calculate percentages of an employee's sales for the last six-month period. If the table is maintained in the third normal form of the logical data model, this information is maintained in a History Table with a multiple component PK of Employee Number and Sales Date. History tables tend to grow over time, and calculations involving both detail and totals are not only somewhat complex, but will inevitably involve at least one full scan of a potentially large table.

The most popular answer to this common problem involves a violation of the first rule of normalization, by maintaining repeating sales data columns, month-by-month, side-by-side for each employee. While this may deliver excellent performance for the some applications, it has three major drawbacks:

1. Providing each repeating column with a meaningful name, such as January Sales, February Sales, etc. would require the SQL to be changed each month.

2. Use of non-meaningful column names, such as Month 1, Month 2, etc. requires a monthly roll-over routine which if delayed, for any reason, must inevitably lead to confusion and error.

3. No matter how many repeating columns are provided, it will never be enough. If the table has 6 repeating columns, human nature ensures that 12 will be needed. If 12 are provided, 24 will soon be considered absolutely essential, and so on, ad infinitum.

There is however, a much simpler and more reliable solution. If the original table continues to be maintained in 3rd normal form and an *additional* temporary table is created or refreshed on a monthly basis, the performance advantages are fully realized and the results are reliable. Moreover since the denormalization now takes place outside of the logical model and the original table remains properly implemented in third normal form, no other applications are penalized.

Temporary Tables

While the creation and maintenance of temporary tables requires an additional investment in disk space, it offers a number of important advantages over denormalization of the logical data model, in that it:

> Avoids "skewing" the model while reaping performance benefits.
>
> Simplifies application code.
>
> Reduces spool usage.
>
> Can be used to store the intermediate results of a query.
>
> Avoids denormalization of frequently joined tables which affect other applications.
>
> Eliminates a large number of joins.
>
> Provides the designer with the ability to choose a Primary Index more suitable to the needs of the specific application.

Temporary tables can be generated as a start-up to month-end processing and deleted when no longer needed.

Pre-Joins

While the Teradata RDBMS is capable of performing 64-table joins, this does not imply that the operation is performed without significant cost. The more tables to be joined at one time, the greater the workload and the slower the performance. Thus, significant improvements in application performance can often be achieved by the use of Join Indexes or by eliminating joins to minor entities by carrying their attributes in the parent table *(Figure 18-2).*

NORMALIZED

EMPLOYEE

EMPLOYEE NUMBER	LAST NAME	STORE NUMBER
PK,SA		
1225	SCROOGE	911
1227	MARLEY	911

STORE

STORE NUMBER	STORE NAME
PK	
911	SAN FRANCISCO
912	LOS ANGELES

DENORMALIZED

EMPLOYEE

EMPLOYEE NUMBER	LAST NAME	STORE NUMBER	STORE NAME
PK,SA			
1225	SCROOGE	911	SAN FRANCISCO
1227	MARLEY	911	SAN FRANCISCO

Figure 18-2

With Teradata's implementation of the Join Index, the user becomes able to pre-define a frequently needed equality join, and have the RDBMS avoid the cost of duplication or redistribution of data for the specified join by maintaining the relevant Row IDs in the Join Index. This effectively prevents data anomalies, but requires an additional WRITE transaction to the index whenever a change occurs to the join columns in either table.

The alternative, carrying the Store Name column in the EMPLOYEE table, is a violation of third normal form, since the column Store Name qualifies Store Number and not Employee Number. If the table is denormalized in this way, and an employee is subsequently transferred to another store, care must be taken to ensure that both columns in the EMPLOYEE table are updated at the same time, or a data anomaly will result. The risk of data anomaly may however be minimized if, in spite of the pre-join of the EMPLOYEE table, the STORE table is permitted to remain in place. Thus, maintaining the Store Name in the EMPLOYEE table requires an additional READ of the STORE table for each change of the Store Number column, which is marginally less expensive than using a Join Index, but requires some degree of on-going user maintenance.

Derived Data

NORMALIZED

EMPLOYEE

EMPLOYEE NUMBER	LAST NAME	STORE NUMBER
PK,SA		
1225	SCROOGE	911
1227	MARLEY	911
1228	WILKINS	912
1228	CRATCHIT	912

STORE

STORE NUMBER	STORE NAME
PK	
911	SAN FRANCISCO
912	LOS ANGELES

DENORMALIZED

STORE

STORE NUMBER	STORE NAME	EMPLOYEE COUNT
PK		DERIVED DATA
911	SAN FRANCISCO	2
912	LOS ANGELES	2

Figure 18-3

Derived Data is defined as redundant stored data, whose values can be determined or calculated from other column values already present in the model. In *Figure 18-3*, the total number of employees in each store can be calculated by a scan of the EMPLOYEE table but the totals are nevertheless maintained in the STORE table as well.

Proper maintenance of this derived data requires that each time an employee is hired, fired or transferred, both tables must be subject to simultaneous update if data integrity is to be preserved.

NORMALIZED

PART — 200,000 ROWS

PART NUMBER	ON HAND QTY	DESCRIPTION
PK,SA		
10612	1260	
11023	65	

PART PRICE HISTORY — 2,000,000 ROWS

PART NUMBER	EFFECTIVE DATE	PRICE AMOUNT
PK,SA		
10612	970615	99.95
10612	971201	109.95
11023	971101	17.50
11023	980201	20.00

DENORMALIZED

PART — 200,000 ROWS

PART NUMBER	ON HAND QTY	DESCRIPTION	CURRENT EFFECTIVE DATE	CURRENT PRICE AMOUNT
PK,SA				
10612	1260		971201	109.95
11023	65		971101	17.50

Figure 18-4

A less obvious, and perhaps more useful example of Derived Data is shown in *Figure 18-4*. The organization maintains a PART PRICE HISTORY table which carries past, present and future price changes. To calculate the current price for a part, it is necessary to submit a full table scan of the 2 million row PART PRICE HISTORY table:

```
SELECT Current_Price_Amount
    FROM Part_Price_History
    WHERE Effective_ Date IN
        (SELECT MAX(Effective_Date)
        FROM Part_Price_History
        WHERE Effective_Date LE DATE);
```

The cost of this expensive operation is avoided by carrying the Current Price Amount as Derived Data in the PART table. Since PART PRICE HISTORY table covers future price increases, which may change on a daily basis, the Current Price Amount column in the PART table must be subject to daily monitoring.

Integral and Stand-Alone Derived Data

Derived Data falls into one of two categories:

> Integral Derived Data, where all the values needed for the calculation are already accessed by the application, for reasons other than the calculation of the derived data.

> Stand-Alone Derived Data, where column values must be accessed for no other purpose than to perform the required calculation.

Since no additional disk I/O is required to generate Integral Derived Data, it is usually calculated on demand as a normal step of the main application.

Depending on the size of the tables the complexity of the calculation and the frequency of the application, a decision must be made whether to calculate Stand-Alone Derived Data, as and when needed, or whether to process the calculation once and maintain the result in an additional summary table. If the number of tables and rows involved in the calculation is small, the Derived Data is usually calculated on demand. Where the calculation involves the use of larger tables and the access frequency is high, the use of summary tables might well result in a significant performance improvement.

Summary Tables

The use of summary tables *(Figure 18-5)* to avoid frequently executed, expensive aggregate operations against large tables, becomes a valid option only if the summary or roll-up tables are maintained in addition to the detail data, not instead of it.

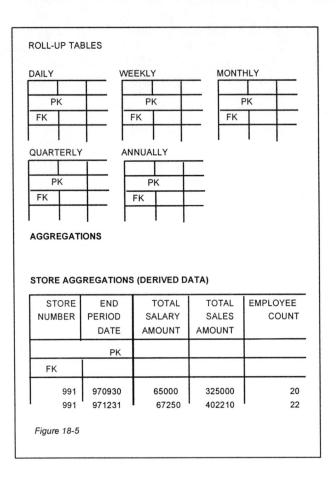

ROLL-UP TABLES

DAILY | WEEKLY | MONTHLY

QUARTERLY | ANNUALLY

AGGREGATIONS

STORE AGGREGATIONS (DERIVED DATA)

STORE NUMBER	END PERIOD DATE	TOTAL SALARY AMOUNT	TOTAL SALES AMOUNT	EMPLOYEE COUNT
	PK			
FK				
991	970930	65000	325000	20
991	971231	67250	402210	22

Figure 18-5

Multiple Primary Indexes

One of the great tragedies of the physical data model is that it permits no table to have more than a single Primary Index. This becomes particularly noticeable in the case an Associative table where both of the FK components of the Primary Key are used, more-or-less equally, for access by two different application groups. Application of the wisdom of Solomon, might well have suggested a Primary Index based on all the components of the Primary Key. However the resulting UPI would be seldom if ever used for access or join and would, in reality serve neither application group.

Figure 18-6 shows the ORDER ITEM table with a Non-Unique Primary Index defined for the Order Number. As a result, the application group which uses this column for access and joins will be favored with excellent performance. Conversely, the group which accesses the same table by way of "Item Number" can only sadly contemplate a tedious lifetime of full table scans.

NORMALIZED

ORDER ITEM

ROW COUNT: 170K

Order Number	Item Number	Quantity	Status Code
PK,SA			
FK	FK	NN	NN
NUPI			
2002	23905	100	X
2002	24001	25	O
2005	23910	500	S

DENORMALIZED

ORDER ITEM

ROW COUNT: 170K

Order Number	Item Number	Quantity	Status Code
PK,SA			
FK	FK	NN	NN
NUPI			
2002	23905	100	X
2002	24001	25	O
2005	23910	500	S

ORDER ITEM

ROW COUNT: 170K

Order Number	Item Number	Quantity	Status Code
PK,SA			
FK	FK	NN	NN
	NUPI		
2002	23905	100	X
2002	24001	25	O
2005	23910	500	S

Figure 18-6

One possible solution is to maintain a second copy of the ORDER ITEM table, identical to the original, but with the Primary Index based on the "Item Number" column instead of "Order Number". While this solution involves no additional I/O for READ operations, it would cost double the disk space for storage and twice the I/Os for WRITE operations. For this reason the Database Administrator might wish to drop the second copy for data maintenance operations and recreate it, using Teradata's highly efficient INSERT/SELECT capability (Chapter 19), as needed for transaction processing and decision support.

Sub-Entities

Maintenance and access of entity tables with huge numbers of rows or columns generally consumes a significant proportion of system resources and may be broken up into a number of sub-sets or Sub-Entities, each with the same Primary Key and Primary Index as the original.

The division of an Entity table into Sub-Entities does not offend any of the rules of the relational database, is perfectly valid in the logical data model and is not considered as a denormalization. As such, the use of Sub-Entities carry no risk of data anomaly and require very little additional storage space.

Sub-Entities may be used to divide complete rows of a larger table into more manageable units, or into a smaller number of columns. *Figure 18-7* shows an Entity with a large number of columns subdivided into:

Frequently used columns

Occasionally used columns.

Seldom used columns.

This permits the RDBMS to work with smaller rows and deliver improved performance as a result.

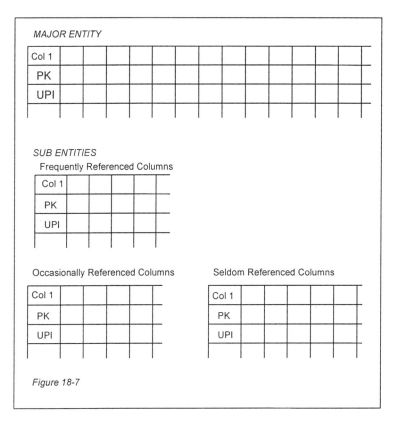

Figure 18-7

In *Figure 18-8*, employees are paid on three different bases:

Salary.

Hourly Rate.

Commission.

Each different pay type requires mutually exclusive columns, such that if there is an amount for Salary, the Hourly and Commission columns are NULL. Wherever there is a significant number of mutually exclusive columns in a table, the table becomes a strong candidate for performance enhancement using Sub-Entities.

BEFORE

EMPLOYEE

EMPLOYEE NUMBER	NAME	HIRE DATE	JOB CODE	SALARY AMOUNT	HOURLY AMOUNT	COMMISSION AMOUNT
PK,SA			FK			
UPI						
11027	DICKENS	621107	001		12.00	
11029	MARLEY	640301	105	25,000		
11030	CRATCHIT	650630	100		5.00	
11035	WILKINS	650810	100			99.00
11040	SCROOGE	660606	105	25,000		

AFTER

EMPLOYEE

EMPLOYEE NUMBER	NAME	HIRE DATE	JOB CODE	EMP TYPE
PK,SA			FK	FK
UPI				
11027	DICKENS	621107	001	H
11029	MARLEY	640301	105	S
11030	CRATCHIT	650630	100	H
11035	WILKINS	650810	100	C
11040	SCROOGE	660606	105	S

SALARIED EMPLOYEE

EMPLOYEE NUMBER	SALARY AMOUNT
PK,UPI	
11029	25,000
11040	25,000

HOURLY EMPLOYEE

EMPLOYEE NUMBER	HOURLY AMOUNT	
PK,UPI		
11027	12.00	
11030	5.00	

COMMISSION EMPLOYEE

EMPLOYEE NUMBER	COMMISSION AMOUNT
PK,UPI	
11035	99.00

Figure 18-8

Thus, each payroll operation for each distinct class of employee is now required to deal with only a small subset of the rows and may safely ignore large numbers of columns, salary deductions, benefits, etc., which are specific to each particular type of employee.

One Teradata bank customer maintained a complete list of current credit card numbers on-line for a complete period of three years. The table was primarily used for validation purposes and was typically accessed on a row-by-row basis using the Unique Primary Index. On occasion however, the bank needed a complete customer list.

New customers were added to the table on a monthly basis and each existing number was changed every three years to reduce the opportunity for credit card fraud. Once every month therefore, the user was obliged to undergo two excessively time-consuming operations which involved the global delete and new insert of 1/36th of the rows of the very large table.

The Teradata Database features a brilliantly-conceived utility called "FastLoad". This utility is used to insert large numbers of rows into a an initially empty table at ultra-fast speeds by writing data to disk a complete block at a time. At the same time, the Teradata RDBMS can globally delete complete tables of any size with no more than a small number of disk I/Os, by simply returning all the data blocks back to the Free Block List of the Cylinder Index.

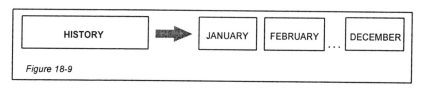

Figure 18-9

Although the solution might initially sound somewhat bizarre, the user decided to sub-divide the large table into 36 sub-entities - one for each of 36 months *(Figure 18-9)*. Each month, the user would globally delete the respective monthly table and repopulate it using FastLoad. In this way the time needed for the complete insert and delete operation was reduced from hours to a few minutes. Although the programming needed to locate individual rows now had to identify the relevant sub-entity table by expiration date, the cost was considered minimal. While additional complexity involved in producing the periodic list was seen by some as a disadvantage, this was simply solved by a minor rewrite of the SQL using the "UNION"clause:

```
SELECT * FROM JanuaryTable
    UNION
    SELECT * FROM FebruaryTable
    UNION
    SELECT * FROM MarchTable
    UNION . . .
    ORDER BY Card_Number, Expiration_Date ;
```

Conclusion

No matter how saintly the intention, any denormalization of tables which causes them to part company from the purity of the logical data model, always limits the over-all effectiveness and scope of the data warehouse. It reduces data flexibility, introduces the potential for data anomalies and generally increases programming costs by making new applications more difficult to implement.

A denormalization is not a denormalization however if it occurs *outside* of the data model itself. The creation of denormalized and summary tables in addition to, rather than instead of, existing tables in the 3rd normal form of the logical data model, may require additional maintenance, but substantially reduces the risks associated with data corruption and interference with other applications. In any event, it is important to remember that however tempting, alluring, enticing or seductive denormalization opportunities may initially appear to be, such solutions should only be considered when *all* the trade-offs are known.

19	# Multiple Sessions, Multiple Users and Partitions

Apart from being able to deliver impressive performance for Decision Support and Online Transaction Processing applications against the largest databases in the world, the Teradata Database must also be capable of loading and maintaining that data, swiftly and accurately, in a reasonable time frame that does not materially interfere with the day-to-day operations of the production environment.

SQL operations which access data by a NUSI or full table scan are always all-AMP operations and require a full table lock. (Locks are discussed in more detail later in this Chapter.) SQL access by Primary or Unique Secondary Index requires fewer than all AMPs, and many such operations can execute on different AMPs in the same elapsed time frame using multiple concurrent sessions.

A session is defined as a single LOGON to the Teradata Database, which is used to submit a consecutive stream of job requests to the data warehouse, until a specific LOGOFF command is received. Since the Teradata RDBMS permits multiple users to LOGON to the system with the same User ID and password, it becomes unable to distinguish between multiple users, each with the same User ID, or one user executing multiple sessions. As a result, data maintenance applications, which access data by Primary or Unique Secondary Index, are often able to reap significant performance advantages by using multiple concurrent sessions and executing in parallel.

While users can write their own parallel-processing applications in third generation languages such as COBOL or C, the programming is complex and the maintenance costly. Fortunately, with a tool box of powerful application utilities, a few carefully prepared SQL-like utility statements are all that is required to perform sophisticated, multiple table, multiple session, data maintenance operations with the quiet simplicity and high performance characteristic of the Teradata Database.

To achieve the levels of performance needed to process millions of insert, update and delete operations on a daily basis, within the rigid time limits of the evening "batch" window, Teradata must literally reach inside itself to seize every advantage from its unique architecture.

As with everything else in life, there is no "one-size-fits-all". By aggregating and sorting all the insert, update and delete operations for a single table in memory and rewriting them to disk, a 32K data block at a time, with a single write I/O, Teradata is often able to overcome the performance limitations inevitably imposed on the system by physical hardware constraints. On occasion however the number of inserts, updates and delete operations per data block of an existing table is sufficiently diffuse as to require a complete data block to be accessed for each row changed. Thus, Teradata must provide its users with a variety of power tools to cover each and every eventuality. These include such application utilities as:

> BTEQ.
>
> FastLoad.
>
> MultiLoad.
>
> FastExport.
>
> TPump.
>
> Archive and Recovery.

Regardless of the difference in their internal processing methodologies however, each and every application utility takes full advantage of multiple sessions which can execute in parallel across the entire Teradata system. If the data is evenly distributed amongst all the AMPs on the system, it is reasonable to suppose that streaming data maintenance transactions will also be evenly distributed.

Apart from time-sharing considerations, no single AMP can execute more than one task at a time. Maximum performance levels are therefore only achieved when all AMPs are fully involved, all of the time.

The optimum number of sessions required to keep all AMPs busy, varies with the application utility being used. BTEQ and TPump, for example, submit optimized, but otherwise normal SQL transactions. The optimum number of sessions varies with the hardware platform being used, the nature of the input data and the distribution of processing amongst the AMPs. FastLoad and MultiLoad require no more than one session per AMP, plus a maximum of two additional sessions for parsing the SQL and maintaining the restart log tables. Multiple-session FastExport was not designed to improve the performance of the Teradata RDBMS. It does however, take full advantage of the multiple channel connectivity characteristic of large Teradata systems, to return huge volumes of data to the user in a shorter time frame. Consequently, the optimum number of sessions needed for FastExport is calculated not on the basis of the number needed to keep the AMPs busy, but on the number of main frame channels available.

BTEQ .IMPORT and .EXPORT

BTEQ (Basic Teradata SQL) is the oldest, but still perhaps the most widely used, of all the Teradata application utilities. BTEQ supports a full range of DDL, DCL and DML functions, including multiple-statement SQL operations with full transaction integrity. It is particularly favored for the single-session, day-to-day pseudo-interactive communications with the data warehouse needed by system administrative staff, for SQL testing by the application development group, and for the production of casual reports. In its convenient .EXPORT mode, BTEQ uses a single session to return data to the user in a variety of file, data and report formats. In .IMPORT mode, BTEQ provides an efficient tool for the "batch" processing of multiple similar DML transactions, using multiple sessions, based on input from a host-based data set or file.

BTEQ is particularly adept in defining multiple statement transactions in such a way as to ensure that if one statement in a transaction fails, all statements fail. BTEQ scripts are free form. They may contain operational commands, such as ".LOGON", ".LOGOFF", and ".QUIT" as well as a rich vocabulary of output format instructions and report writing options.

In determining transaction boundaries, BTEQ continues reading additional SQL requests until it encounters a semi-colon followed by blanks to the end of the line of script. Hence, in the following example, since the terminating semi-colon from the first insert is on the same line of script as the beginning of the next SQL request, both statements are recognized by BTEQ (*only by BTEQ*) as a single transaction:

```
USING   CustNo      (SMALLINT)
        , CName      (CHAR(25)),   BLocNo (INTEGER)
        , ACode      (SMALLINT),   Phone  (INTEGER)
        , Street     (CHAR(25)),   City   (CHAR(22))
        , State      (CHAR(2)),    Zip    (INTEGER)

    INSERT INTO Customer VALUES (
        :CustNo, :CName, :BLocNo, :Acode, :Phone)

;   INSERT INTO Location VALUES (
        :BLocNo, :Street, :City, :SCode, :Zip) ;
```

Since they are defined as a single transaction, both inserts are included in the same request parcel, and this becomes the parsing unit. Moreover since BTEQ .IMPORT insists upon inclusion of the "USING" statement, it is able to take full advantage of the economies provided by the Statement Cache and the late-binding parser.

While the Teradata RDBMS delivers impressive performance in its regular SQL insert/select function, which is used to populate one table with columns from another, its performance becomes nothing short of "spectacular" when one of the tables is initially empty and both tables have identical Primary Indexes. This special case is known as the

"Optimized Insert/Select". Since data rows are already sorted by the hash of the (common) Primary Index, each AMP can easily assemble complete data blocks in memory and write them to the new table a complete data block at a time. Data blocks can be up to 32K in length and properly normalized rows are often less than 100 bytes. As a result, the number of disk I/Os needed to populate the new table, block-by-block, is perhaps reduced to as little as three tenths of one percent of the I/Os needed to store data a row at a time. The disk is typically the slowest element of the Teradata physical architecture. By limiting its use and effectively eliminating it as a performance constraint, Teradata is able to employ the full might of its considerable processing power, AMP-by-AMP, over the entire system and the new table is populated with lightning speed.

It was inevitable that, with the success of the Optimized Insert/Select, users would soon demand the ability to insert rows into an already populated table with the same incredible performance. This was brilliantly solved by the marriage of BTEQ's multiple statement request capability and the Optimized Insert/Select. In the following example, all tables have a Primary Index based on columns in the same domain, and TableA is initially empty. Each AMP is then able to build complete blocks for TableA in memory from the combined rows of TableB, TableC and TableD, and write them back to disk, block-by-block:

```
INSERT INTO TableA SELECT * FROM TableB
; INSERT INTO TableA SELECT * FROM TableC
; INSERT INTO TableA SELECT * FROM TableD;
DELETE FROM TableB;
DELETE FROM TableC;
DELETE FROM TableD;
```

Since rows from different tables are never mixed within the same data block, the global delete of a table requires only that all the previously populated data blocks for the table are returned to the Free Block List of the appropriate Cylinder Index. In this way, the delete of TableB, TableC and TableD is completed in almost instantaneous fashion.

The combination of the optimized insert/select and the global delete provide an excellent solution to the challenge of adding rows to an already populated table. It does however presume that the rows to be added have already been downloaded from the user's host to the Teradata Database using Teradata's high performance data load utility, known as "FastLoad".

FastLoad

FastLoad is a single purpose utility designed to load new tables to the Teradata Database at high speed. Although FastLoad uses utility commands instead of pure SQL, they are syntactically much alike. Input records for FastLoad are read into a "DEFINE" field rather than a "USING" clause, but the function is similar:

```
DEFINE CustNo (SMALLINT),
       CName  (CHAR(25)),    BLocNo (INTEGER),
       ACode  (SMALLINT),    Phone  (INTEGER)
FILE = infile.dat ;

INSERT INTO Customer VALUES (
:CustNo, :CName, :BLocNo, :Acode, :Phone);
```

FastLoad insert statements always generate data parcels and this permits the DML to be parsed once for the entire data load (independently of the data values), and the plastic steps to be stored in AMP memory.

With the parsing complete, FastLoad logs on to the Teradata Database with one session per AMP (or fewer if insufficient memory is available in the user's host server). It then reads the input file and builds a series of 32K blocks of raw data which are distributed amongst the AMPs in round-robin fashion. Upon receiving a 32K block, each AMP:

Resolves the data block into individual records.

Provides each record with a Row ID based on the hash of the Primary Index value.

Returns all rows to the Communications Layer for redistribution to the AMPs responsible for the particular hash bucket referenced in the Row ID.

Accepts its own rows from the Communications Layer and writes them to the target table in unsorted 32K blocks.

For very large tables, the load procedure may be continued on successive evenings until the final end-of-file is reached for all the input data. When each AMP has been notified that all the data has been transmitted, it then:

Sorts all the rows in the target table ascending by Row ID.

Builds data blocks of up to 32K in memory.

Rewrites the sorted data blocks to the target table.

Removes all locks and makes the table available to other users.

By limiting the workload of the Parser, by maximizing the use of the channel or network and by largely eliminating the constraint of the disk, FastLoad is able to utilize the full power of the AMPs, working in parallel, to ensure the hardware is utilized to its limits and delivers near-perfect performance. In addition to performance, FastLoad offers:

Full restartability under all conditions (although this requires minor changes in the restarted FastLoad script, depending on the nature of the interruption).

User-defined error tolerance limits.

Error capture and reporting.

Performance Statistics.

Support of user-prepared INMOD (Input Modification) routines for pre-processing input data in a seamless operation, prior to passing it to FastLoad.

MultiLoad

Beginning with MultiLoad, the Teradata Database entered a new phase of application utility development by introducing a standard front-end for all future such products. This standard front-end, known as the "Support Environment", provides MultiLoad, Fast Export and TPump with a number of sophisticated features, including:

> Completely automatic restart from any interruption without any user intervention other than simply resubmitting the job.

> Full SQL support (except for SELECT).

> Preliminary syntax check prior to execution.

> Conditional processing of commands with a full ".IF", ".ELSEIF", ".ENDIF" capability.

> Support of user-defined input and system variables.

MultiLoad was designed to support up to 100 insert, update and/or delete operations operating on up to 5 pre-populated target tables as a single coordinated unit with full transaction integrity. It does so by logging on with one session per AMP, plus 2 additional sessions for parsing the SQL and maintaining the restart log table. The multiple sessions are used in much the same way as FastLoad. Like FastLoad, all insert, update and delete transactions are eventually written to the target table, a full data block at a time. Unlike FastLoad, MultiLoad carries the burden of additional overhead and requires the creation of one work table for each target table. This work table is required for temporary storage and sorting of the individual DML transactions prior to processing, to ensure they are applied to the target table in the precise order specified in the job script.

Application Utility performance is usually measured in terms of rows changed per AMP per second (RAS). As a result, since FastLoad affects all the rows of the table being loaded, it delivers reasonably predictable performance based primarily on the length of the input records and the number of rows committed to disk with each data block write.

MultiLoad operations, on the other hand, may affect between one and all the rows of the target table for each data block write. At one row per block, it may perform no better than BTEQ. At multiple DMLs per target table row, MultiLoad can exceed the performance of FastLoad. MultiLoad performance therefore depends, not so much on the inherent efficiency of the utility, but more on the density or number of rows changed per data block of the target table(s).

FastExport

FastExport has been described as a "reverse FastLoad", in that it uses multiple sessions to return massive volumes of response data to the user. By sorting the data in and between numbered 32K blocks, FastExport is able to take full advantage of the multiple sessions to transmit response data across multiple main frame-connected channels in parallel. As a result, while FastExport is available from all supported hardware platforms, the full benefits are only realized by larger systems exporting many millions of rows.

FastExport syntax is similar to that of MultiLoad, with all the advantages provided by the Support Environment, including the ability to be automatically restarted after any failure condition, by simply resubmitting the job. However, it is worthwhile to note that since this is a select operation, the Teradata RDBMS will only restart the export from the very first record. To avoid duplicate response records being collected in the host file as the result of a restarted select operation therefore, users should be careful to close and reopen the response file before restarting FastExport.

TPump

TPump (Teradata Transaction Pump) is the newest of the Teradata application utilities, and was primarily designed to fill the performance niche left vacant when the density of MultiLoad transactions is too low to provide satisfactory performance.

Like MultiLoad, TPump is designed to provide a continuous feed of inserts, updates and deletes to as many as five target tables in the data warehouse with all the sophisticated restart and other pre-load facilities provided by the Support Environment. Unlike MultiLoad however, TPump relies on the normal SQL protocol, and a powerful combination of multiple sessions and internally created macros to "pump" transactions "under pressure" to the Teradata RDBMS.

Archive/Recovery

The Teradata Archive/Recovery is used to commit an archive of all, or part, of the data warehouse to moveable media for off-site storage as the ultimate protection against irrecoverable hardware or software failure. Since a typical data warehouse tends to store a massive amount of data, the Archive/Recovery utility allows users to devise convenient and flexible procedures to protect their data:

> As a complete system.
>
> By database.
>
> By table.
>
> By divisions of a table into AMP clusters.
>
> By Permanent Journal (changes to data).

In order to archive data, the utility requires one session per AMP (or fewer depending on available memory). Each session is assigned to a specific AMP and aggregates relevant data (still in Teradata internal format), into 32K blocks for write to the user-defined archive. Recovery of data from archive requires two sessions per AMP. If the AMP configuration of the recovered system is identical to that of the system from which the archive was taken, the data blocks can be rewritten without change and the recovery is accomplished with impressive performance. If the configuration of the new system is different from that of the original, the Archive/Recovery utility must redistribute the rows according to the new hash maps, but since the data is already in internal DBC format, the recovery should still out-perform FastLoad.

Partitioning of Data or Processing

Users new to the Teradata Database, but experienced in other vendor RDBMS products frequently attempt to "tune" the Teradata Database by seeking to partition the data or insulate the transaction-processing users from those responsible for report generation and decision support. They try, for example:

> To partition the data by defining a table with a Non Unique Primary Index based on a column with a tiny number of distinct values, so that rows hash to a small group of specific AMPs.

> To insulate high profile, transaction processing users on a specific host from all others by assigning them to different TDP programs which interface with the RDBMS using different priority levels.

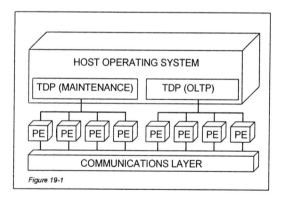

Figure 19-1

Figure 19-1 shows multiple TDPs (Teradata Director Program) executing on a multiple user host to separate data maintenance activities from OLTP (Online Transaction Processing).

The TDP application communicates directly with one or more dedicated Parsing Engines. For systems with multiple Parsing Engines dedicated to a specific TDP, the maximum number of sessions which execute on behalf of that TDP is calculated on the basis of the following formula:

Maximum Sessions per TDP = 120 * (Dedicated PEs -1)

By partitioning the TDPs in this way, during periods of low activity, the user is paying for hardware which is not being used and, during periods of high activity, performance is constrained by the limited number of Parsing Engines available to each TDP. As a result, both groups must eventually suffer the cost in terms of poor performance.

In the Teradata Database, as with any other RDBMS, the final completion of any task by a system must await the completion of its slowest constituent part. The Teradata architecture is designed to make maximum use of the entire system at all times and does not support data partitioning on the AMPs. As a result, despite the use of multiple sessions, any disparity in the distribution of the work load caused by unequal partitioning of the data, will inevitably slow the performance of some processors to the detriment of all.

Pre-Sorting Input Data

Records from an input data set or file which are ordered by a very Non-Unique Primary Index value, tend to serialize AMP operations and will adversely affect the performance of batch inserts, updates and deletes. In *Figure 19-2*, the first example shows an input data set sorted by a Unique Primary Index value, which results in an even distribution of data amongst the AMPs and allows them to process the transactions in parallel.

In the second example, the input data is sorted by a Non-Unique Primary Index value of the table. Since a succession of equal values input to the hashing algorithm will produce an identical result, all input records hashed on a similar value will be sent the same AMP. If the degree of non-uniqueness is great enough therefore, the distribution of data and processing amongst the AMPs will be "lumpy" or highly uneven, will inhibit parallel processing and will largely eliminate any advantage gained from the use of multiple sessions.

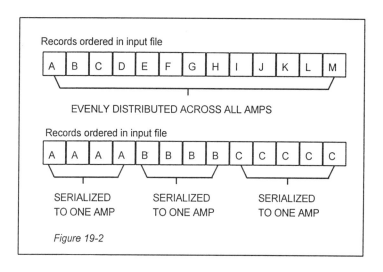

Figure 19-2

Transaction Locks

Multiple sessions can only execute in parallel, subject to the locks placed on the data by the RDBMS on behalf of other users or competing sessions. It is, for example, unwise to allow one user to read the data that another is trying to update. Each user of the system and each executing session needs to be insulated from all other users and sessions by a system of locks which effectively protect against the simultaneous, and possibly contradictory, activities of others.

LOCK REQUEST	LOCK TYPE HELD				
	NONE	ACCESS	READ	WRITE	EXCLUSIVE
ACCESS	Granted	Granted	Granted	Granted	Queued
READ	Granted	Granted	Granted	Queued	Queued
WRITE	Granted	Granted	Queued	Queued	Queued
EXCLUSIVE	Granted	Queued	Queued	Queued	Queued

Figure 19-3

Figure 19-3 shows the four types of transaction locks which are automatically placed by the Teradata RDBMS in response to user requests for access to data. Appropriate locks are immediately granted to any user or session, provided the kind of lock required is fully compatible, or does not conflict, with pre-existing locks. Any lock request which is not immediately compatible with locks currently held on the data must wait in a queue until the previous lock is released.

There are four levels of locks. In ascending order of magnitude they are:

ACCESS   Read the data even if another user has a WRITE lock, and may be updating the same data at the same time. Access may be granted more speedily, but may result in unreliable information. An ACCESS lock is never queued unless it encounters a previously placed EXCLUSIVE lock.

READ   Read data unless someone else has a WRITE or EXCLUSIVE lock. Multiple users may *read* data at the same time. Users requiring a WRITE or EXCLUSIVE lock must wait in the queue.

WRITE   Write to disk. Other users may read the data with an ACCESS lock, but users requesting a READ, WRITE or EXCLUSIVE lock must wait their turn in the queue.

EXCLUSIVE   Used for changing the structure of a database, table view or macro. This lock is incompatible with any other transaction lock and must wait in the queue until all previous lock requests have been fulfilled.

In *Figure 19-4*, a READ lock is held on the data, and a WRITE lock is waiting in the queue. The WRITE lock cannot be granted until the READ lock is removed. A new request for a READ lock is received. This READ lock cannot be granted until the WRITE lock has been satisfied. The new READ lock is therefore queued behind the WRITE lock. Had the new request been for an ACCESS lock rather than a READ lock, it would have been immediately granted.

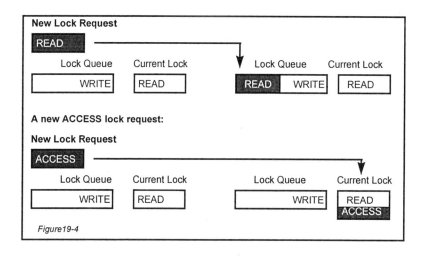

Figure19-4

Automatic Locks

The Teradata RDBMS attempts to lock objects at the least restrictive level necessary to preserve data integrity *(Figure 19-5)*. The level of lock depends on the type of SQL statement being processed. If the SQL supplies a Primary Index or Unique Secondary Index value, the data is locked at the row level (Row Hash). If the required access is other than by Primary or Unique Secondary Index, the entire table must be locked.

ROW HASH The least restrictive lock. Locks all rows in a table which hash to one, and only one, specific value. Other rows, even in the same data block are available to other users.

TABLE Locks all rows in the table.

DATABASE Locks all tables in the database including secondary index subtables.

Tables should be designed so that transaction processing applications access data only by a Primary or Unique Secondary Index to ensure that data is locked at the row hash level. Only row hash locks permit concurrent access to the same tables.

SQL STATEMENT	TYPE OF LOCK		
	ACCESS TYPE		
	PRIMARY OR USI	NUSI OR FTS	
SELECT	Row Hash	Table	READ
INSERT	Row Hash	N/A	WRITE
UPDATE	Row Hash	Table	WRITE
DELETE	Row Hash	Table	WRITE
CREATE, DROP OR ALTER TABLE	N/A	Table	EXCLUSIVE
CREATE, DROP OR MODIFY DATABASE	N/A	Database	EXCLUSIVE

Figure 19-5

Users are permitted to upgrade locks to a higher level (READ to WRITE, WRITE to EXCLUSIVE or READ to EXCLUSIVE), or to a lower level, (READ to ACCESS), using the SQL "LOCKING FOR" command *(Figure 19-6)*. What is often overlooked however, is that the ACCESS lock, granted as a result of the SQL "LOCKING FOR" command, always results in the lock being granted, not at the row hash level, but at the table level. Moreover, while the Teradata Lock Manager may upgrade locks to a higher level during a multiple statement transaction, it always holds locks to the "high watermark", and never down-grades them.

If the user's intention is to read from the table, requesting an ACCESS lock, the data may be less reliable (other users may be writing to it), but the user will generally avoid waiting in the queue. If, on the other hand, the user requests an ACCESS lock for a write transaction, the result is considerably less favorable.

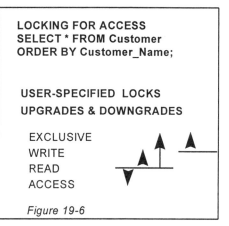

```
LOCKING FOR ACCESS
SELECT * FROM Customer
ORDER BY Customer_Name;


USER-SPECIFIED  LOCKS
UPGRADES & DOWNGRADES

 EXCLUSIVE
 WRITE
 READ
 ACCESS
```

Figure 19-6

For example, the Teradata Lock Manager will not abort a transaction which attempts to write to the tables with a ACCESS lock, but it will recognize that the lock requested is inappropriate for a WRITE operation. Without notifying the user therefore, the Lock Manager will automatically upgrade the ACCESS lock (which is a table-level lock) to a (table level) WRITE lock. A WRITE lock at the table level effectively prevents all other user access to the entire table until the current transaction completes.

Preventing Deadlocks

Deadlocks occur when two users compete with each other for the same data and each is forced to wait in line for the other's lock to be resolved. If, as part of a multiple statement transaction, the user insists upon selecting a data row using a READ lock, before making a decision to update it, the necessary upgrade from a READ to a WRITE lock, which must occur within the transaction can, in competition with other users, occasionally result in a deadlock:

>User A begins a transaction (BT).

>User A SELECTS a row using a UPI, NUPI or USI value.

>User A gets a READ lock on the ROW HASH.

>User B begins a transaction (BT).

User B SELECTS a row using the same UPI, NUPI or USI value.

User B gets a READ lock on the ROW HASH.

User A then attempts to update or delete the row, but cannot be granted a WRITE lock, because User B already has a READ lock.

User B also attempts to update or delete the row, but cannot be granted the WRITE lock, because User A already has a READ lock.

Both users are forced to WAIT . . . **DEADLOCK**

Deadlocks of this kind become preventable in two ways:

1. Instead of reading a row first, the update or delete is made on a conditional basis. For example:

   UPDATE . . . WHERE UPI_Column = :value ;
   DELETE . . . WHERE UPI_Column = :value ;

   The SQL insert syntax does not permit a WHERE clause. In its native mode however, Teradata does not accept duplicate rows, and so any attempt to insert a row identical to any pre-existing row will be automatically rejected.

2. Users could still read a row prior to performing an insert, update or delete by using the SQL LOCKING modifier at the row hash level to perform the initial select:

   BT;
   LOCKING ROW FOR WRITE
   SELECT . . . . ;
   UPDATE . . . . ;
   ET;

Conclusion

Multiple Sessions can only execute in parallel provided there are no conflicting locks placed by any other session or user on the object being accessed. Access to tables by value or join using anything other than a Primary or Unique Secondary Index will always result in a full table lock and will inhibit competing sessions.

The Teradata Database provides a number of elegant and sophisticated tools designed to provide the user with a number of easy-to-use, powerful options for multiple session processing. Each of these occupies a specific performance niche, and within that niche each becomes a top performer in its class.

Opportunities for multiple session processing include:

Export of large volumes of data to the host.

Fast loading of new tables from an input file on the host.

Data Maintenance operations.

Data Archive and Recovery.

The particular utility selected for any particular purpose should be selected not only on the basis of high performance alone, but with additional consideration of:

Ease of implementation.

Ease of Maintenance.

Recoverability.

Resource Cost.

Availability of the Data.

Transaction Integrity.

All the Teradata application utilities place normal transaction locks at the row hash level, provided the data is accessed by Primary or Unique Secondary Index values. FastLoad and Archive/Recovery however, place special utility locks on the table header. FastLoad locks are only released when the FastLoad completes or when the table being loaded is dropped. Since both archive and recovery operations may involve a complex sequence of multiple steps, Archive/Recovery locks must be manually released when the operation is complete using a parameter on the utility statement itself or a "RELEASE LOCKS" utility statement.

In the Teradata Database, the best solution is always the most parallel solution and nothing is more parallel than multiple sessions executing concurrently.

20   The Road Ahead

For those with the fortitude and devotion to duty to have survived the last nineteen chapters, I would like to take a brief time out to share two of my favorite stories. The first concerns one of the greatest artists in history, whom I have not met. The other comes from a delightful and charming, but otherwise unremarkable, elderly lady, to whom I was recently introduced.

Legend has it, that the great Michelangelo was once asked how he could visualize the sublime image of David in a large block of undressed stone. He is said to have replied, "I don't have to visualize him. David is there already. All I have to do is to chip away the parts which are not David, and set him free".

In the other story, the lady was being effusively congratulated on celebrating her 80th birthday. She demured by saying it was really a rather small achievement. "All it means", she said, "Is that for 4/5ths of a century I have been careful to look both ways before crossing the road, and have avoided being hit by a bus".

Whether or not these stories are considered amusing, they are both particularly relevant to the Teradata Database. Like Michelangelo's stone, when the Teradata Database system is delivered from the factory as a series of slightly embellished, but otherwise unremarkable metal boxes, pre-loaded with software, all the performance of which Teradata is capable is already built in. Unlike the data warehouse products of almost all other vendors, the Teradata Database requires little or nothing in the way of pre-tuning, or other heroic measures, to deliver the performance as advertised. Like the elderly lady, the primary function of the physical implementation team is not necessarily to devise interesting ways of improving the performance of the system, but rather to avoid the kind of errors which, through ignorance or carelessness, prevent the Teradata Database from performing to its true potential.

Application Analysis

Implementing applications on the Teradata Database without proper analysis is analogous to stepping off the pavement without looking both ways. Without proper planning, the likelihood of applications performing to expectations is diminished and there is little support for poorly-conceived decisions. A small amount of Application Analysis, on the other hand, not only provides statistical back up for index choices and becomes a preliminary blueprint for application design, but is also helpful in determining the nature, degree and performance effect of future change.

Tables and Spool

Relational tables properly normalized in third normal form should typically have no more than twelve columns and usually fewer than one hundred bytes per row. The larger the row, the fewer the number which can be written to disk with a single I/O. Since the disk is always the slowest element of the hardware system, keeping the number of disk I/Os to the necessary minimum becomes the most important consideration for preserving performance.

Make sure the system has sufficient available spool space to serve the maximum number of users the system must support at any one time. Insufficient spool space causes the system to resort to large numbers of mini-Cylpacks to free up available space. Each user of the system who is permitted to perform complex joins must have enough spool to accommodate redistribution of data or duplication of smaller tables on each AMP.

Non Equality or "Outer" Comparisons

While the ability to perform full table scans, with a speed which no other RDBMS vendor can match, is fundamental to the Teradata architecture, it may not represent the most efficient way possible of fulfilling a request.

With Teradata's recent addition of Value-Ordered and Join Indexes to its already rich Secondary Index support, many of the acceptable reasons for full table scans, such as range testing and computation of aggregates, can be fulfilled from index access alone without resort to the base table rows. In its innovative use of the hashing algorithm, parallel and common steps, the Optimizer is able to negate many of the potentially performance-crippling effects of non-equality comparisons.

Some types of query can only be resolved by full table scan, and no amount of tweaking or tuning will change that. These include string searches using such SQL constructs as "INDEX", "SUBSTR", "LIKE", etc. Queries which involve searching tables by partial column values always indicate that part of the value in a column has a meaning independent of the remainder and demonstrates that the concept of domains is not well understood. Full table string searches can be eliminated if all column values are decomposed to the finest level of access. While selecting rows by partial column values is usually a costly undertaking, string manipulation of the output is relatively inexpensive, and users should remain constantly aware that the concerns of data storage are vastly different to the issues of output.

Denormalization

Any denormalization of tables which deviates from the purity of the logical data model will, sooner or later, exact a heavy cost. While denormalization techniques such as repeating column groups, summary tables, pre-joins, etc., can admittedly result in impressive performance improvements for some applications, they may seriously inhibit others, now or in the future. This need not be a problem however, if denormalized tables are maintained *in addition to* the tables in the logical model, not *instead of* them.

Derived Data

Integral Derived Data is that which can be calculated with no additional I/O required by the application. Stand-Alone Derived Data is defined a calculation which requires access to columns and/or rows not otherwise touched by the application. Based on the complexity of the calculation and the frequency of need, the storage of Stand-Alone derived data can result in a significant performance boost. Against this, the additional cost in coding complexity and potential data anomalies must be carefully weighed.

Referential Integrity and Macros

Implementation of automatic referential integrity by defining Primary and Foreign Keys in the SQL is expensive since it generally involves the permanent maintenance of a number of Secondary Indexes which cannot be easily dropped for data maintenance operations.

SQL macros, on the other hand, represent one of Teradata's more impressive contributions to application performance. They provide impressive benefits such as data and referential integrity checks which can often be executed in parallel, along with inserts, single row updates and deletes for as little as one lapsed I/O. Macros serve to reduce programmer coding time and coding errors and, with the inclusion of an SQL "USING" clause, allow Teradata to take full advantage of its late-binding Parser.

On-Going Maintenance

No matter how well current Primary and Secondary Index choices benefit performance of the applications, future change is inevitable. Collected Statistics may, or may not, help the Optimizer in developing the optimum access plan, but each application should be periodically reviewed to ensure that all indexes are still being used. Statistics on volatile tables should be re-collected whenever five to ten percent of the rows change and regularly tested to ensure that they still have a positive effect on performance. Maintenance of statistics, which do not affect the Optimizer's plan, are both expensive and unnecessary. Keep all EXPLAIN output, supplemented by step diagrams as a normal part of application maintenance for trend analysis to ensure that unanticipated changes become readily apparent and quickly addressed.

Conclusion

The Teradata Database was designed from the ground up, to support massive relational databases in third normal form. Indeed its over all performance may be significantly constrained by the kind of over-tuning and massive denormalizations required by other RDBMS products. With the sophistication of its Optimizer, Teradata now comfortably supports multiple table joins involving as many as 64 different tables in a single operation.

The more tables the data warehouse has, the more Primary Index choices, the better the data distribution, the fewer the full table scans and the greater the opportunity for data mining and detailed decision support. Large numbers of fully normalized tables are an advantage, not a disadvantage. They improve the chances for efficient Nested Joins, provide more data separation, better application control, more efficient blocking and less physical I/O.

The fundamental principles which govern Teradata's well proven capacity for massive parallel processing of huge relational data structures were properly recognized from the beginning. While other major vendors have only recently demonstrated a grudging acceptance of Teradata's genius by attempting to retrofit and redesign their own products in order to compete, the Teradata Database has been able to devote itself to well ordered, properly planned, product development rather than frantic experimentation. In a famous WW2 speech, Winston Churchill pleaded with President Roosevelt, "Give us the tools, and we will finish the job". Teradata has provided its users with the best and most sophisticated tools available in the data warehouse industry. The rest is up to you.

INDEX

F

G

H

I

K

L

P

R

S

T

W

X

Y

Glossary

3550 - NCR UNIX-based mid-range, single node, computer system. Supports Teradata Database Version 2.

3600 - NCR UNIX-based massively parallel computer system. Runs Teradata Database (Version 1) on proprietary architecture.

3rd Normal Form - A state where all columns in tables obey the first three rules of normalization . See Normalization.

Access Module Processor - The physical processor or Vproc in the Teradata Database responsible for data maintenance and retrieval.

Account String - A subset of Teradata logon ID.

Application Processor - A UNIX server to the Teradata Database for Version 1 machines, which facilitates user access, network or channel connections to the Teradata Database.

Application Utilities - Data maintenance utilities which includes BTEQ, BulkLoad, FastLoad, MultiLoad, FastExport and TPump, used for large-scale data loading and maintenance.

Attribute - Technically any column in a table, but generally limited to non-key columns.

BTEQ - Basic Teradata Query facility. A program that allows end-users to access the Teradata Database in interactive, background and report-writing mode from all supported platforms.

BulkLoad - AKA **Bulk Data Load** or **BDL**. An application utility available only from an MVS or VM environment for large-scale data maintenance.

Bynet - High speed scaleable interconnect between multiple SMP Units for the Teradata Database Version 2 running in the WorldMark 5100M environment.

Call-Level Interface - A library of routines that reside in the User's address space, and provides the interface between the application program and the TDP or Gateway.

Clique - A collection of SMP Nodes with shared access to disk arrays using SCSI interfaces.

Cluster - A group of AMPs, usually four in number, which cooperate to protect each other's data in the event of hardware failure. The level of protection afforded by clusters is known as FALLBACK.

Communications Layer - Collective term for Ynet, Vnet and/or Bynet.

COP - Communications Processor - One kind of interface processor (IFP) on the database computer Version 1. A COP contains a gateway process for communicating with workstations via a LAN.

DD - Data Dictionary - The automatically maintained information about all of the databases, tables, views, macros, and users known to the Teradata Database, including information about ownership, space allocation, accounting, and access right relationships among those objects.

Data Type - Variations of alpha, numeric and byte data recognized by the Teradata Database.

Data Warehouse - Major data storage facility for current and future decision support applications.

DBC/1012 - The hardware of the Teradata Database Computer. The DBC/1012 stores data and responds to queries about the data.

Data Control Language - A collection of SQL statements that deal with the transfer of ownership and granting and revoking of access rights.

Data Definition Language - A collection of SQL statements that deal with the creation, drop and modification of database objects.

Deadlock - A condition in which two or more transactions are unable to continue because each is waiting for computer resources held by the other. Deadlock resolution calls for the youngest transaction to be rolled back.

Disk Array - An physical array of disks. The most common configuration supported by the Teradata Database involves 20 disks arranged as 4 ranks of 5 disks each. See RAID.

Data Manipulation Language - A collection of SQL statements comprising Select, Insert, Update and Delete.

Domain - A logical data modeling concept for grouping together all columns in the data base which refer to the same real-world person, place, thing or idea.

Disk Storage Unit - A physical disk.

Entity - A real-world person, place, thing or idea of interest in the data model. Each entity becomes a separate and distinct table.

FastLoad - AKA **Fast Data Load**. - An application utility for loading data from a file on the host to a new table on the Teradata Database at high speed. Available from all Teradata supported platforms.

Foreign Key (FK) - A column or columns in a table that directly reference the primary key column or columns of the same or another table.

Graphical User Interface - A windows-based application language or interface oriented towards graphical screen presentation.

Hash or Hashing - A method of transforming an index value from a table into an address of a physical storage area. The purpose is to store and retrieve data efficiently, minimizing average search time. In the Teradata RDBMS, one result of hashing calculates a hash bucket value which is used to identify the AMP responsible for any given data row.

Hash Bucket - See Hash.

Hashing Algorithm - The arithmetical calculation to which data values are input which results in a hash bucket value plus a remainder. See Hash.

Hierarchical Database - Non-relational database which requires the user to navigate top to bottom through the tables in hierarchical fashion until the required data is located.

Interface Processor - A physical processor on the DBC/1012 or the NCR 3600 responsible for interface between the host and the Teradata hardware. The IFP parses the SQL, generates AMP instructions and interfaces with the AMPs across the Ynet.

Index - A means of ordering and locating rows on disk for efficient access and processing. See Primary Index, Secondary Index and Join Index.

Input Modification Routine - A user-written routine, generally in COBOL or C which pre-processes input data before passing it to BulkLoad, FastLoad, MultiLoad or FastExport, resulting in a single seamless utility operation.

Join Index - A type of Secondary Index which automatically maintains the results of a join between two or more tables.

Journals - Tables maintained by the RDBMS to protect against various kinds of failure. The journals of most interest to the user include system journals, such as the Transient Journal, which protects against transaction failure, the Recovery Journal for fallback-protected tables, and user defined Permanent Journals as an archive option.

Logical Data Model A collection of tables in 3rd normal form which model a business enterprise. The logical data model is constructed according to the rules of SET mathematics and is independent of the RDBMS on which it might eventually be implemented.

Macro - One or more SQL statements that are stored in the Teradata RDBMS and can be executed by a single EXECUTE statement. A macro can have multiple statements and substitutable parameters. Each macro execution is treated as an implicit transaction.

Massively Parallel - A term used to describe Teradata's implementation of dividing the workload amongst large numbers of loosely coupled processors (or CPUs) in such a way that each processor can perform its portion of a task in parallel with all the others.

MultiLoad - Teradata's most sophisticated application utility which permits up to 20 DML statements to be applied to up to 5 target tables under various conditions, at speeds generally exceeding those of BulkLoad and BTEQ.

Node - See Symmetric MultiProcessing Node.

Normalization - A number of rules (generally 3) which determine the correct table for an attribute or column based on the relationship between that attribute and the primary key.

NULL - An SQL keyword. The state of missing or unknown data as distinct from zeros or spaces.

Open Database Connectivity - A standardized protocol and set of calls for portability of SQL database applications between participating vendors.

Parallel Database Extensions, see TOS

Parser - A collective name for a number of Teradata programs which are resident on the IFP, COP or PE and are responsible for the syntax check, object resolution, optimization, and generation of AMP instructions for SQL processing.

PE - Parsing Engine - A physical processor in Teradata Version 1 machines, or a Vproc in Teradata Version 2. Responsible for parsing the SQL, generation of AMP instructions and interface with the other processors across the Communications Layer.

PERM - AKA **Permanent Space** or **MaxPerm**. The amount of space, expressed in bytes, allocated to a database or user for permanent storage of data in tables.

Physical Data Model - The collection of tables with Primary and Secondary Indexes assigned, which is actually implemented on the RDBMS. The logical model usually differs from the logical model for performance reasons.

Primary Index - The column or group of columns in a table most often used for access. The Teradata Database uses the primary index as a distribution index.

Primary Key - A column or group of columns which uniquely identifies each row of a table. A Primary Key must be unique, not null and never changed.

RAID - Redundant Array of Inexpensive Disks . A method of sharing and duplicating the data between the elements of a Disk Array for protection against hardware failure. Teradata presently supports two varieties of RAID, RAID 1 which uses mirroring of data, and RAID 5 which uses parity.

Referential Integrity - The strict observance of PK/FK relationships amongst relational tables optionally maintained automatically by the Teradata RDBMS. If values (other than NULL) in all columns identified as FK have identical counterparts in PK columns of the same or another table, the database is said to observe referential integrity.

Relational Database - A collection of tables with PK and FK relationships which model a business enterprise, and are constructed according to the rules of set mathematics.

Secondary Index - A subtable which references a column or group of columns in a table as an alternate access path to the primary index. Secondary indexes may be unique or non-unique.

Session - A logical connection, or Logon, to the Teradata Database.

SET - A collection of related fields that may take the form in SQL of a list of values or an imbedded SELECT.

Symmetric MultiProcessing Node - A group of CPUs which are tightly-coupled to mutually cooperate and function as a single super-powerful CPU. The Teradata Database Version 2 PEs and AMPs run as virtual processes (Vprocs) in UNIX, on one or more SMP Nodes.

Spool - A temporary file on the Teradata DBS used to maintain the interim or final results of an SQL query.

Subset - A smaller set within a larger set. (see SET).

Subtable - A functional subset of a table, such as a header or index which is maintatined by the RDBMS.

Terabyte - A trillion bytes of data.

TDP - Teradata Director Program AKA **Traffic Director Program**. Host-based software responsible for the registration and transmission of SQL between a user and the Teradata Database. In a channel-connected environment, TDP becomes responsible for ensuring the correct delivery of requests and responses between all the users on the host system and the Teradata Database. In a network environment, a smaller version of TDP known as Micro TDP or MTDP provides a similar service to a single user.

TOS - Teradata Operating System. Developed for the DBC/1012 and the NCR 3600 (Version 1) machines. Teradata Version 2 runs on a standard UNIX platform, and does not require TOS. It does however require a small number of minor modifications to the standard UNIX, known as PDE - Parallel Database Extensions.

Version 1 - The original implementation of Teradata on the DBC/1012 and NCR 3600 which required proprietary hardware and TOS.

Version 2 - The Teradata Database as a purely software product running in the UNIX environment with virtual instead of physical processors. Teradata Version 2 is presently supported on the NCR 3550, 4100 and the Worldmark 5100.

View - An alternate way of organizing and presenting information in the Teradata DBS. A view, like a table, has rows and columns. However, the rows and columns of a view are not stored but are selected from the base table whenever the view is referenced. Views may be used to simplify SQL or to enforce security at the row or column level.

Virtual Table See View.

Vproc - Virtual Processor. Distinct from the physical processors needed by Teradata Version 1. In Teradata Version 2, PEs and AMPs run as separate programs on top of the UNIX operating system in SMP units. Vprocs communicate with each other within an SMP using a memory-sharing protocol known as the Vnet (virtual net), and between SMPs by the scaleable high speed interconnect known as the Bynet.

WorldMark 5100M - The massively parallel computer system using micro-channel technology for internal communications and the Bynet for communications between SMP units, introduced by NCR in late 1995 for the Teradata Database (Version 2). The World Mark 5100 was succeeded by the WorldMark 5150M in 1997.

WorldMark 5150M - The massively parallel computer system using the PCI bus for internal communications. Equipped with a Bynet, the WorldMark 5150M represents the most powerful engine yet for the Teradata Database (Version 2).

Ynet - The original proprietary, high-speed intelligent interconnect at the heart of Teradata's Version 1 implementation of massively parallel architecture. The Ynet was substantially redesigned for Teradata Version 2, and it was replaced by the Vnet within an SMP unit, and the Bynet between SMP units.

List of Acronyms

2GL	2nd Generation Language
3GL	3rd Generation Language
4GL	4th Generation Language
ABEND	Abnormal Program End
AMP	Access Module Processor
ANSI	American National Standards Institute
AP	Application Processor
ATM	Application Transaction Modeling
BT	Begin Transaction
BTEQ	Basic Teradata SQL
Bynet	"Banyan" Net
CLI	Call Level Interface
COP	Communications Processor
CPU	Central Processing Unit
DBC/1012	Data Base Computer
DCL	Data Control Language
DD	Data Dictionary
DDL	Data Definition Language
DML	Data Manipulation Language
DSU	Disk Storage Unit
ER	Entity Relationship
ET	End Transaction
FK	Foreign Key
FTS	Full Table Scan
GUI	Graphical User Interface
IFP	Interface Processor
INMOD	Input Modification Routine
LAN	Local Area Network
LUN	Logical Unit (Disk Arrays)

MIPS	Millions of Instructions per Second
MTDP	Micro Teradata Director Program
NUPI	Non Unique Primary Index
NUSI	Non Unique Secondary Index
ODBC	Open Database Connectivity
PDE	Parallel Database Extensions
PE	Parsing Engine
PJ	Permanent Journal
PK	Primary Key
RAID	Redundant Array of Interactive Disks
RDBMS	Relational Database Management System (or Software)
SMP	Symmetric Multi-Processing Node
SQL	Structured Query Language
TDP	Teradata Director Program
UPI	Unique Primary Index
USI	Unique Secondary Index
V2R2	Teradata Version 2 Release 2
V2R2.1	Teradata Version 2 Release 2.1
Vnet	Virtual Net
Vproc	Virtual Processor
XOR	EXLUSIVE OR calculation

Other books about the Teradata Database by the same author:

The Teradata Database - Introduction

A practical and comprehensive guide to the Teradata Database, its history, its objectives, how it works, and why many of the world's largest business enterprises depend so heavily upon it to maintain their leadership in the market place.

The Teradata Database - SQL

A detailed analysis of Teradata Release 2 Version 2 SQL. An invaluable resource, this book leads the novice and experienced SQL programmer alike using extensive hands-on exercises, through the intricate and delicate steps by which Teradata adopts new ANSI standards on the one hand, while retaining its traditional values on the other.

The Teradata Database - Application and Archive/Recovery Utilities

Following on from the first volume in the series, "The Teradata Database - Introduction and SQL", this book continues the fascinating journey into the world of large-scale data maintenance and disaster recovery. In doing so, it becomes an irreplaceable guide for those who can afford the luxury of a classroom education in the Teradata Database, and essential reading for those who cannot.

With hundreds of easy-to-follow examples and practical exercises, the reader is gently but firmly led to the discovery of how to create efficient and powerful data maintenance applications quickly and effortlessly.

As an added bonus, the book includes a detailed examination of the Teradata Archive and Recovery options needed to protect the data against catastrophic hardware or software failure.

Published by
Education in Parallel
(310) 373 5058

You are invited to E-Mail the author at:
brianmar@netcomuk.co.uk

Visit our Web Site: www.EducationInParallel.com